WOMEN'S RESERVATION AND POLITICS

About the Editor

Dr. Mayanglambam Lilee is the Head, Department of Sociology and Director, Women's Studies Centre at Manipur University, Canchipur (A Central University) in Imphal, Manipur. Previously, she was an Assistant Professor at the Centre for the Study of Social Exclusion and Inclusion Policy (CSSEIP), M.U. She earned B.A. Honours, M.A. and Ph.D. in Sociology from Panjab University, Chandigarh. She has completed a research project sponsored by Indian Council of Social Science Research (ICSSR), New Delhi. She is the author of some selected books 'Gender, Women and Society: Discourse and Praxis in North-East India' (Edited), 'Dimensions of Women's Empowerment: Media, Politics and Reservation' (Edited) and 'Adjustment amidst Multicultural Environment' (Single authored). She can be reached at lileem@manipuruniv.ac.in

WOMEN'S RESERVATION AND POLITICS

Past, Present and Future

Edited by

Mayanglambam Lilee

CONCEPT PUBLISHING COMPANY PVT. LTD.
NEW DELHI - 110 059

ISBN: 978-93-6344-677-9

First Published 2026

Published and Printed by

Concept
Since 1974

Concept Publishing Company Pvt. Ltd.
A/15-16, Commercial Block, Mohan Garden
New Delhi-110059 (India)
T: +91-11-41101460
E: publishing@conceptpub.com, *W*: www.conceptpub.com

Cataloging in Publication--Courtesy: D.K. Agencies (P) Ltd. <docinfo@dkagencies.com>

National Seminar on "Reservation for Women: Past, Present and Future" (2024 : Canchipur, India)

Women's reservation and politics : past, present and future / edited by Mayanglambam Lilee.

pages cm

"... National Seminar on "Reservation for Women: Past, Present and Future" held on 30-31 May, 2024. This seminar was organised by the Department of Sociology, Manipur University, Canchipur (A Central University) under the sponsorship of ICSSR, New Delhi and Manipur University, Canchipur"--Preface and acknowledgements.

Includes bibliographical references and index.

ISBN 9789363446779

1. Women--Political activity--India--Congresses. 2. Women--Legal status, laws, etc.--India--Congresses. 3. Reverse discrimination in employment--India--Congresses. 4. India. Women's Reservation Act, 2023--Congresses. I. Lilee, Mayanglambam, 1985- editor. II. Manipur University. Department of Sociology, organizer. III. Indian Council of Social Science Research, sponsoring body. IV. Manipur University, sponsoring body. V. Title.

LCC HQ1236.5.I4N38 2024 | DDC 320.0820954 23

Preface and Acknowledgements

Women's Reservation and Politics: Past, Present and Future is one of the most momentous outcomes in an edited volume from the National Seminar on "Reservation for Women: Past, Present and Future" held on 30-31 May, 2024. This Seminar was organised by the Department of Sociology, Manipur University, Canchipur (A Central University) under the sponsorship of ICSSR, New Delhi and Manipur University, Canchipur. Despite natural disasters (floods) and Manipur Violence, this Seminar could have been successfully conducted in the State with their financial and moral support. Therefore, I am very thankful to the sponsors, invited resource persons, delegates and other participants for their cooperation and patience across the State.

We immensely thank the keynote speaker, Professor Rajesh Gill (Retd.), Department of Sociology, Panjab University, Chandigarh, for delivering an insightful perspective on the theme of the Seminar by emphasizing the question of why women need a reservation even after seven decades of India's Independence. Following the Keynote address, Prof. Shweta Prasad, Secretary of the Indian Sociological Society (ISS), New Delhi, delivered her speech as a guest of honour. Subsequently, Prof. Rajendra Kshetri, former Head of the Department of Sociology, Manipur University, Canchipur, also delivered his guest of honour speech. Therefore, I am very thankful for their support and update regarding the importance of the Women's Reservation Act of 2023. My sincere gratitude also goes to Prof. Naorem Lokendra Singh, Vice-Chancellor of Manipur University, Canchipur, for delivering valuable speeches on their respective experiences on gender issues concerning the need for women's reservation in India. We thank Professor L. Memcha, Dean, School of Social Sciences, Manipur University, Canchipur, for her valuable suggestions and support in the Department's academic activities. Thanks to the chairpersons or moderators of technical sessions for their suggestions and insight for the paper presenters. Furthermore, I am grateful to all paper contributors for their scholarly papers based on secondary sources and empirical findings on the relevant themes of the seminars. Most importantly, I thank our organising committee, especially Dr. Yumlembam Khogen, Department of Sociology, M.U., co-convener of the Seminar, for his never-ending support. I am also very thankful to Mr. Nitin Mittal and his team, Concept Publishing Company (P) Ltd., New Delhi, for trusting my work and publishing this volume.

This book offers a nuanced and comprehensive exploration of the challenges and opportunities in advancing gender equality in political representation. Therefore, it is an essential read for scholars, activists, politicians, and policymakers aiming to create a more inclusive and equitable society. Through its interdisciplinary approach, this edited book illuminates the past and current state of women's political representation across the county. Most vitally, this volume demonstrates the disempowering factors, the ways forward and the changing reservation policies or Acts concerning the political empowerment of women in mainstream politics.

Mayanglambam Lilee

Contents

Section-II
Women's Reservation, Representation and Legal Regime

Section-III
Reservation Act, Politics and Empowerment

List of Contributors

Bhavana Devi Tekcham, Ph.D. Scholar, Department of Ancient History and Archaeology, Manipur University, Imphal (Manipur).
Email: bhavanadevitekcham786@gmail.com

Chinglen Maisnam (Bobo), Professor, Department of Economics, Manipur University, Imphal (Manipur).
Email: mchinglen@gmail.com

Chungkham Chingkheinganbi, Assistant Professor, Royal Academy of Law, Oinam (Manipur).
Email: cchungkham1@gmail.com

Elangbam Priyokumar Singh, Ph.D. Scholar, Department of English and Cultural Studies, Manipur University, Imphal (Manipur).
Email: pkelangcha98@manipuruniv.ac.in

H. Sudhir, Professor, Department of History, Manipur University, Imphal (Manipur).
Email: sudhirbam4@gmail.com

Hidam Ajit Meetei, Assistant Professor, Department of Ancient History and Archaeology, Manipur University, Imphal (Manipur).
Email: hajitmeetei@gmail.com

Indranil Chattopadhyay, Associate Professor, Department of History, B.K.C. College, Kolkata (West Bengal).
Email: indranilhist@gmail.com

Kaustav Choudhoury, Assistant Professor of Law, St. Xaviers' University, Kolkata (West Bengal).
Email: lawkaustav@gmail.com

Kh. Jitenkumar Singh, Scientist E, Indian Council of Medical Research – National Institute of Medical Statistics (ICMR-NIMS), (New Delhi).
Email: jitensinghkh@gmail.com

Komol Singha, Professor, Centre for Economic Studies and Planning, SSS-II, Jawaharlal Nehru University, (New Delhi).
Email: hijamkomol@gmail.com

Konsam Romabati, Assistant Professor, Department of Philosophy, Manipur University, Imphal (Manipur).
Email: konsam.romabati@manipuruniv.ac.in

Lucy Mishra, Assistant Professor of Sociology, School of Liberal Studies, KIIT University, Bhubaneswar (Odisha).
Email: lucy.mishra2000@gmail.com

M.C. Arunkumar, Professor & Head, Department of Anthropology, Manipur University, Imphal (Manipur).
Email: mcarun60@yahoo.com

Mayanglambam Lilee, Associate Professor & Head, Department of Sociology, Manipur University, Imphal (Manipur).
Email: lileem@manipuruniv.ac.in

Moirangthem Dolly, Assistant Professor, Department of English, Manipur College, Imphal (West Manipur) and Ph.D. Scholar, Srinivas University, Mangalore (Karnataka).
Email: alizeeraj@gmail.com

N. Bangkim Singh, Associate Professor, Sharda School of Law, Sharda University, Knowledge Park-III, Greater Noida (Uttar Pradesh).
Email: julie22nd@gmail.com

Naresh Kumar, Assistant Professor, Department of Political Science, HNB Garhwal University (A Central University), Srinagar (Uttarakhand).
Email: nks1070@gmail.com

Ph. Jayalaxmi, Assistant Professor, Department of English and Cultural Studies, Manipur University, Imphal (Manipur).
Email: jphurailatpam@gmail.com

Rajesh Gill, Professor (Retd.), Department of Sociology & Former Dean Research, Panjab University, (Chandigarh).
Email: rajeshgill09@yahoo.com

Rajni Bala, Associate Professor and Head, Department of Sociology, Baring Union Christian College, Batala, Gurdaspur District (Punjab).
Email: drrajnibala@gmail.com

Sandeep Gupta, Associate Professor, Department of Sociology, Nagaland University, Lumami.
Email: sandeepgupta@nagalanduniversity.ac.in

Sukanya Sarkar Sasmal, Associate Professor, Department of History, Sarojini Naidu College for Women, Kolkata (West Bengal).
Email: indranilhist@gmail.com

Suraj Beri, Assistant Professor, Department of Sociology, Nagaland University, Lumami.
Email: criticalsun@gmail.com

Swati Akshay Sachdeva, Professor, Department of Sociology, Sikkim University, Gangtok (Sikkim).
Email: sasachdeva@cus.ac.in

Sylvia Yambem, Assistant Professor (Guest), Department of History, Manipur University, Imphal (Manipur).
Email: sylvia.yambem@gmail.com

Takhellambam Menaobi Chanu, Ph.D. Scholar, Department of Economics, Manipur University, Imphal (Manipur).
Email: takhellambammenaobichanu@gmail.com

Thingnam Rajshree, Ph.D. Scholar, Department of Sociology, Manipur University, Imphal (Manipur).
Email: kb.thingnam@gmail.com

Uddhab Pyakurel, Associate Professor of Political Sociology, Kathmandu University, Kathmandu (Nepal).
Email: uddhab.pyakurel@ku.edu.np

Yumlembam Khogen, Assistant Professor, Department of Sociology, Manipur University, Imphal (Manipur).
Email: ykhogen@gmail.com

1

Introduction

Mayanglambam Lilee

History has witnessed numerous unresolved women's issues and the rise or fall in the status of women across human civilisations. However, academic interventions or studies on women's issues, especially reservations about women in the political system, do not have a long history. Women's reservation, as a policy of concern, has been realised as recently as in the 1990s. Globally, electoral gender quotas or political representation of women could be broadly divided into three types—reserved seats (constitutional and/or legislative), legal candidate quotas (constitutional and/or legislative), and political party quotas/voluntary (Ojha, 2009; International Idea, n.d. etc.). Among South Asian countries, reservation of seats for women at the Parliamentary level had already been introduced in India's immediate neighbours, Bangladesh, Nepal and Pakistan, in the 2000s. One of the first and foremost steps to empower women in politics was to reserve seats for women candidates since they could not strengthen their candidature in mainstream politics. Women's political intervention ranges from ruling in the local bodies to ruling in the states and the centre. From India's first proposal of the Women's Reservation Bill (WRB) in 1996 to today, many academicians, social activists, politicians etc., debate the pros and cons of women's reservation or quota in political parties, local legislation and the Parliament. Further, it has been debated whether reservation for women in politics is the solution to eliminating gender inequality and discrimination against women. Therefore, there was no consensus on women's reservation in India. Though many have opined that reservation of seats for women could empower them in all domains, others believe that it is meant for educated and urban women only. In this context, supporting relevant literature on women's representation in politics and their reservation bills or acts is briefly discussed below:

In the mid-twentieth century, the major argument on 'personal is political' was widely debated and criticised statements like—'Men are naturally rational and thus suited to politics and public life'. Moreover, women are irrational and, thus, more suited to the emotional life of the home. Such discourses or criticisms of the public/private divide led the second wave feminists to declare that 'personal is political' by challenging the traditional views on family and their respective gender roles (Bal, 2016: 20). Scholars explored several arguments on women's non-participation in decision-making bodies and politics at national and international levels despite implementing women's reservation policy at local governance. In DN's article on 'Reservations for Women in Panchayats' (EPW: 10th June, 1989), he said that 'reservation for women and that too only in minor political bodies, touches merely the surface of the problem of women'. Singla (2007: 229) explained that the lack of 'competencies of the women candidates' or competency factors was due to first-time entrants to the field, low political awareness, and even low participation in the meetings. Similarly, Dhavan

(2008) explored the case for representation for women in the Constitutional framework in India by analysing various factors that have contributed to women's low political representation. Further, he rejects the objections to reservation for women and argues why reservation of seats in legislatures would facilitate women's empowerment. He suggested the best solution is to enact the Bill and allow Parliament or the political parties to evolve the mechanism to distribute seats across the social and economic spectrum and end, once and for all, the perpetuating political procrastination on the proposal. Teltumbde (EPW: May 2010) viewed reservation as a part of national life, which is governed by stereotypes where the women's reservation bill can benefit the significant political parties, with the relatively larger feudal hold on the population, to get their own elected to a disproportionately large number of reserved seat and improve their tally. Likewise, Srivastava (2013) studied the multiple roles and challenges of women political entrepreneurs in India and recalled the sincere efforts from all areas to develop and empower women political entrepreneurs. Singh and Bakshi (2016) explored the impact of the 73rd Amendment Act on women's empowerment in Punjab and Haryana. The authors found that the awareness level among women about PR bodies and their function is inferior; therefore, women, in general, played no significant role in the decision-making process in Panchayat meetings and were not instrumental in initiating new schemes or measures. Further, if we look at the statistics of female representatives in Parliament, less than 15 per cent of female MPs are in the Lok Sabha. By and large, the gender disparity is evident in many States, including Andhra Pradesh, Assam, Goa, Madhya Pradesh, Maharastra, Manipur, Meghalaya, Sikkim etc., where the women's representation is below 10 per cent (PRS, 2023). Though many countries have a quota of women in political parties, the percentage of elected women is below 50 per cent, except in Rwanda (Lilee, 2024: 12). In Rwanda's Constitution in 2003 set a 30 per cent quota for women in elected positions, and ten years later, the country became the world's leader for gender equality in politics, with women occupying 64 per cent of parliamentary seats (UN Women, 2023). Overall, women's representation compared to men remains underrepresented in political institutions globally and it is clear that there is no substantial impact of the first women's reservation in India or the 73rd Amendment on women's political empowerment at Panchayati Raj Institutions across the State.

Meanwhile, the ongoing debate on the pros and cons of the implementation of *The Women's Reservation Act, 2023* may pose several new challenges to female candidates, especially uneducated women, women in rural areas etc. Having considered the importance, it is high time to discuss the opportunities and challenges of 'Reservation for Women' across the historical background, present scenario, and the way forward by analysing the Acts, Policies, and Programmes to empower women of all regions, community, caste, class, religion and creed. Before we jump to the conclusion, we need in-depth discussion or fruitful dialogue through seminars to achieve the goals of empowering women through reservation. Against this backdrop, the Department of Sociology, Manipur University, Canchipur, organised an ICSSR, New Delhi-sponsored National Seminar on 'Reservation for Women: Past, Present and Future' on 30-31 May, 2024. Though this National Seminar was interdisciplinary, it focused mainly on policy perspective by bringing together academicians, researchers, policy-makers, entrepreneurs, politicians etc., across the country. It seeks to fill the gaps between the knowledge or research and policy-making and its implementation on women-centric issues. The present volume is one of this seminar's outcomes and major sub-themes. The chapters in this book highlight facets of women's reservation in the past debates, present scenarios and the ways forward in empowering women in politics.

Chapter Outlines

Most of the chapters in this volume emphasise particular issues of reservation policy specific to women's reservation and their representation in Indian politics, around which the Women's Reservation Bill/Act has been extensively debated for the last three to four decades. After the introductory chapter, the remaining chapters are thematically divided into four sections. The first section focuses on the historical journey of women's reservations across the globe. The second section emphasises the conflicting debate on the linkages of women's reservation and their representation in politics in the context of legal frameworks. The third section deals with the reservation Acts, politics and empowerment. The last and fourth section analysed the gender-specific policies and their challenges to move forward. This section also reveals the ways forward to bring gender equality and equity in decision-making bodies at grassroots level politics to the parliamentary level.

Section—I: History of Women's Reservation and Global Scenario

In this section, there are four chapters dealing with the emergence of reservation policy or quota system specific to women politicians in Afro-America, India, Nepal etc. Chapter 2 is an invited paper from India's neighbouring country, Nepal, to understand the status of women in mainstream politics since there has been a gender quota of 33 per cent since 2008. **Uddhab Pyakurel's** paper explains the state of women in Nepal's politics. This chapter explores how the 2006 People's Movement (also called *Jana Andolan)* brought institutionalised gender equality within the political framework by mandating women's representation in political bodies through the Interim Constitution 2007 and the Constitution of Nepal in 2015. This movement led to one of the most significant socio-political transformations in the Himalayan nations. Though these constitutional provisions have been instrumental in enhancing women's visibility in politics, the persistent socio-cultural norms continue to limit women's full participation in politics. Given the context, this chapter further argues that Nepal needs to continue to move towards a political system that genuinely reflects its population's diverse voices and needs. Moreover, the continuation of creating a more inclusive and equitable political landscape through new narratives about inclusive politics is essential for all the country.

In the case of India, **Sukanya Sarkar Sasmal** and **Indranil Chattopadhyay's** chapter on 'From No Reservation to Reservation: The Welfare Legacy of the First Phase of Women's Movement after Independence' explained how the movement's in early stages have been intentionally overlooked in the academic discussion on women's reservation in India. This chapter further puts emphasis on laying the groundwork for subsequent advancements. Understanding historical context is essential for comprehending the trajectory and achievements of the women's movement in modern India as the women's movement and the freedom struggle were limited to advocating for women's suffrage, right to education, and welfare before independence. The authors draw attention to the influence of the women's movement leaders on National Congress leaders, highlighting their active involvement in policy-making processes through the implementation of pre-Independence legacy or welfare principles into practice. The All-India Women's Conference (AIWC), the most significant association representing the women's movement in modern India, did not consider reservations necessary to bring about gender equality.

The fourth chapter, 'Reservation for Women in Parliament: A Global Perspective' by **Naresh Kumar**, examines the current debate about women's reservations through the prism of international politics. Additionally, it seeks to evaluate the condition of female representation in the legislative bodies of various countries and outline the major challenges to women's participation in political processes. Among many countries, India has enacted legislation to provide specific reservations for women in parliamentary elections. This breakthrough has important ramifications for the global society. The campaign for women's reserves attempts to improve government and empower women by giving them more representation. This is a global problem that aims to establish an inclusive society where men and women have equal political rights. It also aims to tackle broader global issues, including human rights and gender justice. Historically, women have been underrepresented in politics. Therefore, marginalisation of women in political processes has prompted calls for specific measures.

Last chapter of Section-I, contributed by **Moirangthem Dolly** on 'Voyage of Change: Exploring Women's Reservation in Afro-American and Indian Literature' explores how women's reservation in leadership roles influences societal attitudes and helps eradicate social prejudices against women and bring about social reforms. It was reviewed by using Kimberle Crenshaw's intersectional feminist theory and critical discourse analysis, as reflected in Afro-American and Indian literature. By examining the literary works of various Afro-American and Indian writers, this chapter highlighted the transformative power of women's reservation policies in challenging social prejudices and promoting gender equality. On in-depth analysis of the writings of Afro-American and Indian authors, it is found that emphasis was given on representation, countering stereotypes, addressing discrimination's interconnectedness, and advocacy of inclusive leadership. This underscores literature's transformative role in advancing gender equality, inspiring social change, and fostering a more equitable world for all, regardless of gender. Women's reservation policies offer a transformative route to combat gender prejudices to some extent.

Section—II: Women's Reservation, Representation and Legal Regime

This section comprises seven chapters that explore the representation or participation of women in media, politics and the Indian Judiciary in the context of reservation policies. The first chapter of this section by **M.C. Arunkumar's** chapter titled 'Woman's Reservation in Representations: A Sociological Consideration' explains how Manipuri women could be understood with the three models, *Imoinu, Khamnu* and *Panthoibi*, and their dynamics. On the one hand, *the Imoinu* model is about the ideal womanhood in a traditional system; on the other hand, *the Panthoibi* model is about free and independent womanhood. Between the two models, there is *Khamnu* model in which women are taking part in economy, trade and commerce; but not free as that of the *Panthoibi*. Traditionally, individual Manipuri women are part of their *Imoinu* model; collectively, they act in various social and political movements, such as *Panthoibi*. The collective *Panthoibi* should be transformed into individual personhood so that the woman can make an independent decision as a voluntary woman, free from traditionalism. However, woman representatives are less in number in decision-making bodies in political institutions. For equitable woman representatives in decision-making institutions, reservation should be a means; and on the other hand, woman's liberation from traditionalism, operating in every aspect of life, is required. A new personhood should also be created on the principle of equality. Woman Reservation should be thus a means of equalizing gender; and should also be a part of larger social change to bring a new personhood irrespective of gender question. The seventh chapter by **H. Sudhir** and **Sylvia Yambem** on 'Women's Political Participation and Representation: Manipur Experience' reviews the history of women's reservation movement in India since its inception during the Constituent Assembly debates to the present day, reflecting the nation's struggle to ensure political equality for women. Subsequently, authors look at the role of women in the electoral process in Manipur.

In **N. Bangkim Singh's** chapter on 'A Discourse on Legal Regime and Political Reservations for Women in India', an attempt has been made to track the evolvement of the reservation of seats, especially for women in alignment with the legal regime in India. It resorts to untangle the political discourse and legal regime on 'reservation' and its effects on the reservation of seats for women in the political bodies in India, especially the Women's Reservation Bill/Act, 2023 (*Nari Shakti Vandan Adhiniyam*). Though the Indian government has initiated many affirmative actions to ameliorate women's conditions, reservation has remained a political domain in assertion and activation for women in the political bodies. The author further explores that although, the Champakam Dorairajan (AIR 1951 SC 226) judgement led to the first Amendment of the Constitution to uphold the caste-based reservation in Independent India showing an incongruous relationship between lawmaking and law interpretation on 'reservation' in turn, which is also reflected in the reservations of seats for women in India.

The ninth chapter on "Limits of 'Gender' as a Political Category: Reflections on Women Reservation Debate in India" by **Suraj Beri** argues that a nuanced understanding of gender, one that is sensitive to the intricacies of caste, class, and religion in the Indian context, is essential if the concept of gender is to retain its radical potential for democratic values and progressive politics. The notion of intersectionality of gender with caste, class, and religion in the Indian context argues that a unidimensional understanding of gender fails to capture the complexities of women's lived experiences and struggles. This chapter aims to juxtapose gender as a differentiated category *vis-à-vis* the women's reservation discourses in contemporary India and makes a point that an unqualified ahistorical 'abstract' notion of gender has fundamental limits in terms of its representational claims as well as political meanings and practices. The debate around women's reservation in India highlights the need for a more nuanced understanding of gender, one that takes into account the intersectionality of caste, class, and religion. Only by embracing such a contextualised and historically grounded notion, including both representation and redistribution dimensions of gender politics, can we hope to realise its full potential for progressive politics in India.

Kaustav Choudhoury's chapter on 'Women's Representation in Indian Judiciary: A Case for Women Reservation' examines the intricate interplay between women judges and their representation within the Indian judicial system. With a focus on understanding the historical evolution, current status, and prospects of women judges' representation in the Indian Judiciary, this chapter adopts doctrinal research methodology based on secondary sources to advocate for women judges' reservation in the Indian Judiciary. It critically examines the challenges and barriers encountered in implementing reservation policies, including societal attitudes, institutional biases, and structural impediments. Further, the chapter explores the impact of women's representation on the functioning of the judiciary, analysing the correlation between diversity on the bench and judicial decision-making. In addition, this chapter also probes into the ongoing debates and reform initiatives aimed at strengthening women's reservation in the judiciary, including calls for legislative amendments, policy interventions, and institutional reforms. The chapter concludes by offering insights into the complexities and nuances of women's reservation in the Indian judiciary, advocating for a holistic approach that integrates legal, institutional, and societal dimensions to advance gender justice and uphold the principles of equality before the law.

The eleventh chapter, contributed by **Lucy Mishra** on 'Feminist Perspectives on Media Representation of Women in Politics' discusses gender inequality that often begins with power dynamics, particularly concerning women in politics. The media serves as a vehicle for conveying stories about the world. Through education, news reporting, entertainment and advertising, the media delivers messages to audiences in a narrative form. These narratives send both explicit and implicit messages to media consumers, reflecting social, cultural and political discourses that influence how audiences understand these systems. Media messages often align with dominant ideologies, reinforcing the *status quo*. This does not mean all media contents are homogenous, as alternative viewpoints do exist. However, the dominance of mainstream ideologies is a concern for minority groups, whose voices are frequently marginalised in mainstream media.

The last part of Section II (Chapter 12) is jointly contributed by **Bhavana Devi Tekcham** and **Hidam Ajit Meetei** on 'Pioneering Equality: Media Narratives and the Progressive Representation of Women in Indian Politics'. Authors examine not only how media have manifested women in Indian politics but also historical happenings, yet impending changes and legal measures are undertaken to encourage participative, inclusive, and gender equality. Additionally, this chapter deals with recurring problems that female politicians experience, including underrepresentation and sensationalism, as well as online abuse. It highlights the promise of social media as a pathway to public engagement and narrative shaping. Legislative actions like the 73rd Constitutional Amendment Act and the Women Reservation Act of 2023 are viewed as laudable means of achieving gender parity in political representation. The chapter calls for a strategy that combines media literacy with increased attention to increasing female leadership in the sector and public awareness campaigns.

Section—III: Reservation Act, Politics and Empowerment

The first two chapters of Section III are focused on women's empowerment-related issues, challenges and possible measures to uplift them. Chapter 13 is an exception in that it addresses the linkages between women's empowerment and fertility issues in Sikkim. The chapter 'Women's Empowerment and Dwindling Fertility in Sikkim' by **Komol Singha, Kh. Jitenkumar Singh** and **Swati Akshay Sachdeva** found that the majority of existing studies on the relationship between the two found it to be inversed. On the one hand, women's empowerment is increasing as the economy and society grow. However, the fertility rate has been sharply declining on the other hand, causing fear in many developed economies around the world today, including Japan, Hong Kong, and South Korea. Similarly, Sikkim, one of the highest ranks in women empowerment states, now has the lowest fertility rate in the country, far below the replacement rate. This led to a serious apprehension that Sikkim's indigenous population might become extinct within a few decades. Using primary data collected through a well-structured schedule from 2400 ever-married women (aged 15-49) across all districts of Sikkim and secondary data gathered from the National Family Health

Survey reports, authors examined a major research question and found that no clear and logical relationships between the two (empowerment and fertility rate) were discovered. However, Sikkim's exceptionally low fertility rate is expected to be balanced shortly, as the economy grows rapidly and people recognise the importance of a higher fertility rate.

The fourteenth chapter is on 'The Women's Reservation Act, 2023: A Leap towards Women's Empowerment'. **Chungkham Chingkheinganbi** examined whether the Women's Reservation Act is a transformative step towards bridging the gender gap in political representation, which aimed at increasing women's representation in India's political landscape, thereby fostering gender equality and empowering women in leadership roles so as to a leap towards women's empowerment. The fifteenth chapter by **Konsam Romabati** on 'Women Reservation Act, 2023: Fair Equality of Opportunity through a Rawlsian Lens' examines the Reservation Act through the lens of American political philosopher John Rawls' Theory of Justice. It puts Rawls' principle of 'fair quality of opportunity' into perspective and explains how it can justify the Act, arguing that it is compatible with his concept of affirmative action. Further, the chapter explored that affirmative measures, when tailored towards the marginalised sections of a community who have been denied fair opportunities, will provide the impetus for attaining social justice. Conclusively, it reinstates that the Women's Reservation Act is one practical approach to combat the patriarchal culture and give the due opportunity that Indian women rightfully deserve and challenge the exclusion, discrimination, oppression, invisibility, and stereotyping faced by women.

Last but not the least, the next chapter on 'Performance of Power in Politics and Administration in Royal Court: Women in B.M. Maisnamba's *Ningthemnubee*' is contributed by **Elangbam Priyokumar Singh** and **Ph. Jayalaxmi**. Authors critically examine the role played by Manipuri women in times of war, power politics, and the maintenance of peace and harmony in society. The contentious question is why the circumstances of women changed drastically and why the question of reservation arises in Manipur, where women have been engaging in politics and economy since time immemorial. To reveal the authority and power of Meitei women in the political framework and to outline their potential in administration and conflict management about the royal court, B.M. Maisnamba's celebrated novel *Ningthemnubee* (2006 and 2024) was examined precisely.

Section—IV: Gender-based Policies, Challenges and Ways Forward

By acknowledging the systematic underrepresentation of women in political arenas, six chapters in Section IV deal with gender-based policies and their challenges, grievances, critiques etc., across classes, castes, regions, genders, and so on. The first paper (Chapter 17) of Section IV is contributed by **Rajesh Gill** on 'Women in Decision-making: Current Scenario & Issues Ahead' offers the women's current status and issues ahead in education, health, and political aspects. The author states that gender equality as a concept has turned out to be the most commonly used but still most misunderstood by virtue of the immense complexities involved. Women's sudden disappearance from employment after their overwhelming proportion in education at all levels and in all streams has been conceptualised as a '*Leaky Pipeline*' phenomenon and has been noticed in STEM, i.e. Science, Technology, Engineering and Mathematics. Following the worldwide trend, women in India, too, are overrepresented at lower levels of the professional hierarchy, thus leaving a huge gender gap in the decision-making positions at the higher echelons. Persistence of structural gender bias is one major deterrent, which has been underscored in several judicial pronouncements in cases, where gendered rules and practices have been challenged in Honourable Courts. Unless a large number of women enter into decision-making positions, gender equality shall remain a mirage. Subsequently, **Chinglen Maisnam (Bobo)** and **T. Menaobi Chanu** contribute their chapter on 'Gender Responsive Budgeting: A Small Reflection'. Authors highlight that the rationale for Gender Budgeting (GB) arises from recognising that national budgets impact men and women differently through the pattern of resource allocation. It is also one of the critical tools to tackle the mounting violence against women. Many state governments in India have also prepared a Gender Budget Statement and have started reflecting allocations for women in the GB Statement of the State Budgets. However, the introduction of the system of Gender Budgeting has still been a distant dream for the bulk of the North Eastern States. The chapter concludes by calling for an urgent need for institutionalising gender budgeting in the entire North Eastern region and for making adequate provisions for women with proper gender budgeting by all departments, besides ensuring accountability and transparency in implementing the schemes.

The nineteenth chapter, 'Unveiling Voices: Critiques and Challenges of Women's Reservation Policies in India's Political Arena' by **Sandeep Gupta**, delves into the complexities of the reservation policies, scrutinising their implementation challenges, impact, and the broader context of intersectionality and inclusivity. Despite their noble intent, critiques abound, from concerns about the erosion of meritocracy to fears of tokenism and elite capture. The implementation hurdles range from logistical issues to entrenched cultural norms and political opposition. Moreover, the effectiveness of these policies in addressing marginalised communities' needs remains a subject of debate. This chapter navigates these challenges, advocating for an inclusive approach that acknowledges women's diverse experiences and identities. By addressing intersecting forms of discrimination and empowering marginalised communities, India can realise the true potential of women's political participation, advancing principles of social justice and inclusive governance.

Rajni Bala's chapter 'Beyond Symbolic Representation: Challenges and Opportunities for Women Leaders in Punjab's Panchayati Raj Institutions' examines the intricate dynamics of women's leadership within Panchayati Raj Institutions (PRIs) in Punjab, India, focusing on the disconnection between numerical representation and substantive empowerment. While the 73rd Constitutional Amendment has significantly increased the number of women in governance, many factors like cultural, institutional, and socio-economic barriers continue to hinder their ability to exercise absolute authority. The findings highlight that while women's participation in governance has the potential to foster more inclusive and equitable decision-making, entrenched gender norms and structural inequalities undermine their effectiveness. Despite many challenges, the chapter reveals instances of transformative leadership where women leaders have navigated these barriers to make substantial contributions to their communities. At the same time, the author argues for a multifaceted approach to enhance women's empowerment in PRIs. Recommendations include targeted capacity-building programmes, financial independence initiatives, community awareness campaigns, and institutional reforms to create a more supportive environment for women leaders. By addressing these barriers, the study underscores the need to move beyond symbolic representation towards genuine empowerment, fostering a governance system that reflects and respects gender equality at the grassroots level.

Thingnam Rajshree and **M. Lilee** contribute Chapter 21, titled 'Empowering the Transgender Community in Manipur through Affirmative Action: Opportunities and Challenges'. The authors review the facets of Transgender-based policies/ affirmative actions in India. The 'landmark' judgment of the Supreme Court of India in 2014 allowed transgender persons to self-identification pressing the importance of psychological sex over biological sex, treating them as socially and educationally backward classes of citizens to extend all kinds of reservations in cases of admission in educational institutions and for government jobs. The transgender persons of Manipur are no exception when it comes to discrimination and exclusion. Although their presence has been noted even historically as figures of the royal palace of the erstwhile Manipuri kingdom, the pervading heteronormative gender binary dilutes an inclusive society for the transgender community leading to their discrimination and marginalisation. With a complex history of transgender in the state, be it acceptance or discrimination in the social milieu, this chapter tries to understand how this act has benefited the said community of the state by engaging with the various measures taken up by the government and explore the issues and challenges at the ground level in its implementation and execution of Transgender related policies.

Finally, in Chapter 22, **Yumlembam Khogen** contributes to the title 'Ensuring Women's Political Empowerment: The Women's Reservation Act, 2023 and the Ways Forward'. The author explores the legislative, administrative, societal, and supportive measures necessary for the Act's success and sustainability. These prerequisites are spread across different domains, but all need to coincide in a compatible framework for an effective implementation of the Act. Further, it examines these prerequisites in terms of a clear legal framework with detailed guidelines and rules, judicial support through mechanisms to address disputes, effective governance structures at various levels, capacity building and training for officials, adequate resource allocation, public awareness campaigns, initiatives to address socio-cultural barriers, education and empowerment programmes, mentorship and support networks, monitoring and evaluation mechanisms, legal protections against discrimination, and strong political commitment. The chapter concludes by suggesting that the Act's effective implementation will be a reality only by addressing these coincided prerequisites, leading to substantial improvements in women's political participation and empowerment in India.

Despite having many controversies, women's reservation policies or quota systems have been pivotal in addressing gender disparities in political representation across the globe. Though there is no substantial impact of the first women's reservation in India or the 73rd Amendment on women's political empowerment, its implementation is more than 30 years old and the latest Women's Reservation Act, 2023 is almost ready to implement after the next delimitation. In this situation, some critical questions emerged like—How far have we moved if the Panchayat [Constitution (64th) Amendment] Bill and the 73rd Constitutional Amendment were the beginning? Why should reservations for women be one-by-third or 33 per cent of seats? What is the basis of this figure? Will the recent Women's Reservation Act (*Nari Shakti Vandan Adhiniyam*) 2023 fulfil the aspirations of women? Will the Women's Reservation Act, 2023 bring women's overall empowerment? Why did the issue of reservations for Indian women come up and is still lingering in the Constitutional Assembly? If implemented, what are the ways forward? In this volume, 28 authors attempted to answer some of these critical questions. Undoubtedly, it is high time to analyse the pros and cons of reservation for women in politics from multidisciplinary perspectives. To conclude, it is significant to mention that some scholars have sought to resolve the women-centric reservation Acts and its ways forward for empowering women politically in the decision-making bodies. This volume opened the door for many researchers interested in working on women's empowerment, reservation, and politics.

REFERENCES

Dhavan, Rajeev. (2008). "Reservation for Women: The Way forward", *National Law School of India Review, 20*(1): 1-45. Retrieved from https://www.jstor.org/stable/44283670

D.N. (1989). "Reservation of Women in Panchayats", *Economic and Political Weekly, 24*(23): 1269. Retrieved from https://www.jstor.org/stable/4394922

Bal, G. (2016). *Contemporary Gender Issues: Identity, Status and Empowerment.* Jaipur: Rawat Publications.

International Idea. (n.d.) *Gender Quotas Database.* Retrieved on 10-10-2024, from https://www.idea.int/data-tools/data/gender-quotas-database/quotas

Lilee, M. (2024). "Milestone of Reservation for Women in India', *MUWWA Newsletter 2020-23, 8*(8). Manipur University, Canchipur.

Ojha, Suman. (2009). "Reservation for Women in the Indian Parliament: Lessons from other Countries." *The Indian Journal of Political Science, 70*(2): 471.

PRS Legislative Research. (2023). "Profile of the newly elected 17th Lok Sabha."

*PRS Legislative Research. (*2023). Women's Reservation Bill [The Constitution (108th Amendment) Bill, 2008]. Retrieved from https://prsindia.org/billtrack/womens-reservation-bill-the-constitution-108th-amendment-bill-2008-45

Singh, Swinder and Bakshi, Sumita. (2016). "Impact of 73rd Amendment Act on Women Empowerment: A Study of Punjab and Haryana", in Bal, Gurpreet (Eds.). *Contemporary Gender Issues: Identity, Status and Empowerment.* Jaipur: Rawat.

Singla, Pamela. (2007). *Women's Participation in Panchayati Raj.* Jaipur: Rawat.

Shrivastava, R. (2013). "Political Entrepreneurship of Indian Women: Challenges and Possibilities", *The Indian Journal of Political*

Science, 74(2): 233-244. Retrieved from https://www.jstor.org/stable/24701106

Teltumbde, A. (2010). "One More Reservation", *Economic and Political Weekly, 24*(23):13-15. Retrieved from http://www.jstor.com/stable/25664297

UN Women (2023). *India passes law to reserve seats for women legislators.* Retrieved on 3-9-2024, from https://www.unwomen.org/en/news-stories/feature-story/2023/10/india-passes-law-to-reserve-seats-for-women-legislators

Section-I
History of Women's Reservation and Global Scenario

2

State of Women in Nepal's Politics

Uddhab Pyakurel

Introduction

The 2006 People's Movement, which led to the greatest socio-political transformation in the Himalayan nation, has also solidified political rights for marginalized communities, including women. The movement, also called *Jana Andolan II,* brought institutionalized gender equality within the political framework by mandating women's representation in political bodies through the Interim Constitution 2007 and the Constitution of Nepal in 2015. These Constitutional provisions have been instrumental in enhancing women's visibility in politics, but the persistent socio-cultural norms continue to limit their full participation. The legal frameworks in place have led to significant progress in women's political representation, particularly at the local level. The 2015 Constitution ensures that women have at least one-third representation in the federal and provincial legislatures and 40 per cent representation in local bodies. As a result, Nepal has emerged as one of the Asian countries with the highest levels of female political representation. Despite these advances, the reality of women's political empowerment is complex. While women are increasingly present in political offices, they remain underrepresented in key leadership positions within political parties and the government. Weak implementation and enforcement often undermine the effectiveness of legal provisions. On the one hand, political parties which are largely led by men frequently fail to offer them substantive roles in decision-making processes, relegating them to peripheral positions despite their numerical presence. On the other hand, women in leadership show their patriarchal mindset and do not create a conducive social atmosphere for women to grow. As a result, women have to live with an inferiority complex even if they are big in number in the political position. Given the context, this chapter presents an updated overview of the state of women in Nepali politics, and argues that Nepal needs to continue to move towards a political system that genuinely reflects the diverse voices and needs of its population. And the continuation of creating a more inclusive and equitable political landscape through new narratives about inclusive politics is essential for the country and the region, South Asia.

Nepal: An Historical Overview

Nepal, being a country of more than 148 social groups, including more than a six-dozen ethnic groups, 132 languages, and 10 different religions, has witnessed exclusion, discrimination, and domination of various groups in many spheres including socio-cultural, economic and political (Pyakurel, 2006; Pyakurel, 2021; Pyakurel, 2022). The high caste hill males are numerically a minority; yet, they overwhelmingly dominate the political, social, and economic realms in Nepal, whereas the ethnic groups, Dalit (the traditional 'untouchable' Hindus) and Madhesi (residents of the plains who share culture with North

Indian societies) collectively constitute more than two-thirds of the population, but were discriminated against and excluded from various socio-political realms. Research by Neupane (2000) presented data from 1999 and demonstrated the overwhelming dominance of the above-mentioned communities not only in the executive branch, parliament, judiciary, public administration, and security forces but also in local government, party leadership, academia, industry and commerce, civil society, and cultural associations. Jointly high caste hill community including Newar were 36.37 per cent of the population according to the 2001 Census but held 80 per cent of the State's leadership positions in the central level executive, legislature, judiciary, public administration and state security organizational leadership in 1999. Their domination included holding 95 per cent of the positions in the civil administration, 91 per cent of the judiciary, 80 per cent of positions in the constitutional commissions, 72 per cent of positions in the cabinet, and a 68 per cent representation in Parliament (including House of Representatives and National Assembly). Also, the dominance in the leadership of professional bodies of cultural, academic, science-technology, and civil society was 95, 89, 87, and 91 per cent respectively. Overall, the hill Dalit (7.09 % population) had 0.3 per cent representation in the twelve sectors whereas the indigenous nationalities (21.85%, not including Newar and Tarai indigenous nationalities) and Madhesi (32.33%, including Madhesi Dalit and Tarai indigenous nationalities) had 7 and 11 per cent representation respectively in the twelve influential sectors (Neupane, 2000). The similar situation was applicable even in academia, the media, and civil society.

As far as women are concerned, they were severely underrepresented in the cabinet and the Supreme Court had no female justice during the 1990s. The representation of women in the Parliament and central committees of major political parties never crossed six and ten per cent respectively. Representation in the bureaucracy was around seven per cent and less than one per cent at the first-class officer level and above (The World Bank and DFID, 2006). Even though the first attempts at resistance by women date back to the early twentieth century, the Nari Samiti (Women's Committee), formed in 1918 by the social reformer and religious ascetic Yogmaya, is believed to have played a crucial role in the abolition of *sati*—the tradition of Hindu widows being burned alive on their husbands' funeral pyres—in 1920. Even if restoration of democracy through people's movement of 1990 helped introduce inclusion in some of the socio-political structures, ten-year's Maoist armed insurgency between 1996-2006, and people's movement of 2006 are considered as the significant turning points in Nepalese history to allocate the equality, opportunities and benefits to all suppressed and oppressed groups (Pyakurel, 2007, Pyakurel, 2011[1]; Adhikari, 2008; Adhikari, 2013; Adhikari and Pyakurel, 2015). Also, the indigenous people movement 2007, the Madhesi Movement 2007, the Tharu Movement 2009, all helped ensure equity, integration, and social protection to all marginalized people. The *Comprehensive Peace Accord (CPA)* in 2006 committed the state,

> To carry out an inclusive, democratic and progressive restructuring of the state by eliminating the current centralised and unitary form of the state to address the problems faced by women, Dalits, Adivasi Janajatis, Madhesis, oppressed, neglected and minority communities and backward regions by ending discrimination based on class, caste/ethnicity, language, gender, culture, religion and region (Article 3.5).

In its 'forward-looking' programme, the SPA committed to restructuring the state to make it "participatory, representative and inclusive of the country's social, cultural, geographic, caste/ ethnic and linguistic diversity". It further assured reservations to women, Dalits, 'backward' Janajati groups, Madhesis, and 'backward' regions, and to resolving the citizenship problem. Several legal provisions were enacted around this time to reflect the state's commitment to inclusion. The most significant of these was the Act to Amend Some Nepal Acts for Maintaining Gender Equality, 2006, which resulted in 56 changes to discriminatory provisions in Nepal's legal regime concerning gender. It also led to other progressive steps such as granting statutory status to the National Women's Commission and the enactment of the Nepal Citizenship Act, 2006, considered the most liberal among the country's citizenship laws thus far, in granting equal rights to both mother and father to pass on citizenship to their children. The Election to Members of the Constituent Assembly Act, 2007, laid out procedures to make the Constituent Assembly more inclusive. Likewise, the Civil Service Act was also amended to set aside 15 per cent of all seats to women, 12 per cent to Janajatis, 10 per cent to Madhesis and four per cent to Dalits—along with two per cent for the disabled and two per cent for 10 districts identified as 'backward'.

The Constitution of Nepal (2015)[2] clearly envisions Nepal as an inclusive state and guarantees the right to equality, social justice and freedom from discrimination to all. The Constitution of Nepal is a significant milestone in promoting of GESI to ensure equal rights for women, the poor, persons with disabilities, gender and sexual minorities, people living in geographically remote areas, and people from other excluded or vulnerable groups. A core aspect of the 2015 Constitution is ensuring that the policies and systems of Nepal are inclusive, particularly of the rights of women and historically excluded groups, calling for "ending discriminations relating to class, caste, region, language, religion and gender" and to "create an egalitarian society based on the principles of proportional inclusion and participation, to ensure equitable economy, prosperity and social justice".

The Constitution explicitly provides a broader framework for ensuring GESI, i.e.: (i) The principle of equality and non-discrimination; (ii) Constitutional national commissions and human rights institutions, including the National Women Commission, National Dalit Commission, National Inclusion Commission, National Madhesi Commission, National Muslim Commission, National Indigenous Commission and National Human Rights Commissions; and (iii) various fundamental rights of individuals and groups that address gender inequality and women's empowerment, i.e. Rights to Equality, Rights of women, provisions for positive discrimination towards women and assurance of special measures for women in education, health, employment and social security. Other positive provisions as per the Constitution include affirmative action to address historical disadvantages and a prohibition of any sex or caste/ethnicity-based discrimination. Along with that, Article 38 (3) ensures the protection of women from physical, mental, sexual, psychological and other forms of violence, exploitation or discrimination on grounds of origin, religion, race, caste, tribe, sex, economic condition, language, region, ideology or on other similar grounds. The Constitution identifies specific disadvantaged groups that have the right to participate in the functions of the state and equal access to public services, including socially or culturally backward women, Dalit, indigenous people, indigenous nationalities, Madhesi, Tharu, Muslim, oppressed class, *Pichhada* class, minorities, the marginalized, farmers, labours, youth, children, senior citizens, gender and sexual minorities, persons with disabilities, persons in pregnancy, incapacitated or helpless, backward region and indigent Khas Arya.

The Civil Service Amendment Act, 2014 embraces inclusivity and provides quotas for 45 per cent of all civil service positions. Employees of these allocated 45 per cent positions must comprise 33 per cent women, 27 per cent Adivasi Janajatis, 22 per cent Madhesis, 9 per cent Dalits, 5 per cent persons with disabilities and 4 per cent from other excluded groups. In addition, the provisions of the Local Government Operation Act [Section 24 (3 and 5] make it mandatory to ensure the participation of women, and excluded groups in the planning and implementation of development programmes. While ensuring the representation and participation of women and excluded groups in leadership and decision-making at all levels of society is a goal in itself, it has also been proven to significantly contribute to more equitable and inclusive development outcomes across sectors. The political representation of women and excluded groups has significantly increased following Nepal's federal restructuring in accordance with the 2015 Constitution. The Constitution mandates that 40 per cent of all elected representatives at the local level must be women, and 20 per cent must be Dalit women. Similarly, it mandates that 33 per cent of all elected representatives at the federal and provincial levels must be women, and provides additional representational quotas for other socially excluded groups. Accordingly, the elections of 2017 created a historical milestone for promoting GESI in Nepal's politics, with 14,352 (41%) women representatives elected at the local level, the highest number ever elected to public office. Among these, 6,500 are Dalit women. Similarly, women were elected to 34 per cent of seats in Provincial Assemblies, and 33.5 per cent of the seats in the Federal Parliament, including 32.7 per cent in the House of Representatives and 37.3 per cent in the National Assembly respectively. Dalit representation in the current House of Representatives is 7 per cent, compared to 0.48 per cent in 1991. Adivasi Janajatis and Madhesis made significant progress in the first provincial elections in 2017 with 22 per cent Adivasi Janajatis, 16 per cent Madhesis and 3 per cent Muslims elected to Provincial Assemblies. Likewise, among those elected to the National Assembly, 12 per cent are Dalits, 8 per cent Madhesis and 22 per cent Adivasi Janajati.

The Constitution has ensured 33 per cent representation of women in the state system, which is fully implemented in people's representation. From civil servants and teachers to security agencies, the presence of women is gradually increasing. Women have reached three highly specialized posts. Former Public Service Commission member Bidhya Devi Bhandari states that the reservation system has encouraged women to join the civil service. Initially, the reservation system played a key role in awakening interest among women by creating a desire to participate. This system, along with increased social awareness and literacy, has assured women that they can stand independently, read, write, and compete in the workforce. Moreover, the lack of job security, services, and stability in the private sector has made government service more attractive to women.

Table 2.1: Caste/Ethnic Groups and Women Representation in the HoR, interim Legislature and Constituent Assemblies (in percentages)

	1991	**1994**	**1999**	**2007**	**2008**	**2013**	**2017**	**Population**
Khas Arya	53.7	62.4	58.1	49.4	33.6	40.7	41.8	31.2
Adivasi Janajatis	34.2	24.9	25.9	30.6	34.1	32.8	30.9	35.3
Madhesis	9.3	10.3	14.2	13.6	20.7	16.5	17.1	15.3
Dalits	0.5	0.0	0.0	5.2	8.9	6.8	6.9	13.8
Muslims	2.4	2.4	2.0	1.2	2.8	3.3	3.3	4.4
Women	3.4	3.4	5.9	17.3	32.8	29.5	32.7	

Source: Computed bu author.

The data reflect a significant shift in the composition of Nepal's legislature over time, particularly after introducing the proportional representation (PR) system in 2008. The

Khas Arya group, historically overrepresented in the House of Representatives (HoR) and constituent assemblies, saw a steady decline from 62.4 per cent in 1994 to 33.6 per cent in 2008, aligning more closely with their actual population share (31.2%). This decline is most pronounced after 2008, coinciding with the PR system's introduction, which facilitated greater inclusion of marginalized groups. Adivasi Janajati representation fluctuated but remained close to their population share. Their representation peaked in 2008 (34.1%) and remained stable thereafter. Madhesi representation saw a gradual increase, from 9.3 per cent in 1991 to 20.7 per cent in 2008, reflecting the growing political assertion of Madhesi communities. However, it slightly declined in 2013 and 2017. Dalits, who were nearly absent in parliament before 2007, gained noticeable representation, rising from 0.5 per cent in 1991 to 8.9 per cent in 2008, though still lower than their population share (13.8%). Muslim representation has remained relatively low, despite a slight increase after 2008 (2.8% in 2008 to 3.3% in 2017), still below their population percentage (4.4%). Women's participation was extremely low before 2007 (only 3.4% in 1991 and 1994). A sharp increase occurred after 2007 (17.3%), with the introduction of PR in 2008 boosting women's presence to 32.8 per cent—a significant leap. Although there was a slight dip in 2013 (29.5%), women's representation remained strong in 2017 (32.7%), indicating the continued impact of affirmative policies. This data underscores how Nepal's political reforms, particularly the introduction of PR, have contributed to reducing the historical dominance of the Khas Arya group and increasing representation for marginalized communities and women. While improvements are evident, Dalits, Muslims, and Madhesis remain underrepresented relative to their population share, suggesting that further efforts are needed to ensure equitable political participation.

Table 2.2: Current State of Women in all three Government Bodies

Current	Total	Women
Federal Parliament	334	114
Lower House (HoR)	275	92
Upper House (NA)	59	22
Executive (cabinet)	25	3
Total Provincial	550	193
Provincial Chiefs	8 (all seven deputy Speakers plus speaker in Karnali Pradesh)	
Executive	63	9
Local Government	35221	14465
Municipality (including Metropolitan, Sub Metropolitan, and Municipalities)	Chief 293	13
	Deputy 293	229
Rural Municipality	Chief 460	12
	Deputy 460	335
	Ward Chairs 6713	69
	Ward members: 6713+6713= 13426	13303 (123 Dalit women members vacant)
Dalit Women Ward Member	(6,743)	6594 (123 vacant)
	Normal:	412

Source: Computed by author.

In the local level election 2022, a total number of 25 and 567 women won in Municipality's Mayoral/Deputy Mayoral positions respectively. Similarly, 69 women won the post of ward president, while 442 women won ward member post (other than the reserved women quota). From the reserved women's quota, a total of 6732 women and 6610 Dalit women were elected as ward members. Thus, a total of 14,445 women won the election. In this election, 1,35,409 candidates were registered on behalf of the party, of which 55,719 were women candidates. The comparison between the previous and current data on women's representation in Nepal's government bodies shows both progress and persisting challenges in gender inclusivity. While women constitute 34.1 per cent (114 out of 334) of the Federal Parliament, their representation stands at 33.4 per cent (92 out of 275), maintaining the trend from 2017 (32.7%) in Lower House which is officially called House of Representatives (HoR), and 37.3 per cent (22 out of 59) in the Upper House or National Assembly (NA). As far as Executive is concerned, women remain significantly underrepresented at only 12 per cent (3 out of 25), in the Federal Cabinet signalling the persistent male dominance in key decision-making roles. Women make up 35.1 per cent (193 out of 550) in all seven Provincial Assemblies. However, only 9 out of 63 (14.3%) are women in the provincial executive positions, which is similar to the Federal executive, indicates an ongoing struggle in leadership roles. However, out of 14 Provincial Chiefs (Speakers and Deputy Speakers), women hold 8 positions, showing some improvement in leadership at the provincial level.

Overall women representation in 753 local governments is relatively good in Nepal. A total of 14,465 women hold positions in local governance out of total 35,221 seats, making up 41.1 per cent presence there. However, the scenario looks like higher the position, lower the representation of women; out of 293 municipality chiefs, only 13 (4.4%) are women, and only 12 (2.6%) out of 460 rural municipality chiefs are women. Yes, there is 229 (78.2%) of the 293 deputy mayor positions and 335 (72.8%) of the 460 rural municipality vice-chair positions secured by women. But it is due to compulsory quota[3] to be ensured by political parties if they give candidacy in chief and deputy post. As there are 6,713 ward chairs to be elected, only 69 out of 6,713 (1%) are women. Again women could make up 13,303 (49.54%) ward members out of total 26852. In fact 13,426 should the actual reserved number of women ward members, but 123 positions of women (particularly Dalit women) remain vacant indicating a challenge in finding candidates or structural barriers preventing dalits from taking office. If the representation of women in the latest elections of 2017 and 2022 compared, the Federal (34.1%) and provincial levels (35.1%) have remained fairly stable in 2022 compared to 2017 (32.7%). However, women's presence in the executive remains disproportionately low at local government level, data is found a steady with limited progress in leadership roles. There is a slight increase from the past, but their presence in executive, i.e. mayor of municipalities, chief of rural municipalities and ward chair positions, remains minimal.

Nepal's gender quotas have been effective in increasing women's representation in legislative bodies, but women remain underrepresented in executive roles at all levels. The proportional representation (PR) system introduced in 2008 significantly contributed to improving women's presence in parliament. However, at the local level, while the number of elected women has increased, their roles are still largely confined to quota-based positions, not leadership roles. Dalit women's participation remains a challenge, as evidenced by the 123 unfilled reserved seats in ward committees. To achieve true gender equality, Nepal must move beyond quotas and address systemic barriers that prevent women from contesting and winning top executive positions.

Challenges

Nepal opted for mixed electoral system comprising Proportional Representation (PR) and First-past-the-post (FPTP). Since the

PR is a new system for South Asia, there is still a strong belief that it is not a system equivalent to FPTP. Largely, the perception behind MPs coming from PR is that they are not elected but nominees. Along with this, discriminatory practices, i.e. concerning the CDF etc. could be witnessed. Socio–economic challenges are a major barrier that hinders political participation and empowerment of women (Naz *et al.*, 2011). The extent differs across countries and regions depending on their social and economic context (Naz *et al.*, 2011). These factors include, but are not limited to: poverty, illiteracy, unemployment and gender stereotypes (Nwosu *et al.*, 2012). These factors are further compounded by male dominance in politics and the nature of political systems as it contributes significantly to the invisibility of women in the decision-making process (Kebede, 2020).

From an early age, children go through a process called gender socialization as they learn the culture's gender related rules and expectations (Vinney, 2024). They search for clues about gender and use them to form a constellation of gender cognitions, self-conceptions and stereotypes (Martin & Ruble, 2004). This socialization of young people and its gendered forms is a possible mediating factor in connecting gender and political ambition (Oliver, 2024). The process of gender political socialization lies at the not-yet theorized intersection of political socialization and gendered socialization (Bos *et al.*, 2021). The process of gendered socialization shapes behaviour for years to come, including during the time when young adults are making early career-related decisions (Bos *et al.*, 2022).While the effects of gender socialization can be direct, they can also operate indirectly (Eckes and Trautner, 2012). Gender-bias exists in the community, leading to the formation of gender stereotypes which are culturally shared and reinforced by social institutions and interactions like education, media, and family roles (Heilman, 2012). The existence of these norms is directives to the accepted and expected behaviour. The aspirations and participation of women who exhibit counter-stereotypical behaviour face resistance and backlash (Dworkin *et al.*, 2015).

Bos *et al.* (2022) developed and tested the "gendered political socialization theory," which is a new theory that describes the politics-specific gender socialization of young people. According to the theory, children infer that politics is for men and girls infer political roles with their defined gender roles and teach children to see politics as a male-dominated field. Women who make efforts to break the glass ceiling face leadership-specific bias (Cortina *et al.*, 2021). The glass ceiling, an artificial impediment and invisible barriers, that weighs against women's access to top decision-making positions in public or private regardless of domain (European Institute for Gender Equality, 2024). The gender bias includes negotiating both the 'First generation bias,' i.e. intentional bias created by society and organizations, and the 'second generation bias', i.e. unintentional bias (Grover, 2015). The second-generation bias is an often unconscious and subtle way that manifests in the unfair treatment of employed women in comparison to men (Batara *et al.*, 2018). Furthermore, the effects of compounded gender stereotypes are more evidently seen on a specific group of women, including women from indigenous backgrounds or minority groups, women with disabilities, women from lower caste and/or economic status, migrant women, and LGBTQIA+ women (UN Women, 2020). A glance at the history is enough to affirm the exclusion of women from the political sphere. The feminine characteristic is deemed unsuitable for holding leadership positions, hence affecting political participation (Campbell, 1989). The gender perceptions have always portrayed males as an ideal political figure, being assertive, rough, and rational. In comparison, women are expected to have a warm and caring nature (Lovenduski, 2005). This expectation sets women to fail against both the masculine as well as feminine standards as women are perceived as unlikeable if too assertive and incompetent if too feminine (Vedantam, 2016). The underrepresentation of women in politics is further exacerbated by the resistance of men to the participation of women. Women find greater acceptance only when they adhere to the patriarchal norms of the society (Cruz & Coronel, 2023).

In addition, the perception that men make better leaders than women significantly impacts electoral outcomes. The effects of these stereotypes are also seen on the discriminatory, sexist and biased media coverage that discourages women from entering politics (Trabelsi, 2023). This enforces further gender disparities in political representation (Franklin, 2004). Furthermore, this is compounded by misogyny and sexism that manifests in the social systems increasing the hostility against women simply based on their gender. This is done to restrict their participation in the political sphere (Manne, 2018). Cruz & Coronel (2023) analyzed Leni Robredo's activities, as a woman in politics who stood in the national elections of Philippines. This was done by the analysis of various posts and comments from selected Facebook pages containing gendered disinformation about her. The study concluded that longstanding societal, cultural, and political structures are not challenged, and this is why male leaders remain empowered to uphold the gender-based inequalities. In this way women in politics remain to be targets of threats, intimidation, and violence and scorn.

A survey conducted by the Pew Research Centre in 2023 states that Americans identified the need for women to prove themselves more than men as a major obstacle in politics. Additional barriers include gender discrimination, insufficient support from party leaders, societal reluctance to elect women to higher office, and a lack of early encouragement for women to assume leadership roles (Howowitz & Goddard, 2024). Most women are newcomers to the field of politics, and there is a need to establish themselves. This puts them at a disadvantage against the male politicians who are already well known. Women still have to fight the stereotype that they are less capable for roles traditionally expected to be for men. This disadvantage is even more prominent when a person who has already held a position in office does not need to fight for recognition (Gómez & D'Antonio, 2023).

Table 2.3: People's Views on Gender Roles and Gender Equality in Nepal

Indicator	**Year**	**Strongly agree**	**Somewhat agree**	**Somewhat disagree**	**Strongly disagree**
Women should not be encouraged to work outside the home	2022	2.5%	5.2%	16.4%	75.7%
It is not suitable for women to engage in politics		2.5%	4.8%	17.7%	74.9%
Women should not have control over her income, movement and other decision-making process		9.9%	11.1%	14.4%	64.4%
If a wife does not obey her husband, he has the right to punish her		3.9%	13.0%	17.3%	65.7%
When job opportunities are limited, men should have more right to a job		3.1%	8.8%	18.3%	69.5%
Male members of family other than husband (father in law, brother in law) have right to punish the daughter in law if she disobeys them		2.7%	8.6%	19.0%	69.6%

Source: SNP 2022.

The report titled *'A Survey of the Nepali People in 2022'*, conducted and published by the School of Arts, Kathmandu University, also shows a similar trend, where a certain percentage of people still believe that women remain at home with traditional household chores; according to the data collected from sampled 7056 households in Nepal, more than 7 per cent respondents state saying it is unsuitable for women to engage in politics. While 21 per cent Nepalis were off the view that women should not have control over their income, movement, and other decision-making processes, almost 17 per cent respondent encourages a husband to have his right to punish wife if he does not obey him. Still 12 per cent Nepali want men to get job opportunity as and when there is limited job opportunity. In Nepal, the gender attitudes are ingrained in the social lives of people, where family is the primary setting for the transmission of gender status. The decision-making at both the domestic and national level is dominated by patriarchy and it extends to and intersects with forms of discrimination beyond gender (Upreti *et al.*, 2020; Pyakurel, 2023). A common misconception is that males are patriarchal thinkers, and this is not necessarily true. While most people continue to see men as the problem of patriarchy, it is important to understand that patriarchal thinking and action may be as ingrained in women as in men (Gavroche, 2023). While the majority of the people are of the view that women should be empowered to participate in politics, some still perpetuate sexist attitudes and beliefs about specific issues related to gender in politics (Kwame, 2023).

Both religious/traditional practices and culture have contributed to the creation of an environment that favours the preference for sons in Nepal. Sons are valued for carrying on the lineage and performing the ancestral worship, which is believed to bring peace to the deceased parents. Sons are also seen as a parent's support for old age. In addition, having a son increases a woman's autonomy in the household decisions (Adhikari,

2023). The preference that begins here extends its effects on other spheres of life, including access to education, work, and domestic responsibilities. Even though the Constitution of Nepal guarantees free basic education for all, the reality is that boys are clearly favoured when it comes to education (Maharjan, 2023). The data from the government suggests that even today most parents send their sons to private schools for better education, while enrolling their daughters in government schools. All this occurs despite parents recognizing the importance of educating daughters. This occurs due to the reluctance to invest in a daughter as a result of patriarchal attitudes. Furthermore, especially in Madhesh, this problem is compounded by poverty and household responsibilities and early marriages that prevent many girls from attending schools.

Education, in this regard, is seen as a privilege in the case of girls. This issue, rooted in the patriarchal thinking pattern of society, severely impacts the economic condition of women in the future, as education ensures better chances of employability. This increases a woman's financial independence and economic stability, which leads to their empowerment (Kamau, 2021). This is further confirmed highlighting the importance of plugging the gap between higher education and employment to resolve the quest of women's declining employment. Education is a key to empowering women's participation in politics and civic life. Educational inequality limits women's participation in politics and decision-making, therefore, reducing diversity in leadership. Additionally, it also limits women's ability to organize and advocate for their rights effectively (Singh, 2024).

Economic condition is a major determinant in the level of participation of women in politics. While the preference of son poses a major disadvantage for girls in education, that has its effects on employability and income, the problem is not limited to this sphere. In Nepal, like in many parts of South Asia, women receive a smaller share of property in comparison to men (Bhandary, 2017). They also frequently experience inequality in terms of access to healthcare and nutrition, limited chances to generate revenue and little authority over productive resources (Acharya *et al.*, 2010). These issues, coupled with traditional household responsibilities and limited access to resources, reinforce women as dependent and vulnerable and perpetuate discrimination, exploitation and domination (Adhikari and Sharman, 2022; International Labour Organization, 2018).

The laws in Nepal have historically been discriminatory towards women. This is also applicable in terms of property rights (Subedi, 2024). '*Manusmriti*' is an authoritative text in the Hindu religion that is believed to have been written by the first mythical man and lawgiver Manu. The text outlines the set of duties that each individual must follow based on their social caste and stage in life (Encyclopedia Britannica, 2024). The '*Manusmriti*' also outlines specific guidelines regarding women's right to property through the concept of '*stridhan*' that translates to women's property in English. '*Stridhan*' encompasses various types of property that women can own independently. It includes the gifts by women from her family, relatives, and husband during and after marriage (Jha, 1920). However, on the other hand, it also states that a wife and a slave have no property and should use the belongings of the person to whom they belong, referring to the father, husband, and son (Subedi, 2024). This has had a lasting impact on the social construction and norming as well as the traditional property rights of women. It established women as secondary owners of property (Razdan & Sharma, 2022). In the context of Nepal, there were no clear provisions regarding property rights for women in 1975 (IOM, 2016). Before the amendment of Civil Code (Muluki Ain) in the year 1997, women were not considered eligible to claim parental property. While this amendment allowed unmarried women to claim property after they cross 25 years of age, it was conditional as the property would have to be returned if they decided to get married.

To date, the majority of women do not have land ownership certificates and rarely get involved in productive activities. They heavily depend on the male members of the family to meet their needs (Rimal, 2023). According to the National Statistics office (2024) the data from the National Population and Housing Census of 2011 state that women enjoy ownership over land and property in only 19.71 per cent of the households in the country although the Government of Nepal has introduced measures to help women gain ownership over land and property. The efforts include a 25 to 50 per cent tax discount on land registration in the name of women and 35 per cent tax exemption for single woman and joint land registration in the name of husband and wife with a fee of Rs. 100. This shows that women's ownership to property is still limited (IOM, 2016). This is further supported by IOM Nepal Chief of Mission, Maurizio Busatti, who highlights the irony that even though women make up 51.5 per cent of Nepal's population and 75 per cent work primarily in agriculture, many do not own the land that they have been farming in for years (IOM, 2016).

Groups that occupy a more marginal position in the society have fewer forms of capital and usually find the costs of running for office prohibitive. Even when they run, they have a harder time being elected. Women fall into this group as a consequence of the persistent existence of the public/private gender divide, which relegates women primarily to the private sphere (Feo *et al.*, 2021). This significantly affects women's participation in politics. Research indicates that granting property inheritance rights to women can enhance their political participation. A study conducted in India found that when women have equal inheritance rights, there is a rise in female candidacy and an increase in the likelihood for electoral success of women (Nandwani, 2024). Despite the legal advancements, the challenge persists as the cultural norms have been deeply ingrained. Women's rights to inherit, own and control property are primarily determined by the values and norms that are socially acceptable in addition to the mechanisms of intra-household decision-making and distribution (Acharya, 2021). This calls for a corresponding shift in social attitudes as legal provisions alone are insufficient (Dhungana, 2021).

The economic vulnerability is further aggravated by the domestic and unpaid care work that women are involved in on a day-to-day basis. This is one of the main reasons for lack of progress towards achieving gender equality. As per the definition of The International Labour Organization (2018) set by the 19th International Conference of Labour Statistics (ICLS) in the year 2013 and the International Classification of Activities for time use Statistics (ICATUS) in 2016. Unpaid care work is non-remunerated work carried out to sustain the well-being, health and maintenance of other individuals in a household or the community. These activities are often considered to be a part of women's responsibilities. In the context of Nepal, women's work is largely confined to the household and is unaccounted for by both the family and the state (Forum for Women, Law and Development, 2023). This connects to women's political participation as the disproportionate burden of time and unpaid care work results in negative social and economic consequences for women and limits their opportunities for education, career advancement, and political participation (UN Women, 2022).

Conclusion

This chapter emphasized the complex ways in which women of Nepal have navigated political systems, often facing the dual challenge of gender discrimination and political marginalization.

Despite having these challenges, women continue to fight back as powerful agents of change, pushing for policies that address not only gender equality but also broader social, economic, and environmental concerns. This very impact of women in politics is undeniable, as they bring unique perspectives and experiences that often lead to more inclusive and holistic governance. The journey of women in politics has been through many challenges and it reflects both progress and setbacks in the ongoing pursuit of gender equality. Throughout history women have fought against many societal norms, institutional barriers, and cultural limitations to assert their rights in the arena of politics. While significant strides have been made in many parts of the world, the journey remains incomplete for Nepal, with women still underrepresented in leadership roles, policy-making positions, and political decision-making processes.

For Nepal to completely realize the potential of its legal provisions, a more inclusive and supportive political culture must be incorporated in the system. This chapter argued that continued efforts are the requirements to ensure that women's political empowerment is not only a matter of legal representation but also a reflection of genuine participation and leadership. Furthermore, Nepal must embrace new narratives of inclusive politics that extend beyond mere quotas, creating a political system that effectively reflects the diverse voices and needs of its population. The path towards gender equality in politics is quite long, but with sustained commitment and transformation, Nepal can set a powerful example for its neighbouring countries and beyond. The idea of progressiveness is dynamic and constantly evolving. What appears impossible now may be possible within a decade or longer, as humans continue to push boundaries and expand the scope of what is achievable. A decade ago, the idea of a woman leading a country or holding a high position politically might have seemed out of reach especially in Nepal. But today,

Nepal welcomes more women in positions of power than ever before. This is a result of legal reforms, such as constitutional provisions that mandate gender quotas, as well as changing societal attitudes that recognize women's capabilities as leaders.

> "Something which we think is impossible now is not impossible in another decade."
>
> —Constance Baker Motley

NOTES

1. Pyakurel, U.P. (2011). The vision of the Jana andolan II for a future of Nepal. in Upteti *State and democracy in Nepal: Emerging paradigm, issues and challenges.* Delhi: Kalinga Publications.
2. The Constitution of Nepal, 2015, Constituent Assembly Secretariat, Singhdurbar.
3. The Section 17(4) of the Local Level Election Act 2017 states that a political party must fill a woman in either the mayor/chairperson or deputy mayor/vice-chairperson position. It is also legally mandatory to appoint a female ward member and a Dalit female ward member at the ward level.

REFERENCES

Adhikari, I. (2006). "Women in Conflict: The Gender Perspective of Maoist Insurgency" in Lok Raj Baral (ed.), *Nepal: Facets of Maoist Insurgency*, Delhi: Adroit Publishers, pp. 60-85.

Adhikari, I. (2008). "Democracy and Problems of Democratization in Nepal." In V.A. Pai Panandikar and Rahul Tripathi (eds.), *Towards Freedom in South Asia: Democratization, Peace and Regional Cooperation*, New Delhi: Konark Publishers, pp. 65-80.

Adhikari, I. (2013). "Nepal: Women in Army (Research Report)", Kathmandu: SNV Nepal.

Adhikari, I. & Pyakurel, U. (January-December 2015). "Coping with Disaster: Nepal's Devastating Earthquake and State Response." *Nepali Journal of Contemporary Studies*, *XV*(1-2).

Adhikari, I, Pyakurel, U. & Ulvila, M. (2010). "Decades of Political Upheaval in Nepal: People's Movement and People's War" in Tove Selin & Kristiina Vainio (eds.), *Oligarchy by Elections: The State of Democracy in Asia*, Helsinki: LIKE and Suomen Rauhanpuolustajat.

Acharya, C. (2021). "Parental Property Equal Right Policy of Nepal: A Focus Group Discussion of Students of Law Faculty of Kathmandu". *Research Nepal.*

Acharya, D.R., Bell, J.S., Simkhada, P., Van Teijlingen, E.R. & Regmi, P.R. (2010). "Women's autonomy in household decision-making: a demographic study in Nepal". *Reproductive Health, 7*(1). https://doi.org/10.1186/1742-4755-7-15

Adhikari, R. & Sharma, J. (2022). "Les riches possibilities de l"étude genrée du changement social au Népal". *European Bulletin.*

Adhikari, S. (2023, November 21). "Examining the Role of Female Education on son Preference among Nepalese Women". *International Institute for Applied Systems Analysis.* Retrieved from https://pure.iiasa.ac.at/id/eprint/19207/1/WP-23-010.pdf

Batara, M.A., Ngo, J.M., Sy, K.A. & Erasga, D. (2018). "Second Generation Gender bias: The Effects of the Invisible bias among Mid-Level Women Managers". *Asia-Pacific Social Science Review, 10*(2).

Bhandary, S. (2017). *Understanding Some Cultural Barriers to Women's Access to Education: A Case Study in Rural Nepal.* [MA Thesis, MF Norwegian School of Theology]. Retrieved from https://mfopen.mf.no/mf-xmlui/bitstream/handle/11250/2458602/AVH5035-1509-Bhandary-navn.pdf?isAllowed=y&sequence=1

Bos, A.L., Greenlee, J.S., Holman, M.R., Oxley, Z.M. & Lay, J.C. (2021). "This One's for the Boys: How Gendered Political Socialization Limits girls' Political Ambition and Interest". *American Political Science Review, 116*(2): 484-501. Retrieved from https://doi.org/10.1017/s0003055421001027

Campbell, K. (1989). *Man cannot Speak for Her.* London: Greenwood Press.

Cortina, C., Rodríguez, J. & González, M.J. (2021). "Mind the Job: The Role of Occupational Characteristics in Explaining Gender Discrimination". *Social Indicators Research, 156*(1), 91-110. Retrieved from https://doi.org/10.1007/s11205-021-02646-2

Cruz, S.D. & Coronel, F.N. (2023). *More Than a Woman: A Critical Discourse Analysis of Cyber Misogyny towards Women in Politics on Facebook* [University of the Philippines System].

Dhungana, R.K. (2014). "Nepali Hindu Women's Thorny Path to Liberation". *DOAJ (DOAJ: Directory of Open Access Journals)*. Retrieved from https://doi.org/10.9771/104

Dworkin, S.L., Fleming, P.J. & Colvin, C.J. (2015). "The Promises and Limitations of Gender-transformative Health Programming With Men: Critical Reflections from the Field". *Culture, Health & Sexuality, 17*(Sup 2): 128-143. Retrieved from https://doi.org/10.1080/13691058.2015.1035751

Eckes, T. & Trautner, H.M. (2012). "Developmental Social Psychology of Gender: an Integrative Framework". in *Psychology Press eBooks* (pp. 17-46). Retrieved from https://doi.org/10.4324/9781410605245-7

European Institute for Gender Equality. (2024, December 10). *Glass ceiling*. Retrieved from https://eige.europa.eu/publications-resources/thesaurus/terms/1099?language_content_entity=en

Feo, F., Fiorelli, C. & Piccio, D.R. (2021). "Gendered Patterns in Candidates Campaign Fundraising: The Case of Italy". *International Political Science Review, 44*(1): 43-58. Retrieved from https://doi.org/10.1177/01925121211049106

Franklin, B. (2004). "Packaging Politics: Political Communications in Britian's Media Democracy" (2nd edn.). London: Arnold.

Gavroche, J. (2023, March 7). *Bell Hooks: Understanding Patriarchy*. Autonomies. Retrieved from https://autonomies.org/2023/03/bell-hooks-understanding-patriarchy/?

Gómez, C.P. & D'Anutono, F.R. (2023, January 27). *How Unequal Access to Funds Hinders Women's Participation in Politics*. GLOBSEC. Retrieved from https://www.globsec.org/what-we-do/commentaries/how-unequal-access-funds-hinders-womens-participation-politics#_ftn2

Grover, V. (2015). "Second Generation Gender Bias: Invisible Barriers Holding Women Back in Organizations." *International Journal of Applied Research, 1*(4):1-4.

Gupta, A.K. (2019). "Significance of Girl Education: Parents Perception from Rural Madhesh of Nepal." *Journal of Management and Development Studies, 29*: 61-68.

Heilman, M.E. (2012). "Gender Stereotypes and Workplace Bias". *Research in Organizational Behaviour, 32*: 113-135. Retrieved from https://doi.org/10.1016/j.riob.2012.11.003

ILO. (2018). "Care Work and Care Jobs for the Future of Decent Work". *International Labour Organization.* Retrieved from https://www. ilo.org/wcmsp5/groups/public/---dgreports/---dcomm/---publ/documents/publication/wcms_633135.pdf\

International Organization for Migration. (2016). "Barriers to Women's Land and Property Access and Ownership in Nepal". in *IOM.* Retrieved from https://www.iom.int/sites/g/files/tmzbdl486/files/our_work/DOE/LPR/Barriers-to-Womens-Land-Property-Access-Ownership-in-Nepal.pdf

Jha, G. (1920). *Manusmriti Verse 9.194 [Strīdhana (Property of the Wife)].* Retrieved from https://www.wisdomlib.org/hinduism/book/manusmriti-with-the-commentary-of-medhatithi/d/doc201574.html?utm

Kebede, A. (2020). "Opportunities and Challenges of Women's Participation in Decision-making at Local Government Administration: The Case of Debre-Tabor City Administration, South Gondar Zone, Amhara Regional State, Ethiopia". *Advance.* Retrieved from https://doi.org/10.31124/advance.10048160.v3

Kwame, P. (2023, June). *Public Perceptions about Women in Politics in Ghana.* Figshare. Retrieved from https://figshare.com/articles/online_resource/PUBLIC_PERCEPTIONS_ABOUT_WOMEN_IN_POLITICS_IN_GHANA-_Philip_Kwame_Benson_pdf/23556633?file=4132803

Lovenduski, J. (2005). *Feminizing Politics.* Cambridge: Polity.

Maharjan, R. (2023, December 2). *Nepalese Girls Still Don't Have Equal Educational Opportunities | D+C - Development + Cooperation.* Retrieved from https://www.dandc.eu/en/article/lives-young-women-nepal-are-determined-traditions-and-taboos-even-though-constitution

Manne, K. (2018). *Down Girl: The Logic of Misogyny,* 1st edn. New York: Oxford University.

Martin, C.L. & Ruble, D. (2004). "Children's Search for Gender Cues". *Current Directions in Psychological Science, 13*(2): 67-70. Retrieved from https://doi.org/10.1111/j.0963-7214.2004.00276.x

Nandwani, B. &. R.P. (2024). "Property Inheritance Rights and Female Political Participation in India". *ideas.repec.org*. Retrieved from https://ideas.repec.org/p/zbw/glodps/1517.html

Naz, A., Rehman, H., and Alam, A. (2011). "Gender and Development: Socio-cultural, Economic, Religious and Political Impediments in Women's Empowerment and Gender Development (A Case Study of Malakand Division KPK, Pakistan)". *Peshawar University Teachers Association Journal* (PUTAJ), ISSN 2219-245X. Vol 18-2011. p. 45.

Nwosu, E., Nchedo, O. & Onigbo, A.N. (December 2012). *International Journal of Environment, Ecology, Family and Urban Studies* (IJEEFUS). *2*(4): 29-36.

Oliver, T. (2024, September 21). *Socialized for Success: Exploring the Relationship between Gender and Political Ambition among Undergraduates*. LSE Undergraduate Political Review. Retrieved from https://upr.lse.ac.uk/articles/107

Paudel, P.K. & Pyakurel, U. (2018) "Untold Truth of foreign Labour Migration and Increasing Aspiration within Youth in Nepal," *Cultural and Religious Studies*, *6*(8): 479-488.

Pyakurel, U.P. (2018). "Restrictive Labour Migration Policy on Nepalese Women and Consequences", *Sociology and Anthropology*, *6*(8): 650-656.

Pyakurel, U. (July 2006). "Women in Armed Conflict: Lesson to be learn from the Telengana People's Movement," *Contribution to the Nepalese Studies*, *33*(3).

Pyakurel, U. (March 2005). "Micro-credit: The Strong Tool for Women Empowerment and Poverty Alleviation in Nepal," *Nepali Journal of Contemporary Studies*.

Pyakurel, U. (January-July 2006). "Identity Politics in Nepal," *Research Journal*.

Pyakurel, U. (2007). *Maoist Movement in Nepal: A Sociological Perspective*, New Delhi: Adroit Publisher

Pyakurel, U. (September 2009). "Food Globalization and its Impacts: What Development Contributes to the Villages of Nepal?" *Nepali Journal of Contemporary Studies*, *IX*(2)

Pyakurel, U. (2011). "Migration and Changing Family Structure in Nepal" in Wako Asato and Hideko Nakata (eds.). *Migration: Global Reconstruction of Intimate and Public Spheres*, Kyoto: Kyoto University Global COE Programme.

Pyakurel, U. (January 2015). "Nepal: from Caste Society to Multicultural one", *Reflection. 4*(1).

Pyakurel, U. (2021). *Reproduction of Inequality and Social Exclusion: A Study of Dalits in a Caste Society, Nepal.* Brussels: Springer

Pyakurel, U. (2022). "Inner-party Democracy in Nepal: A Study of Major Political Parties in Parliament", in C.D. Bhatta (ed.). *Rooting Nepal's Democratic Spirit.* Lalitpur, Nepal: Friedrich-Ebert-Stiftung Nepal office.

Pyakurel, U. (2023). "Youth in Local Level Planning Processes: Review of Local Impressions". *Social Inquiry,* 5(1).

Pyakurel, U. (2024). "Nepali Way to dealing with the concept of Green and Circular Economy: Some anecdotes", in Preville Claudius & Uddhab Pyakurel (eds.). *Green and Circular Economy in Nepali context.* Kathmandu: EU-Nepal Trade and Investment Programme (TIP), Investment Support Facility (ISF) & Kathmandu University Center for Contemporary Studies (KU-NCCS).

Pyakurel, U., Bhola P. Bhattarai, Sanot Adhikari & Swasti Shrestha (January-June 2017). "Youth Involvement in Community based forest management in Nepal". *Nepali Journal of Contemporary Studies. XVII*(1).

Pyakurel, U. (September 2009). "Food Globalization and its Impacts: What Development Contributes to the Villages of Nepal?" *Nepali Journal of Contemporary Studies, IX*(2).

Pyakurel, U., Khakurel, P. & Singh, A.R. (2022). "Higher Education in Nepal during COVID-19: Prospects and Challenges", in Netswera et.al. (eds.) *Higher Education and the COVID-19 Pandemic.* USA: Center for International Higher Education at Boston College, pp. 213-228.

Rimal, J. (2023, September 20). "Improve Women's Role in Decision-making." *Gorakha Patra.* Retrieved from https://risingnepaldaily.com/news/32808

Singh, R. (2024, December 13). "Educational Inequality of Women: Causes and Consequences: OPED." *Eurasia Review.* Retrieved from https://www.eurasiareview.com/13122024-educational-inequality-of-women-causes-and-consequences-oped/

Subedi, S. (2024). *Historical Progression of Women's Property Right in Nepal: Muluki Ain 1910 to Country Civil Code 2074.* Available at SSRN 4787711.

SOA (2022). *A Survey of the Nepali People in 2022.* Lalitpur: School of Arts.

Trabelsi, M. (2023b, March 3). "Women in Politics and the Media." *International IDEA.* Retrieved from https://www.idea.int/news/women-politics-and-media

UN Women. (2022). "Invisible" Violence, Visible Harms: Violence against Women in Politics in Nepal: The experience of locally elected representatives. In *asiapacific.unwomen.org.* United Nations Entity for Gender Equality and the Empowerment of Women (UN Women).

UN Women. (2024). *Mexico.* UN Women: Americas and the Caribbean. Retrieved November 29, 2024, from https://lac.unwomen.org/en/donde-estamos/mexico

Upreti, B.C. and Pyakurel, U.P. (eds.) (2012). *Contemporary Nepal: Reflections on Emerging Political and Social Issues and Trends.* Delhi: Kalinga Publications.

Vinney, C. (2024, August 13). *What is Gender Socialization? Definition and Examples.* Thought Co. Retrieved from https://www.thoughtco.com/gender-socialization-definition-examples-4582435

3

From No Reservation to Reservation

The Welfare Legacy of the First Phase of Women's Movement after Independence

Sukanya Sarkar Sasmal and *Indranil Chattopadhyay*

Introduction

Before independence, the women's movement and the freedom struggle were limited to advocating for women's suffrage, right to education, and welfare. Hence, Prime Minister Jawaharlal Nehru's initial ideas were inadequate in addressing the broader spectrum of women's rights and concerns. When researching the women's movement, the years from Independence until the 1970s are considered the initial phase. Researchers draw attention to the influence of the women's movement leaders on National Congress leaders, highlighting their active involvement in policy-making processes through the implementation of pre-Independence legacy or welfare principles into practice. As they had previously been involved in the liberation fight, the women's movement leaders could actively collect information and influence the National Congress leaders. The predominance of affluent urban middle-class women in the early women's movement and their focus on constitutional rights made it customary for lower-class women to remain unnoticed. The prioritization of constitutional rights reflected the determination and influence of the women's movement during that period. It was their most outstanding achievement, as women in many other countries had to fight for a long time to achieve these rights. The All-India Women's Conference (AIWC), the most significant association representing the women's movement in modern India, did not consider reservations necessary to bring about gender equality. The movement's early stages have been intentionally overlooked in the academic discussion on women's reservation in India. The essay aims to shed light on the often-overlooked early stages of the women's movement in India and how its efforts laid the groundwork for subsequent advancements. Understanding this historical context is essential for comprehending the trajectory and achievements of the women's movement in modern India.

Major Aim(s)

When researching the women's movement, the years from Independence until the 1970s are considered the initial phase. The movement's early stages have been intentionally overlooked in the academic discussion on women's reservation in India. This chapter explores how the women's movement's stance towards reservation transformed with time.

Theoretical Framework

Radhika Kumar divides the women's movement in India into three phases. The first phase was 1850-1930, when the social reform movement was a precursor to the women's movement. According to her, 1919-1939, or the period between the two world wars, can be considered the second phase as the issue of women's suffrage and legal rights became dominant. The inclusion of women in the national movement from 1930-1947 led to the transition from their image of being others' responsibility to the image of active agents or active members. Radhika felt that women's issues were somewhat overshadowed and lost their importance in the larger social development concept after Independence. She noted that the women's movement gained momentum since the 1970s. When the 'emergency' was withdrawn in 1977, several women's groups developed and prepared the way for the autonomous women's movement. Radhika Kumar notes that feminism in India has seen the focus shift from the needs to women's rights. In other words, she has accepted that there was no influential women's movement until 1970 (Kumar, *The Women's Movement in India*, 2015: 425).

Methodology

This chapter involves meticulous original research work based on archival records, Constitutional laws, and reports of various Committees and Commissions related to women. In addition to these primary sources, a large number of research papers and relevant books have been used as secondary sources. The use of qualitative methods has allowed for the identification of the main pattern of thinking or theme that prevailed in a particular period regarding reservations for women and its evolution with time, along with debate and contradictory ideas. *This chapter relies on historical research methods, i.e. the directed search for relevant data, narrations, and descriptions extracted from the writings have been presented thematically and as far as possible in chronological order.* Primarily, this study has investigated the topic of women's reservation in the context of the progress of the women's movement, ensuring a comprehensive and reliable exploration of the subject.

In our efforts, we aim to integrate both newer research findings and references from that era into our project. The All-India Women's Conference (AIWC) played a crucial part in furthering the women's movement in post-Independence India. We have used Aparna Basu and Bharati Roy's work on AIWC to some extent. Their book frequently refers the AIWC's journal, "Roshni," and so we have relied on the records from the organization's Delhi headquarters and archived sources. Prominent journals have referenced the writings of contemporary leaders of the women's movement such as Vina Majumdar and Renuka Ray. In the same way, only the most relevant works by Madhu Kishwar and Nivedita Menon have been used. This integration of newer research findings ensures that this study is up-to-date and comprehensive, providing the audience with a well-rounded understanding of the topic.

Planning for Women's Development: Early Phase

Before Independence, the women's movement and the freedom struggle were limited to advocating for women's suffrage, right to education, and welfare. Hence, Prime Minister Jawaharlal Nehru's initial ideas were inadequate in addressing the broader spectrum of women's rights and concerns. No report on the status of women was produced during Nehru's tenure. Instead, there was a belief that the socialist model of equality, democracy, secularism and modernization would be able to end all forms of discrimination against women, including caste and religious bigotry (Ghosal, 2005: 799). Nehru felt that women's organizations should remain within the larger political and economic context. By 1936, he observed AIWC (All-India Women's Conference): "functioning in the air" and warned that in the future, they would be "functioning in little coteries and drawing room parties" (Kullar, 2016: 106). In 1939, a sub-committee under the National Planning Committee prepared a report on the role of girls in a planned economy. Several women's organizations and Congress leaders participated in it including Laxmibai Rajwade, Sarojini Naidu, Vijayalakshmi Pandit, Hansa Mehta, Taraben Premchand, Begum Shahnawaz, Begum Hamid Ali and many more. On August 14, 1947, after Nehru's historic Independence speech, Hansa Mehta handed over the tricolour flag to the Chairman of the Constituent Assembly, Dr. Rajendra Prasad, saying that the first national flag was a gift from the women of India (Nair, 2018: 21).

After Independence in 1948, the government published a report on the role of women in the economy, edited by K.T. Shah. This report contained many revolutionary proposals. For example, a woman worker would have full rights over her income. No woman shall be dismissed from work for marriage or childbearing. A woman should not be excluded from participation in work because the working environment or hours are unsuitable for her. However, the emphasis should be placed on changing unfavourable conditions (Banerjee, 1998: WS-3). Emphasis was placed on the necessity of acquiring equal skills for men compared to women in household chores. But hardly any mechanism was adopted to implement these proposals.

Welfare Legacy

Researchers draw attention to the influence of the women's movement leaders on National Congress leaders through the implementation of pre-Independence legacy or welfare principles into practice. As they had previously been involved in the liberation fight, the women's movement leaders could actively collect information and influence the National Congress leaders. One of the aspects of women and child development planning before Independence was an emphasis on birth control planning. This demand was raised in the Lucknow session of the All-India Women's Conference in the 1930s and again from 1950 onwards, family planning became an essential subject in the First and Second Plans under the pressure of Family Planning Association of India. The Community Development Programmes emphasized women's motherhood and family issues. By 1950, the government had initiated the improvement project through the 'Mahila Mandal' programme (Kullar, 2016: 113). Social Welfare, Family Welfare, Health, Education, Women and Child Welfare departments which were less important from the aspects of power, status, decision-making, influence, facilities and allotted funds, came to be known as 'women departments', usually given to women ministers (Srivastava, 2011: 414). After Independence another major ground of welfare activities was refugee rehabilitation. At its Madras Conference (December 1947 to January 1948), the AIWC made proposals for refugees and played an essential role in refugees' resettlement. Rameshwari Nehru and Hannah Sen were in-charge of the Women's Wing of the Union Government's Ministry of Rehabilitation. The initiative of Kamaladevi Chattopadhyay and Kitty Siva Rau to form co-operative societies in Delhi made it possible to build permanent homes for homeless people (Roy Bharati, 1990: 102).

Constitution of India and Women

The prioritization of Constitutional rights reflected the determination and influence of the women's movement. It was their most outstanding achievement, as women in many other countries had to fight for a long time to achieve these rights. The AIWC, the most significant association representing the women's movement in modern India, did not consider reservations necessary to bring about gender equality. Since Independence, the Government has made concerted efforts towards removing various gender biases to ensure that women enjoy equal status with men, in the real sense as enshrined in the Constitution of India (Sreekumar, 2006: 620). The Constitution of India called for ending legal discrimination against women in employment and public places. Article 14 of the Constitution guarantees the equal rights and protection of men and women in the eyes of the law. Sections 1 and 2 of Article 15 prohibit any discrimination based on sex, and Section 3 has said that special care should be taken to protect the rights of women and children (2019: 1). Women are entitled to equal opportunities as per Article 16. The right to equal living conditions and equal pay for equal work has been ensured per Section 39. Even the preamble of the Constitution of India guarantees women's rights, it is said that according to the constitutional law, women will enjoy equal rights with men so that they can take an influential role in the administration of the country (2019: 1).

No to Reservation

In 1950, the AIWC's demands were included in the Constitution of independent India (Kullar, 2016: 112). Since the colonial period, the Women Indian Association and the National Council of Women in India demanded equality of livelihood for all citizens, adult suffrage, the right of women to participate in elections on equal terms with men and above all, no reservation for women (Nair, 2018: 24). In the colonial period the Indian National Congress objected to special electoral rights for Muslims, Sikhs and Christians offered by the British Government. In the 1930s, the AIWC and the WIA followed Congress especially Gandhi, who rejected the reserved seats. The major women's organisations opposed similar proposals for women. Though other Women Organisations associated with political parties other than Congress held a different position. Begum

Shahnawaz, a Muslim activist, supported reservation of women. Along with Mrs. Subbarayan, she submitted a memorandum in favour of reserve seats for women when the Congress boycotted the First Round Table Conference on constitutional reform in 1930. All leading women organisations denounced Shahnawaz and Subbarayan's effort. In 1931, in a joint memorandum of the AIWC, NCWI (National Council of Women in India) and WIA addressed to the British Prime Minister, Sarojini Naidu and others, at the time of the Second Round Table Conference, opined that—"to seek any form of preferential treatment would be to violate the integrity of the universal demand of Indian women for absolute equality of political status" (Dutoya, 2016: 47). Rajkumari Amrit Kaur, on behalf of AIWC to Lord Lothian, Head of the Joint Parliamentary Committee in London on the question of Legislative Reservation, conveyed the message, "By merit and merit alone do we wish to find—and we are confident we shall find—a place in Councils and Federal Legislatures of our country." AIWC demanded "Equality and no privileges, a fair field and no favour" (Nair, 2018: 25).

Muthulakshmi Reddi of the WIA opposed to reservation, even for lower castes, for the sake of a common platform. In spite of their protest against reservation, the Government of India Act of 1935 granted women reserved seats in the provincial and central legislatures. All leading women organisations including AIWC protested that—"the communal award will divide us, Indian women" (Laura, 1999: 61). Sarojini Naidu, as well as Renuka Ray, in July 1947, even before India declared its independence, discarded the reservation of seats in the name of the ideal of equality. Renuka Roy recalled the fact that since inception, the women movement in India opposed reservation (Dutoya, 2016: 50). However, later, in 1955, the Kaka Kalelkar Committee first recommended that women be designated as a 'backward class' and so reservation for them was essential.

Failure of Laws

The Constitution, when enacted, theoretically guaranteed equality to women. In reality, the issue of women was considered so trivial that the right of men and women to equal pay for the same work was enshrined under the Constitution's 'Directive Principles of State Policy' and had not been turned into law. Finally, in 1975, the 'Equal Remuneration Act' was passed. (Kullar, 2016: 107). The Minimum Wages Act of 1948 stated that there could be no discrimination between men and women regarding wages for the same work. For women's safety, The Factories Act of 1948 restricted them from moving machinery and lifting heavy weights. However, there was no system to ensure these regulations were followed correctly. Article 39 of the Directive Principles of the Constitution prohibits all forms of exploitation of women and children. The Prevention of Immoral Traffic in Women and Girls Act was enacted in 1956 to implement this (Lovely, 2004: 257-258). The 1956 Act against the use or trafficking of women or children for sex or other purposes was amended and re-enacted in 1986 (Lovely, 2004: 245). Thus, the failure of the earlier Act was proved beyond doubt.

In the 1950s, during the pre-election period, the Hindu Code Bill became a point of contention among Hindu leaders, along with Prime Minister Jawaharlal Nehru. The purpose of this Bill was to unify, codify, and modernize the laws relating to marriage, divorce, inheritance, ownership of property, and related matters. The context of this Bill was the growing dissatisfaction with the social and legal handicaps of women in Indian society. Many laws were vague and, in many cases, contradictory (John, 1952: 174-175). During the long debate on the Hindu Code Bill, many liberal people and women's organizations supported it. The Bill created controversy not only within Parliament but also in the public sphere. The President of the All-India Women's Conference, Jankibai Joshi, did not favour changing the personal law of Hindus (Sinha, 2012: 94). In 1952, Renuka Roy said that although the Constitution called for the end of gender discrimination and equality, there was a storm of irrational protest when the Hindu Code Bill made social laws on marriage and property the same regardless of gender (Ray, 1952: 268-269). However, the Muslim women's movement is believed to have developed by the 1980s after the *Shah Banu case*. Nevertheless, practically, the Muslim Satyashodaka Mandal, formed in Maharashtra in 1960, contemplated the problems of Muslim women. They marched in Bombay demanding reform of Muslim law and abolition of triple *talaq* in 1966. Apart from that they wanted a uniform law that applied to all.

In the 1960s and 1970s, some of the major enactments passed by the Government to eradicate social evils were the Dowry Prohibition Act of 1961, the Maternity Benefits Act of 1961, the Medical Termination of Pregnancy Act of 1971 and Child Marriage Restraint Act of 1976. A Committee was formed by the Indian government on abortion, and, Masuma Begum and Avabai Bomanji Wadia, members of AWIC, gave a call for liberalizing abortion laws and the law was introduced in 1972 (Roy Bharati, 1990: 110). As the year 1975 was declared as the World Population Year, AIWC conducted various programmes and played an important role in sensitizing village women about family planning (Roy Bharati, 1990: 112). Since 1959, it has followed the initiatives taken by UNO to protect children's rights (Roy Bharati, 1990: 104). Madhu Kishwar claimed that it was comparatively simple to pass laws supporting women in India as compared to many other countries. Without much opposition, the rights to abortion, equal pay for equal work, and maternity benefits—all of which the women's movement in the West had to fight for decades to achieve—were adopted in India (Kishwar, 1996: 2867). Nivedita Menon objected to this, stating that the Medical Termination of Pregnancy Bill was brought up in Parliament in 1971 as a population control measure, and that was the extent of the debate. Contrarily, abortion was being explored as a strategy to achieve slower population increase rather than as a matter of women's autonomy over their bodies (Menon, 2000: 3837).

Women Mass Movement: 1950s to 1970s

Communist women, however, were not optimistic about the terms of the Constitution or the Five-Year Plan. Because of that, in 1954, Vivla Farooqui and some women members of C.P.I. formed the National Federation of Indian Women. Led by several women, including Aruna Asaf Ali, it worked for the rights and empowerment of women. Leftist women realized that they had to fight against the feudal mentality in society and within the party. A section of Gandhian women was dissatisfied with the government's centralization, bureaucratic dependence, and large-scale planning but was forced to accept it (Forbes, 2000: 226). The post-Independence women's movement was decentralized. So basically, two streams can be observed. On one side was the movement related to the livelihood problems of the poor lower-class people, and on the other was the struggle for ending gender discrimination and legal rights. These movements took different forms, influenced by various idealisms and doctrines. In the 1960s, women activists became active for the rural poor and female factory workers. Neera Desai reports that women actively participated in the Naxal Bari movement, the movement against the rise in rice prices, the Nav Nirman Yuva movement in Gujarat and Bihar, the Dhule movement in Maharashtra and the Chipko movement (Forbes, 2000: 242). Gandhian, leftist, and socialist ideologies were active in the Shahada and anti-price hike movements in Maharashtra, Seva, and movements in

Gujarat. The Progressive Organization of Women was formed in Hyderabad. Under the influence of the Maoist Women Organization, the Purogami Stree Sangathana was formed in Pune, and the Stree Mukti Sangathana in Bombay (Kumar, 1993). The first women's day was celebrated in India under their joint initiative. The women's organization of the CPI(M) the party had the most significant mass base, including Dalits and agricultural labourers. In West Bengal, the Democratic Women's Association gained influence among agrarian and middle-class women from the 1970s. The Women's Federation was equally influential in Kerala. Most of the Maharashtra Sramik Mahila Sabha members were tribal women and agricultural labourers from the Dhulia and Thana regions. The National Federation of Indian Women opened branches in Maharashtra, Bangalore, Mysore and Jammu between 1970 and 1973 (Omvedt Gail, 1975: 41). According to Gail Omvedt, those girls who came out of the home and took part in social production, who were exploited both within and outside the family and who had a double burden of work, participated in the women's movement (Omvedt Gail, 1975: 42).

The women's movement in the West and some initiatives of the United Nations gave direction to the women's movement in India. The Ford Foundation, Oxfam, ILO, and some Scandinavian government agencies funded research and organization on women's issues in India. Post-1975 research activities made the participants of movements aware of the problems of women working in agricultural and other unorganized sectors (Majumdar, Fall Winter, 1994: 43). 1975 was the International Women's Year declared by the United Nations. The United Women's Liberation Struggle conference was organized in Pune in October 1975 by women activists of the Lal Nishan Party, labour organizations and a newspaper called Magoa. Farmers, labourers, professors, coolies, bank workers, teachers-students—women from all walks of life participated in it. More than 700 women discussed women's issues ranging from money laundering to clean drinking water for two days. Since then, this type of rally started in different parts of India. This women's movement saw many traditional practices, customs and reforms as a source of exploitation (Forbes, 2000: 244). As a result, the government's declared egalitarian policy faced severe criticism.

Towards Equality Report: Recommendation for Restricted Reservation

Efforts were again made in the mid-1970s to examine the status of girls in India. In 1971, the United Nations took the initiative to find out the status of women in some countries of the world, and in 1974, the Committee for the Status of Women in India (CSWI, 1974) joined the work. The result is the Towards Equality Report, which is still a pioneer in women's research (Kullar, 2016: 109). In 1971, the Ministry of Education and Social Welfare formed a committee to review Constitutional, legal, and administrative frameworks. The Committee, led by Dr. Phularenu Guha, examined how the social status of girls was conducive to their education and employment. This Committee presented the Towards Equality Report in 1974. It was made based on interviews with 500 women in each province and extensive research. The report was significant in determining the status of women in India. One of the essential aspects is the concept of women's equality. It is essential for national, social, economic and political development. Henceforth, equality and self-reliance will be considered necessary conditions for providing women with income opportunities. Marriage and motherhood of women should not be considered an obstacle in the formation of the nation-state. Steps must be taken to fulfil the goals that the Constitution has set up (*De Jure*) into reality

(*De Facto*) (Majumdar, Fall Winter, 1994: 42-43). It showed that the condition of girls has deteriorated instead of improving. The privileges and rights promised by the Constitution remain unknown to most girls. Girls had to be confined to their traditional roles. Most of the revolutionary proposals to ensure gender equality were not implemented. Though most women leaders believed Nehru to be an outstanding champion of women's rights but in a speech at a girl's college in New Delhi in 1950 Nehru mentioned that women's education was important for making better homes, better family and better society. He showed his displeasure at the sloppy way in which Indians kept their houses and said that "Women are chiefly responsible for running the home and should know how to do this in an orderly and aesthetic way." Although he was talking to the students pursuing higher education but there was not a word about their future role in country's progress (Banerjee, 1998: WS-6).

The issue divided the Committee for the Status of Women in India (CSWI, 1974) member was legislative reservation for women. Prof. Vina Majumder personally put emphasis on women reservations in Parliament going beyond the committee's recommendation to restrict them up to the Municipal level. The committee as a whole did not recommend for reservations up to the level of Parliament (Laura, 1999: 63). Regarding reservation, Dr. Phulrenu Guha warned that there was a possibility that reservation of seats would only help women of a particular class who were already privileged and she apprehended that this type of reservation might led other communities or classes to argue for reservation of seats resulted in rise of separatist tendencies and hampering of national integrities (Laura, 1999: 65).Vina Majumder and Lotika Sarkar competed against the national integrity argument and held up the view that women are a category and not a community and therefore, should not be compared with other minority groups (Laura, 1999: 65).

Primary Findings

In the early days of independent India, women's progress was thought to be a natural result of the socialist values of equality, democracy, secularism, and modernization. Despite legal protection and Constitutional guarantees, the intended progress for women did not materialize. Since the colonial period, reservations for women were opposed by leading women's organisations as it was considered contradictory to the notion of equality. This legacy continued to influence early women activists in independent India. The idea of Women's Development evolved from Women's Welfare during the Fourth Plan, as a result of the commencement of a new stage in the women's movement in 1970 (Mitra, 2019: 57). However, reservations for women were later thought to be appropriate to ensure women's representation.

Conclusion

Before the declaration of emergency, women had led the charge in the campaigns against price increases and corruption. The CSWI member secretary, Vina Mazumdar, notes that although her generation had opposed special representation as 'daughters of independence,' 'We have found our understanding of nation-building changing radically' over time (Menon, 2000: 3836). This change of outlook affected policy-making. Since the beginning of the planned development, women have been viewed as a deprived section requiring welfare measures. It was only in 1975 that a UN Declaration compelled the national government to shift the emphasis of its women's programmes from welfare to development (Mohanty, 1995: 3347). In 1957, the Balwant Rai Committee, while recommending the Panchayati Raj System for the country, overlooked women's participation as an issue of significance. It considered the question of women in Panchayats from the perspective of the women and children development programme. The Ashok Mehta Committee in 1974 on Panchayati Raj Institutions emphasised women's role in the decision-making processes of the Panchayeti Raj (Datta, 1995: 66-67). In the 1985 Nairobi International Women's Conference the question of women political participation was highlighted. It was recommended that 35 per cent of the total seats should be reserved for women. The National Perspective Plan (1988) was adopted in India, and it recommended that some posts should be reserved for women at the block and village level administration. With these developments, the issue of reservation, which once had been pushed to the background, again came back to the forefront as the most debated topic in Indian politics. The publication of the Towards Equality Report has led to extensive debates regarding the issue of women's reservations. It was evident within twenty years of independence that women were not achieving equal representation through their advancements, making reservations a necessary consideration.

REFERENCES

AMANA. (2020). *Pheida: Gender at the Periphery.* Imphal: K.K. Printers.

Amnesty International. (2023). *Colonialism and Sexual Orientation and Gender Identity: Submission to the Independent Expert on Protection against Violence based on Sexual Orientation and Gender Identity.* Peter Benenson House, Easton Street London WC1X ODW, UK: Amnesty International Ltd.

Arendt, H. (1958). *The Origins of Totalitarianism.* Ohio: The World Publishing Company.

Arjan Kumar Sikri, J. & K.S. Panicker Radhakrishnan, J. (2014 INSC 275). *National Legal Authority* Vs. *Union of Inida and others.* Digital Supreme Court Reports.

Banerjee, N. (1998). Whatever Happened to the Dreams of Modernity? The Nehruvian Era and Woman's Position. (EPW, Ed.) *Economic and Political Weekly, 33*(17): WS2-WS7.

Chanu, S.B. (2018). *State, Citizenship and Transgender Identity India: A Case Study of the Nupi Manbi Community in Manipur.* New Delhi, India: Sodhganga.

Datta, P. (1995). "Datta Prabhat, Womenand Panchayat Bodies in India, Indian Political Science Association." *The Indian Journal of Political Science, 56*(1/4).

Department of Gender Studies, National Council of Educational Research and Training. (2020-2021). Inlcusion of Transgender Children in School Education: Concerns and Roadmap. New Delhi. Retrieved March 7, 2025, from https://clpr.org.in/wp-content/uploads/2022/01/Inclusion_of_Transgender_Children_in_School_Education.pdf

Deshpande, A. (2023). *Affirmative Action in India.* New Delhi: Oxford University Press.

Dr. Konika Khuraijam, D.R. (2022). "A Study on Violation of Rights of Transgender in Manipur." *International Research Journal of Commerce, Arts and Science, 13*(12), 50-59.

Dutoya, V. (2016). "A Representative Claim Made in the Name of Women? Quotas and the Political Representation of Women in India and Pakistan (1917-2010)." *Revue française de science politique* (English Edition), *66* (1).

Dutta, S.B. (2023, August 26). "Nupi Maanbi: Transgenders of Manipur Who Went from Being Accepted to Ostracised to Now Finding Own Voices." India: *Indiatimes News.* Retrieved June 5, 2024, from https://www.indiatimes.com/news/india/nupi-maanbi-transgenders-of-manipur-who-went-from-being-accepted-to-ostracised-to-now-finding-own-voices-606294.html

Forbes, G. (2000). *Women in Modern India.* Delhi: Cambridge University Press.

Ghosal, S.G. (2005). "Major Trends of Feminism in India." *The Indian Journal of Political Science, 66* (4), 793-812.

Government of India. (2019). *The Transgender Persons (Protection of Rights) Act, 2019.* Government of India, New Delhi.

Government of Manipur. (2024). *Gazette,* Dirtectorate of Printing & Stationary, Government of Manipur.

Government of Manipur. (2023). "The Expert Committee Constituted by the Central Government on Transgender, list of actions shall be taken up by the Department of Higher & Technical Education, Manipur as per the timeline, Gazette No. 563." Directorate of Printing and Stationary, Government of Manipur.

Government of Manipur. (2023). "The Governor of Manipur is pleased to appoint Director, University & Higher Education, Manipur as the Complaint officer to deal with the complaints relating to violation of the provisions of the Transgender Persons." *Gazette*, Directorate of Printing & Stationary, Government of Manipur.

Jain, A. (2024, June 19). "As Calcutta HC orders 1% quota for transgender people, how SC ruling & 2019 law protect their rights." *The Print.*

John, B. (1952). A, The Hindu Code Bill, *Far Eastern Survey. 21*(17), 173-176.

K.G., D. & Keshlata. (2024). "Towards Transgender Inclusion: Apllying Sustainanble Devlopment Goals to Address and Resolve the Transgender Challenges in India." in R. Bala & M. Lilee, *BREAKING BARRIERS: Gender Disparities, Inclusion and Empowerment in India* (pp. 13-30). New Delhi-110068: Mohit Tiwary for M/s. Sunmarg Publishers & Distributors.

Kishwar, M. (1996). "Women and Politics: Beyond Quotas." *Economic and Political Weekly, 31*(43).

Kshetri, R. (2006). *The Emergence of Meetei Nationalism.* New Delhi: Mittal Publications.

Kullar, M. (2016). "Emergence of Women's Movement in India." *Asian Journal of Women's Studies, 3*(2): 106.

Kumar, R. (1993). *The History of Doing: An Ellustrated Account of Movements for Women's Rights and Feminism in India 1800-1990.* New Delhi: Kali for Women.

Kumar, R. (2015). "The Women's Movement in India." *Indian Journal of Public Administration, LXI* (3).

Lairikyengbam, R. (2022, October 19). *Legal Hints.* (W. GuniLeima, Interviewer) Doordarshan Manipur.

Lairikyengbam, R. (2024, May 8). *Legal Hints Live Phone—In Programme | The Transgender Person (Protection of Rights) Act, 2019.* (Chanchalkumari, Interviewer) Doordarshan Manipur.

Laura, D.J. (1999). Competing Inequalities: The Struggle Over Reserved Legislative Seats for Women in India. *International Review of Social History, 44* (Supplement 7: Complicating Categories: Gender, Class, Race And Ethnicity).

Laura, D.J. (2020, May 4). Leibaklei | Transgender in Manipur | Part-2. *Leibaklei |Transgender in Manipur| Part-2.* (A. Huidrom, Interviewer) Doordarshan Manipur.

Laura, D.J. (2020, February 6). Leibaklei Part-I. (A. Huidrom, Interviewer) Doordarshan Manipur.

Lovely, P. (2004, July Paulse Lovely, *International Human Rights Movements and Protection of Women's Rights*, Ph.D. Theses, Cochin University of Science and Technology, Under the Supervision of Prof. K.N. Chandrasekharan, July 2004), India: Sodhganga.

Majumdar, V. (Fall Winter, 1994). "Women Studies and Women Movement in India: An Overview." *Women Studies: A World View, 22*(3/4).

Mehta, D.R. & Sharma, M. (2023). "Transgender's Education in India: Status and Challenges." *International Journal of Novel Research and Development, 8*(1): a248-a246.

Menon, N. (2000). "Elusive 'Woman': Feminism and Women's Reservation Bill." *Economic and Political Weekly, 35*(43/44).

Ministry of Social Justice & Empowerment. (2019, June 25). *Welfare of Transgenders.* Press Information Bureau. Retrieved from February 20, 2025, from https://pib.gov.in/PressReleasePage.aspx?PRID=1575534

Miranda, N. (2021, July 23). *World Literacy Foundation.* Retrieved from March 15, 2025, from https://worldliteracyfoundation.org/early-intervention-reduces-illiteracy/

Mishra, V. (2023). *Transgenders in India : An Introduction.* Abingdon, Oxon; New York: Routledge.

Mitra, S. (2019). "Planning and Budgeting for Women's Empowerment in India: A Historical Process." *ANTYAJAA, Indian Journal Women and Social Change, 4*(1).

Mitra, S. (2019). *Module, Legal Awareness Programme.* New Delhi: National Commission for Women.

Mohanty, B. (1995). "Panchayati Raj, 73rd Constitutional Amendment and Women." *Economic and Political Weekly, 30*(52).

Nair, U. (2018, April 17). *AIWC Archive org.* Retrieved from Archive org.

Ngangom, T. (2024). *Manipur HC issues notice to state edu dept on PIL by transgender medical officer.* Imphal: *Hindustan Times.*

Omvedt Gail, R. O.-D.-5. (1975). "Rural Origins of Women's Liberation in India." *Social Scientist, 4* (4/5 Special Number on Women), 40-54.

Oxaal, Z. & Baden, S. (1997). *Gender and empowerment: definitions, approaches adn implications for policy.* Brighton, UK: BRIDGE(development-gender), Institute of Development Studies, Univeristy of Sussex.

Planning Department, Government of Manipur. (2019, November 11). "Manipur Vision 2030: Leaving No-one Behind: Acheiving Inclusive Growth and the Sustainable Development Goals." Retrieved February 21, 2025, from Planning Department, Government of Manipur: https://planningmanipur.gov.in/media/filer_public/05/b8/05b8621c-943a-4682-ae5f-d02e7db7b5c9/manipurvision2030_fullnew.pdf

Ray, R. (1952). "The Background of the Hindu Code Bill, Pacific Affairs." *Pacific Affairs, 25* (3).

Roy Bharati, B.A. (1990). *Women's Struggle: A History of the All-India Women's Conference 1927-1990.* New Delhi: Monohar.

Sarma, K.S. (2024, January 24). "Just 239 Voters? Manipur Trans Community Raises Eyebrows." Imphal: *The Times of India*. Retrieved from March 2, 2025, from https://timesofindia.indiatimes.com/city/imphal/just-239-voters-manipur-trans-community-raises-eyebrows/articleshow/107098382.cms

Singh, N.I. (1976/2003). *The Manipur Administration (1709-1907)* (First Edition 1976 ed.). Imphal: Ningombam (O) Ibetombi Devi.

Sinha, C. (2012). *Debating Patriarchy: The Hindu Code Bill Controversy in India (1941–1956).* New Delhi, India: Oxford University Press.

Sreekumar, S.S. (2006). "Representationof Women in Legislature: A Sociological Perspectivein: The Indian Context." *The Indian Journal of Political Science, 67*(3).

Srivastava, R. (2011). "Minority Representation of a Political Majority Group,Women in Indian Democratic Process." *The Indian Journal of Political Science, 72*(2), 409-420.

The Transgender Persons (Protection of Rights) Bill, 2019. (n.d.). Retrieved March 8, 2025, from https://prsindia.org/billtrack/the-transgender-persons-protection-of-rights-bill-2019

UNDP. (2016). *Skilling for Livelihood Opportunities for Transgenders in India*. Retrieved February 18, 2025, from https://www.undp.org/sites/g/files/zskgke326/files/migration/in/Skilling-for-Livelihood.pdf

Yumkhaibam, R. (2017). "Beauty Parlour as a Scope for Socio-Economic Status among Transgender Nupi Maanbis of Manipur." *International Journal od Research in Humanities, Arts and Literature*, 5(8).

Yumkhaibam, R. (n.d.). *Gender Inequality, Power, and Resistance: A Study of the Socio-cultural Location of Trangender Nupi Mannbis of Manipur*, pp. 180-191. Kyoto University.

4

Reservation for Women in Parliament

A Global Scenario

Naresh Kumar

Introduction

The marginalization of women in political processes has been a pervasive issue globally, prompting calls for specific measures to ensure gender parity in governance. In response, India has enacted groundbreaking legislation to provide specific reservations for women in parliamentary elections. This move has significant implications not only for India but for the global society at large. Women's reservations aim to improve governance and empower women by increasing their representation in political bodies. This issue surpasses national boundaries, seeking to establish an inclusive society where men and women enjoy equal political rights and address broader global concerns such as human rights and gender justice.

Women Representation and Feminist International Scholars

Feminist Theory International Relation (IR) is a critical approach that helps to deconstruct women's reservations in electoral politics. The theory is an attempt to rebel against mainstream theories of IR, such as realism and liberalism, which, are accused of excluding gender as a valuable unit in world politics. Feminist scholars argue that traditional IR theories are inherently patriarchal as they prioritize male-dominated perspectives and issues. Important variants of feminist IR theory hold that it is patriarchal and there is a need for feminist IR to challenge and break down existing patriarchal structures in world politics towards the making of a more just and egalitarian world. These structures enforce gender inequalities and limit women's participation and influence in political decision-making. Feminist theorists advocate for dismantling these systems to create a more just and equitable global order (Tickner, 1992; Enloe, 2014). Feminist IR emphasizes the importance of including women's perspectives in the international political discourse, policy-making, and leadership roles. This inclusion is seen as essential for addressing women's issues creating more comprehensive and effective policies (Peterson & Runyan, 1999). Unlike traditional IR theories prioritize high-politics issues of state security, feminist IR emphasizes human security, which encompasses economic, social, and political well-being, particularly for women and marginalized groups. This broader approach to security aims to address the root causes of insecurity and promote sustainable peace (Tickner, 2001). Feminist IR recognizes the intersecting identities and oppressions that women face based on race, class, sexuality, and other factors. This intersectional approach helps in understanding the diverse experiences of women and the multiple barriers they encounter in political participation (Crenshaw, 1989; Hill Collins, 2000). This theory emphasizes inclusion, whereby women's voices will be heard as part of political debate, policy, and leadership worldwide. The Critical Mass Theory forms another significant framework regarding women's reservation in politics. It argues that a certain minimum of women is needed to exist within political bodies for them to achieve influence and deliver substantial change. Research shows that once this critical mass, often considered at about 30 per cent, is reached, women are enabled to change political institutions and their cultures to be more sensitive towards gender in policies and practices.

Historical Context of Women's Political Representation

Historically, women have been significantly underrepresented in political arenas across the world (Hughes, 2011). This underrepresentation is rooted in long-standing societal norms and gender roles that have traditionally relegated women to the private sphere. In many cultures, political leadership has been viewed as a male prerogative, with women's contributions often undervalued or overlooked. The struggle for women's suffrage in the late 19th and early 20th centuries marked the beginning of a broader movement towards gender equality in politics (Clarke, 1996). However, achieving actual representation in legislative bodies has been a slow and ongoing process. India's decision to implement reservations for women in parliamentary elections represents a significant legislative milestone. This measure aims to rectify the gender imbalance in political representation and ensure that women have a voice in the legislative process. The rationale for reservations is based on the need to create a level playing field for women in politics. Structural barriers such as patriarchal attitudes, lack of access to resources, and limited political networks have historically hindered women's entry into politics. By reserving seats for women, the legislation seeks to overcome these barriers and provide women with the opportunity to participate actively in governance. Women's reservation in politics is usually operationalized through gender quotas, viewed as one of the essential tools towards gender equality and ensuring the participation of women in decision-making. One of the primary mechanisms for promoting women's political participation is the implementation of gender quotas and affirmative action policies. Gender quotas mandate a certain percentage of political positions to be reserved for women, ensuring their representation in decision-making bodies. These quotas can be legislated at the national level or adopted voluntarily by political parties (Dahlerup, 2006).

Women Reservation in Different Parts of the World and Impact on Policy and Governance

Research indicates that increased female representation in politics leads to more gender-sensitive policies and governance practices. Women politicians often prioritize issues such as healthcare, education, social welfare, and gender-based violence, which are essential for human security and social development (Paxton & Hughes, 2015). For instance, countries with higher female representation have been found to adopt more comprehensive policies on maternity leave, childcare, and domestic violence (Krook & O'Brien, 2010). Gender representation in legislative assemblies varies significantly between developed and developing countries, influenced by socio-economic, cultural, and political factors. This comparison explores gender ratios in legislative assemblies of both categories, examining countries with high and low gender representation.

In Sweden as of 2023, women make up 47.4 per cent of the Riksdag, Sweden's national legislature (IPU, 2023). Sweden has long been a leader in gender equality, with policies and a political culture that promote gender parity. This high representation reflects the country's commitment to egalitarian principles and progressive social policies. In the United States women representation is moderate, as of 2023, women hold 27 per cent of seats in the U.S. Congress (House and Senate combined) (*ibid.*). While there has been significant progress over the years, the U.S. still lags behind many other developed countries in terms of gender representation. The disparity highlights ongoing challenges related to political culture, electoral systems, and societal norms. In Japan women representation is low, as of 2023, women hold 9.9 per cent of seats in the House of Representatives and 23.1 per cent in the House of Councillors (*ibid.*). Japan's low representation of women in politics is influenced by traditional gender roles, societal expectations, and limited support for female politicians. Efforts to increase representation have been slow, reflecting deep-rooted cultural norms and structural challenges. In South Korea women representation is moderate, as of 2023, women hold 19 per cent of seats in the National Assembly (IPU, 2023). South Korea has made strides in improving gender representation, but progress remains uneven. Societal attitudes towards gender roles and the political culture pose significant challenges. However, recent efforts and policies aimed at promoting gender equality show promise.

Rwanda has the highest women representation, as of 2023, women hold 61.3 per cent of seats in Rwanda's lower house of Parliament (*ibid.*). Rwanda stands out globally for its high female representation, a legacy of post-genocide reconstruction efforts that emphasized gender inclusivity. This has been supported by constitutional mandates and societal reforms aimed at gender equality. In Nigeria gender representation is very low, as of 2023, women hold only 6.7 per cent of seats in Nigeria's National Assembly (*ibid.*). Nigeria's low representation reflects deep-rooted socio-cultural norms and structural barriers that hinder women's political participation. Despite various initiatives, progress remains slow, highlighting the need for more robust gender equality policies and advocacy. In India gender representation is moderate to low, as of 2023, women hold 14.4 per cent of seats in India's Lok Sabha (lower house) and 11.6 per cent in the Rajya Sabha (upper house) (IPU, 2023). India's gender representation is influenced by a mix of socio-cultural norms, political dynamics, and economic factors. Despite Constitutional provisions and policies aimed at increasing women's participation, progress remains uneven. Regional disparities and societal attitudes towards women in politics continue to pose significant challenges.

Sweden and Rwanda demonstrate that high gender representation can be achieved through deliberate policies and cultural shifts. Both countries have implemented gender quotas and have political environments that support female participation. However, the paths to achieving high representation differ. Sweden's gradual cultural shift contrasts with Rwanda's post-crisis transformation, illustrating diverse strategies for enhancing gender parity. United States, Nigeria, India, Japan, and South Korea reveal the challenges in achieving gender parity, albeit for different reasons. In the U.S., structural and systemic barriers, such as the lack of proportional representation and socio-political dynamics, contribute to moderate female representation. In Nigeria, entrenched patriarchal norms and inadequate policy frameworks are major obstacles. In India, despite constitutional provisions, socio-cultural norms and regional disparities hinder significant progress. Japan faces traditional gender roles and societal expectations, while South Korea is challenged by societal attitudes and political culture. All cases highlight the need for targeted interventions to address specific barriers within each context. The analysis reveals that both developed and developing countries can achieve high gender representation under the right conditions. Developing countries like Rwanda can surpass developed nations like the U.S. in gender parity through strategic reforms. Conversely, developed countries with advanced democratic institutions, like Sweden, set benchmarks for gender equality. The disparity within categories (e.g., U.S. *vs.* Sweden and Rwanda *vs.* Nigeria) emphasizes that economic status alone does not determine gender representation. Instead, it is the intersection of political will, cultural attitudes, and legislative frameworks that drive gender parity.

The gender ratio in legislative assemblies is a complex interplay of socio-economic, cultural, and political factors. High representation in Sweden and Rwanda shows cases of successful strategies in diverse contexts, while moderate and low representation in the US, Nigeria, India, Japan, and South Korea highlights ongoing challenges. Reservation for women in legislative bodies helps to achieve higher women representation that would eventually lead to greater gender parity. Rwanda stands out as a global leader in gender parity in political representation. Following the 1994 genocide, this increased representation has led to significant policy advancements in gender equality, health, and education (Burnet, 2011; Bauer & Burnet, 2013). The Nordic countries, including Sweden, Norway, and Finland, have successfully implemented gender quotas, resulting in substantial female representation in their parliaments. These countries are also known for their robust welfare systems and societal support for gender equality, which facilitate women's participation in the workforce and politics (Teigen, 2012). India has implemented a policy reserving one-third of seats in local government bodies for women, leading to increased female participation at the grassroots level. This has empowered many women, particularly in rural areas, to engage in governance and advocate for community-specific needs (Buch, 2000 and Rao, 2005).

Southern European countries, such as Spain and Italy, have also implemented gender quotas with varying degrees of success.

While these measures have increased women's representation, challenges related to political culture and party dynamics persist. The effectiveness of quotas in Europe often hinges on the broader socio-political environment and the commitment to gender mainstreaming. Latin America has made notable progress in women's political representation through affirmative action. Countries like Argentina and Bolivia have implemented legislative quotas, resulting in significant increases in the number of women in parliament. Bolivia, for instance, has achieved near gender parity in its legislative body. However, similar to other regions, challenges such as patriarchal attitudes, violence against women in politics, and the dominance of male-dominated political networks continue to pose obstacles. Ensuring the meaningful participation of women requires addressing these structural and cultural barriers.

This change translates into a substantive policy gain in gender equality, health, and education. However, there remain critics who argue that the top-down nature of gender equality cannot be translated fully into empowerment at the grassroots level, especially in rural areas where traditional norms are strong. Moreover, it can result in tokenism and push women further to the margins within political parties, which supersede the effectiveness of such affirmative action; their involvement in substantive policy decisions is often compromised. This has empowered several rural women who can get involved in governance and articulate their needs about service delivery. In these countries, it is evident that the introduction of gender quotas in national legislatures has been low, in countries like Japan and South Korea, which have only recently introduced them. In this respect, cultural factors—such as traditional gender role expectations and societal expectations from women and men—are critical to such outcomes. The practice in these contexts depends largely on political will and the commitment to see through proper implementation. One area where gender equality is a sign of progressiveness is among Nordic countries, which possess the most robust forms of affirmative action. Both Sweden and Norway are found to have the lowest percentage of female members in their respective parliaments among the OECD countries, mainly due to voluntary party quotas, followed by Finland. This is supplemented with societal solid support for gender equality and well-established welfare systems that not only aid women in their work but also assist them in politics. In the case of Southern European countries, like Spain and Italy, gender quotas have also been applied to ensure female representation to date. Although increasing female representation, the approach does not appease political culture and other party-related pressures. In the case of Europe, gender quotas work in most cases because of the broader socio-political environment in promoting gender mainstreaming. Latin America has been at the forefront of affirmative action in women's political representation. Institutionalized quotas, like in Argentina and Bolivia, have increased the parliamentary representation of women in leaps and bounds. Bolivia boasts near gender parity in its legislative chamber. However, as in other areas, there are still many stumbling blocks, including patriarchal attitudes, political violence against women, and the resistance of male-dominated political networks. Doing away with these structural and cultural barriers is pivotal for the meaningful participation of women.

The implementation of reservation policies for women will impact international politics very much. Through gender equality and women empowerment, such policies render governance better, more inclusive, and representative. This would, therefore, be expected to result in effective and responsive policy-making, especially with issues that tend to affect women and marginalized groups the most. Feminist IR theory centres on human security, which includes economic, social, and political well-being. Including women in politics might also hold the key to changing public policy in such a way as to increase interest and focus on issues dealing with human security, like health, education, and social welfare. For example, in Rwanda, the sharp increase in female politicians has been related to improvements in gender-based violence and land rights. There are signs that gender-inclusive governance has positive effects on peace and stability. Very often, women bring in different perspectives to processes of conflict resolution and peace building by emphasizing dialogue, collaborative process, and sustainable resolution. For instance, following the genocide in Rwanda, women have formed the backbone of national reconciliation and reconstruction. Despite the enormous benefits of reserving policies for women, there have been several challenges and criticisms. These have ranged from concerns about tokenism to the quality of representation.

Increasing female participation in politics has profound implications for global governance. It can lead to more inclusive and representative decision-making processes, enhance the legitimacy of political institutions, and contribute to more effective and responsive policymaking. Firstly, women's reservation will lead to inclusive decision-making, as female participation ensures that diverse perspectives are included in the decision-making process, leading to more comprehensive and holistic policies. This inclusivity is particularly important in addressing complex global issues such as climate change, conflict resolution, and sustainable development (True, 2013). Secondly, it will foster legitimacy and trust in the governance as the inclusion of women in political processes enhances the legitimacy and trust of political institutions. When political bodies reflect the diversity of the population, they are more likely to be perceived as fair and representative, which can strengthen democratic governance and social cohesion (Mansbridge, 1999). Thirdly, it will lead to effective policymaking because women in politics often prioritize policies that address human security and social welfare, leading to more effective and responsive governance. For example, research shows that female legislators are more likely to introduce and support Bills related to healthcare, education, and gender-based violence (Thomas, 1994; Swers, 2002). Fourthly, gender-inclusive governance can also contribute to peace and stability. Women bring different perspectives to conflict resolution and peace building processes, emphasizing dialogue, collaboration, and sustainable solutions. Studies have shown that peace agreements and post-conflict recovery efforts are more successful and lasting when women are involved (O'Reilly, Súilleabháin & Paffenholz, 2015).

Implementing policies that promote female political participation can significantly enhance the power stature of countries on the global stage. Countries that prioritize gender equality and women's empowerment are often viewed as progressive and forward-thinking, which can improve their international reputation and influence. Countries with strong records on gender equality can leverage this as a form of soft power in international relations. Gender equality can enhance a nation's diplomatic standing, allowing it to build alliances and partnerships based on shared values and principles (Nye, 2004). Promoting women's participation in politics is also linked to economic competitiveness. Gender equality in the workforce and political spheres can lead to more innovative and effective policies that drive economic growth and development. Research shows that countries with higher levels of gender equality tend to have stronger and more sustainable economies (World Economic Forum, 2017). Countries that implement gender quotas and other affirmative action policies often experience significant social development gains. These gains include improvements in health, education, and social welfare, which contribute to overall societal well-being and stability (Sen, 1999). Increasing women's representation in politics is essential for promoting gender equality, enhancing global governance, and improving the power stature of implementing countries. While significant progress has been made, challenges and criticisms remain, highlighting the need for continuous efforts to address structural and cultural barriers. By incorporating feminist perspectives and advocating for inclusive and representative governance, we can create a more just and equitable global order.

Women's Reservation and Feminist Foreign Policy

Women's reservations in political assemblies are a strategic tool to increase female representation in governance structures. By ensuring a minimum number of seats for women, these policies aim to rectify gender imbalances and foster more inclusive decision-making processes. When women are adequately represented in legislative bodies, it creates a foundation for the development and implementation of feminist foreign policies (FFP). Institutionalizing gender parity through women's reservations ensures that women's voices are not only heard but also heeded in legislative processes, fostering a political culture that values and promotes gender-sensitive policies both domestically and internationally. Women legislators often bring attention to issues traditionally overlooked in male-dominated assemblies, such as human rights, social justice, and gender equality. This elevation of previously marginalized issues shapes foreign policy agendas to be more inclusive and equitable, prioritizing women's rights in international agreements and treaties and reflecting feminist foreign policy principles. Diverse representation in assemblies ensures that a wider range of perspectives is considered in policymaking.

Women from varied backgrounds offer unique insights and solutions to global challenges, which is crucial for feminist foreign policy that addresses issues through an intersectional lens. Women's perspectives often emphasize human security over traditional notions of state security, focusing on the well-being of individuals and communities, including economic security, health, and education. Integrating these priorities into foreign policy helps create more holistic and sustainable approaches to international relations, aligning with feminist foreign policy's core objectives of protecting and promoting human rights and social justice globally. Women's participation in assemblies can enhance advocacy for peaceful conflict resolution and the inclusion of women in peace processes. Studies have shown that peace agreements involving women are more likely to be durable and effective, ensuring that female legislators play a significant role in shaping foreign policy strategies that prioritize dialogue, reconciliation, and long-term peacebuilding. Additionally, women in legislative bodies are often strong advocates for development and humanitarian efforts, prioritizing issues such as education, healthcare, and economic empowerment, essential components of feminist foreign policy. By pushing for these issues in international development agendas, women legislators help create foreign policies that are more responsive to the needs of vulnerable populations.

Conclusion

The feminist mandate to make for gender-sensitive international relations and ensure equitable gender representation is critical to both developed and developing countries. It is essential to implement these goals to make political equality more gender-just, reservation in representative institutions becomes an important tool to address the deep-rooted disparities in political and social structures. The reservation bill by the Indian government marks an important milestone in this direction that aims to ensure that women are at the center of policymaking processes. This move is not a foundational step towards realizing the broader objective of women-led development, which is crucial for the overall progress of society. Without meaningful representation in political spaces, women cannot effectively promote their rights or influence policies that impact their lives. To achieve this just legislation would not be enough, this demands a whole-hearted political commitment from all the political parties and society at large and a broader societal shift, where males actively support and accept increased female participation in governance. There is a need to address the most significant challenge to gender representation, particularly in countries, like India, where the patriarchal nature of socio-political dominates the decision-making. A good number of studies have repeatedly illustrated that patriarchal norms marginalize women in various spheres of life, including politics. To overcome these barriers, it is important to sensitize the population about the importance of gender-equitable representation. Education and awareness campaigns can change societal attitudes and break down the barriers to women's full participation in political life. By adopting and implementing reservation policies, India, by setting a precedent for gender equity has the potential to assume a leadership role in the Global South, particularly among Asian countries. This move not only strengthens countries position in world politics but also paves the way for more inclusive and representative governance structures globally. In the long run, such efforts can contribute to more balanced and fair international relations, where women's voices and perspectives are adequately represented and valued.

REFERENCES

Bauer, G. & Burnet, J.E. (2013). "Gender Quotas, Democracy, and Women's Representation in Africa: Some Insights from Democratic Botswana and Autocratic Rwanda." *Women's Studies International Forum, 41*: 103-112.

Buch, N. (2000). "Women's Experience in New Panchayats: The Emerging Leadership of Rural Women." *Centre for Women's Development Studies.*

Burnet, J.E. (2011). "Women Have Found Respect: Gender Quotas, Symbolic Representation, and Female Empowerment in Rwanda." *Politics & Gender, 7*(3): 303-334.

Childs, S. & Krook, M.L. (2009). "Analysing women's substantive representation: from critical mass to critical actors." *Government and Opposition, 44*(2): 125-145.

Clarke, N. (1996). "Becoming a Woman and other Essays in Nineteenth and Twentieth Century Feminist History." *Feminist Review, 53*(1): 109-111.

Crenshaw, K. (1989). "Demarginalizing the Intersection of Race and Sex: A Black Feminist Critique of Antidiscrimination Doctrine, Feminist Theory and Antiracist Politics." *University of Chicago Legal Forum, 1*: 139-167.

Dahlerup, D. (2006). *Women, Quotas and Politics.* Routledge.

Enloe, C. (2014). *Bananas, Beaches and Bases: Making Feminist Sense of International Politics.* University of California Press.

Franceschet, S., Krook, M.L. & Piscopo, J.M. (eds.). (2012). *The Impact of Gender Quotas.* Oxford University Press.

Hill Collins, P. (2000). *Black Feminist Thought: Knowledge, Consciousness, and the Politics of Empowerment.* Routledge.

Hughes, M.M. (2011). "Intersectionality, Quotas, and Minority Women's Political Representation Worldwide." *American Political Science Review, 105*(3): 604-620.

Inglehart, R. & Norris, P. (2003). *Rising Tide: Gender Equality and Cultural Change Around The World.* Cambridge University Press.

Krook, M.L. (2016). 'Contesting Gender Quotas: Dynamics of Resistance'. *Politics, Groups, and Identities, 4*(2): 268-283.

Krook, M.L. & O'Brien, D.Z. (2010). "All the president's men? The appointment of female cabinet ministers worldwide." *Journal of Politics, 72*(3): 733-744.

Mansbridge, J. (1999). "Should Blacks Represent Blacks and Women Represent Women? A Contingent 'Yes'." *Journal of Politics, 61*(3): 628-657.

Nye, J.S. (2004). *Soft power: The Means to Success in World Politics*. Public Affairs.

O'Reilly, M., Súilleabháin, A. Ó. & Paffenholz, T. (2015). 'Reimagining Peacemaking: Women's Roles in Peace Processes'. *International Peace Institute.*

Paxton, P. & Hughes, M.M. (2015). *Women, Politics, and Power: A Global Perspective*. CQ Press.

Peterson, V.S. & Runyan, A.S. (1999). *Global Gender Issues*. Westview Press.

Powley, E. (2007). "Rwanda: The Impact of Women Legislators on Policy Outcomes Affecting Children and Families." *UNICEF.*

Rao, N. (2005). *Women in Local Government: Gender and Governance in India and South Asia.* Manohar.

Sen, A. (1999). *Development as Freedom*. Alfred A. Knopf.

Swers, M.L. (2002). *The Difference Women Make: The Policy Impact of Women in Congress*. University of Chicago Press.

Teigen, M. (2012). "Gender Quotas on Corporate Boards: on the Diffusion of A Distinct National Policy Reform." *Comparative Social Research, 29*: 115-146.

Thomas, S. (1994). *How Women Legislate*. Oxford University Press.

Tickner, J.A. (1992). *Gender in International Relations: Feminist Perspectives on Achieving Global Security*. Columbia University Press.

Tickner, J.A. (2001). *Gendering World Politics: Issues and Approaches in the Post-cold War Era*. Columbia University Press.

True, J. (2013). *The Political Economy of Violence Against Women*. Oxford University Press.

Waylen, G. (2014). "Informal Institutions, Institutional Change, and Gender Equality." *Political Research Quarterly, 67*(1): 212-223.

World Economic forum. (2017). "The Global Gender Gap Report 2017." *World Economic Forum.*

5

Voyage of Change

Exploring Women's Reservation in Afro-American and Indian Literature

Moirangthem Dolly

Introduction

In pursuit of creating an ideal and inclusive society, one cannot overlook the pivotal role of women's reservation in leadership positions. Women's reservation refers to the allocation of a certain percentage of seats or positions specifically for women in political, educational, or other government bodies. As such, the 106th Indian Constitutional Amendment Act, 2023 was passed in sync with women's reservation in the Lok Sabha and the Legislative Assemblies across states and NCT Delhi. These reservation policies are more than just administrative measures. They will be effective and instrumental in eradicating long-standing prejudices and systemic biases against women in the country. By examining Afro-American and Indian literature, the complex web of gender dynamics can be understood thereby revealing how women's reservation can significantly transform a society. Some of the literary works taken into consideration for the study include Toni Morrison's "The Beloved", Alice Walker's "The Color Purple", Mahasweta Devi's "Draupadi", Anita Desai's "Clear Light of Day", Arundhati Roy's "The God of Small Things", Jumpa Lahiri's "The Namesake", Rabindranath Tagore's "Gitanjali", Zora Neale Hurston's "Their Eyes Were Watching God", Nikki Giovanni's "Black Feeling, Black Talk" etc.

Review of Literature

Reddy and Wilson (2016) examine gender stereotypes and the impact of women's reservation policies based on Afro-American and Indian literary narratives. The study gives us an insightful account of the role of literature in challenging societal norms and advocating for gender equity. Sharma and Davis (2017) present a comparative analysis of women's reservation in political leadership, with special reference to Afro-American and Indian literary perspectives. The study explores the nuances of women's representation and the challenges faced in achieving gender parity in leadership roles. Patel and Green (2017) discuss collaborative leadership in the context of women's reservation policies, drawing lessons from Afro-American and Indian literature. The study emphasizes the importance of inclusive leadership practices in promoting gender equality and social justice. Singh and Harris (2020) explore the theme of eradicating social prejudices through meticulous study on women's reservation from Afro-American and Indian literary perspectives. The study highlights the role of literature in challenging stereotypes and advocating for inclusive policies. Gupta and Williams (2019) examine representation and advocacy in Afro-American and Indian literature, offering insights for women's reservation policies. The study underscores the significance of literature as a tool for promoting gender equity and empowering marginalized voices. Patel and Jones

(2020) analyze intersectionality through Afro-American and Indian literature. Their study discusses implications for women's reservation policies and highlights the interconnected nature of oppression and the need for policies that address plurality in identity and experiences. Kumar and Thompson (2018) analyze the role of literature in advocating for women's reservation, comparing Afro-American and Indian literary works. The study emphasizes the transformative potential of literature in shaping societal perceptions and promoting gender equality. Smith (2018) explores women's reservation in political leadership, drawing insights from Afro-American and Indian literature. The study discusses the challenges and opportunities for women in leadership roles and the role of literature in addressing gender disparities. Gupta and Robinson (2019) examine the theme of challenging patriarchal constructs through Afro-American and Indian literary narratives on women's reservation. The study highlights the role of literature in challenging oppressive norms and advocating for social change. Williams and Gupta (2018) investigate intersectionality and women's reservation through a comparative study of Afro-American and Indian literary perspectives. The study underscores the complexity of gender inequality and the importance of inclusive policies that address intersecting forms of discrimination.

Research Gap

While some valuable insight has been found in the reviewed literature regarding the role played by literature in advocating for reservation policies for women and challenging gender inequality, there are still research gaps that ought to be covered. First and foremost, there is a need to have more comprehensive comparative analyses between the Afro-American and Indian literary perspectives on women's reservation, covering the exploration of similarities and differences and the implications this may have for the implementation of typically formulated policies. Moreover, secondly all the literatures are focused on discussing the representation of women's experiences and activism, with a lack of discussion on evaluating the effectiveness and impact of women's reservation policies in practice. Thirdly, there is little research done on the intersectional dimensions of women's reservation concerning both Afro-American and Indian societies, particularly about women from their respective marginalized groups. Future research can be conducted on the contribution or role literature plays in influencing public perception and attitudes towards reservation policies for women and the barriers and challenges that exist within different cultural societies to the implementation of such policies. Such research would add valuable dimensions to understanding the complex dynamics surrounding women's reservation and its implications for gender equity and social justice.

Women's Reservation through Literary Lens

This study entitled "Voyage of Change: Exploring Women's Reservation in Afro-American and Indian Literature" addresses the need to explore the Afro-American and Indian literary landscapes concerning women's reservation policies and their potential for fostering societal reforms. By investigating the representation and treatment of gender equity in literature from both cultures, this research seeks to uncover insights into the role of literature in advocating for women's rights and political empowerment.

Fostering Collaborative Leadership in Policy Formulation on Women Empowerment

In both Afro-American and Indian literary traditions, a resonating call for collaborative leadership, rooted in inclusivity and community engagement, echoes through the works of renowned authors. Toni Morrison's monumental novel, "*Beloved*", conveys the importance of communal support through the line, "*Freeing yourself was one thing, claiming ownership of that freed self was another*". This statement expresses the idea that true liberation requires not only individual emancipation but also communal recognition and solidarity. Likewise, Rabindranath Tagore's timeless poetry collection, "*Gitanjali*", embodies the spirit of collective harmony, advocating for a life devoted to service and interconnectedness. Tagore's words, "*I slept and dreamt that life was joy. I awoke and saw that life was service*" emphasize the significance of selflessness and community engagement in fostering a harmonious society. These literary masterpieces inspire readers to champion inclusive leadership practices that honour diverse perspectives with tolerance and acceptance. Not only that, they also prioritize the well-being of the collective over individual pursuits. In the realm of Afro-American literature, writers such as Octavia Butler and Audre Lorde emphasize the imperative of holding institutions accountable for promoting gender equity and social justice. Butler's assertion, "*The only way to keep a broken world from turning you into a broken person is to love the broken in it,*" underscores the importance of empathy and compassion in effecting positive change within society. Similarly, Lorde's powerful declaration, "*There's really no such thing as the 'voiceless'. There are only the deliberately silenced, or the preferably unheard*", sheds light on the systemic barriers that silence marginalized voices and advocates for amplifying those voices through inclusive leadership practices. In Indian literature, authors like Anita Desai and Arundhati Roy advocate for policies that challenge discrimination and injustices against women by confronting societal norms and institutionalized biases. Desai's works often delve into the complexities of identity and belonging, while Roy's writings explore the political and social realities of contemporary India. Both authors highlight the importance of inclusive leadership practices that prioritize gender equity and social justice. Women's reservation policies emerge as a critical mechanism for addressing systemic inequalities and advancing inclusive leadership practices. By ensuring equal representation and participation in decision-making processes, these policies create opportunities for marginalized groups, particularly women, to have a voice and influence in shaping the future of their communities and societies.

Ending Gender based Stereotyping and other Multi-faceted Social Prejudices

In 'The Color Purple', Alice Walker introduces strong female characters who defy stereotypes about women's capabilities. Through Celie's transformation, Walker challenges societal norms and illustrates the potential for women to excel in leadership roles. Celie's proclamation, "*I'm poor, I'm black, I may be ugly, but dear God, I'm here. I'm here!*" highlights her resilience and determination to overcome adversity. Similarly, in "*The God of Small Things*" by Arundhati Roy, strong female characters like Ammu challenges societal constraints. Ammu's defiance against societal norms is captured in her words, "*Things can change in a day. They can change in a moment.*" These quotes demonstrate the transformative power of strong female characters in dismantling stereotypes and align with the goals of women's reservation policies to provide equal opportunities for women in leadership roles. In advocating for policy prioritization, Afro-American writers like Audre Lorde stresses the significance of intersectionality, urging policymakers to address issues of women particularly the prejudices against women of colour. Lorde's assertion, "*There is no such thing as a single-issue struggle because we do not live single-issue lives*", underscores the interconnectedness of various forms of oppression faced by marginalized women such as gender prejudice, sexism, colour prejudice, political prejudice, and so on. Similarly, Indian author like Kamala Das highlights the urgency of addressing women's concerns in policymaking. Das' reflection, "*My body is my garden, my will is my gardener*", speaks to the importance of agency and autonomy for women. Through these quotes, Lorde and Das express the necessity of policy measures, including women's reservation, to address the intersecting challenges faced by women and promote gender equality and social justice.

Redefining Women's True Identity and Potential

Toni Morrison's famous novel "*Beloved*" intricately gives us an insightful account on experiences of black women, spotlighting the crucial significance of representation in confronting systemic injustices. Through the character of Sethe, a resilient black woman protagonist, Morrison vividly illustrates the profound struggles endured within an unjust society. Sethe's remark *"Freeing yourself was one thing, claiming ownership of that freed self was another"*, captures the rigorous journey towards self-liberation and the subsequent challenge of asserting agency in a world plagued by systemic inequities. This quote serves as a sharp reminder of the dual burdens faced by women of colour in their pursuit of freedom and self-determination. Furthermore, within "*Beloved*", Morrison skilfully projects the pivotal role of political representation through Sethe's lament: "*Definitions belong to the definers, not the defined*", thereby illuminating the imperative for women to actively participate in shaping the narratives and frameworks that govern their existence. By highlighting the disparity in power dynamics and the monopolization of definitions by dominant societal forces, Morrison stresses on the urgent need for marginalized voices, particularly those of women, to be included in the discourse and decision-making processes that impact their lives. This emphasis on political representation serves as an effective and instrumental tool in challenging and subverting prevailing societal prejudices and norms. Similarly, in Mahasweta Devi's compelling short story "*Draupadi*", the character of Draupadi emerges as a symbol of resistance against injustice and patriarchal oppression. Draupadi's bold declaration, "*I will not let my voice be silenced. I will speak out against oppression*", encapsulates the spirit of defiance and resilience exhibited by women in the face of systemic marginalization. Devi portrays Draupadi as a fearless advocate for change, unyielding in her determination to assert her rights and demand recognition for her voice in a society plagued by gender-based discrimination. In both "*Beloved*" and "*Draupadi*", the authors masterfully weave narratives that illuminate the enduring struggles of women against systemic injustices. Through their respective characters, Morrison and Devi underscore the imperative for women to not only attain freedom but also actively participate in reshaping societal narratives and structures. These literary works serve as powerful testaments to the resilience, courage, and unwavering determination of women in their relentless pursuit of equality and justice through their meaningful representation across spheres.

Addressing Intersectionality and Challenging Patriarchal Construct

In Toni Morrison's novel "*Sula*", the character Nel bravely declares, "*I want to make sure I'm the only one of us who ever dies*", encapsulating a profound sense of individuality and agency amidst complex social dynamics. Similarly, Indian authors like Shashi Deshpande and Bapsi Sidhwa advocate for women's empowerment and gender equality through their literary works.

Deshpande's novel "*The Dark Holds No Terrors*" follows the journey of a woman reclaiming her identity and agency, wherein, the protagonist boldly asserts, "*I will not be made to feel guilty for being what I am.*" This quote embodies the spirit of resistance against patriarchal oppression and reflects the protagonist's determination to assert her autonomy and self-worth. Likewise, Bapsi Sidhwa's "*Cracking India*" pursues the intricacies of gender dynamics in a patriarchal society. In this novel, the character Lenny questions, "*What does it mean to grow up? To have power over your own life?*", thereby emphasizing the struggle for autonomy and self-determination faced by women in the face of patriarchal structures, and highlights the quest for empowerment and agency. Through these Afro-American and Indian literary works, it becomes evident that women's reservation policies represent a crucial step towards challenging patriarchal constructs and fostering a more inclusive society. Afro-American literature, as exemplified by Zora Neale Hurston and Nikki Giovanni, deals with women's intersectional experiences, advocating for policies that embrace diversity and inclusivity. Hurston's "*Their Eyes Were Watching God*" portrays the protagonist Janie's journey towards self-discovery and empowerment, symbolized by the imagery of her being "stretched on her back beneath the pear tree." Similarly, Giovanni's poetry celebrates the inherent worth and strength of women, as she proclaims, "*I am so perfect so divine*", challenging societal norms that seek to diminish women's value. Likewise, through their writings, Indian authors like Nayantara Sahgal and Mridula Garg amplifies intersecting oppressions faced by women and puts forth the importance of policies that address discrimination and promote inclusivity. Sahgal's "*Rich Like Us*" explores the resilience of women in the face of political turmoil and societal constraints, highlighting their capacity to rise above adversity. As such, Garg's works emphasize the resilience of women, resembling their perseverance to a lotus blooming in a swamp. It symbolizes hope and resilience in the face of adversity. Both literary traditions stress the urgent need for inclusive policies that recognize and embrace diverse identities, advocating for a society where every individual, regardless of gender, race, or background, has the opportunity to thrive and contribute to the collective progress. Women's reservation policies, by ensuring equal representation and participation in decision-making processes, serve as a vital mechanism for dismantling patriarchal structures and advancing towards a more equitable and inclusive society.

Promotion of Equity

In the Indian literary landscape, Anita Desai's "*Clear Light of Day*" deals with the intricacies of women's lives, as illustrated by the character Bim's remarkably bold statement, "*In India, there is no place for an unmarried woman*" thereby encapsulating the societal pressures and expectations imposed on women, on one hand, and highlighting the urgent need for societal change and gender equality, on the other hand. Similarly, Jhumpa Lahiri's "*The Namesake*" explores the theme of identity and belongingness through its protagonist character Ashima, who reflects, "*For being a foreigner, Ashima is beginning to realize, is a sort of lifelong pregnancy*". This profound observation speaks to the perpetual sense of displacement and cultural disconnection experienced by immigrant women, and reveals the complexities of their experiences in navigating between multiple worlds. In the Afro-American literary landscape, Langston Hughes' poem "*Mother to Son*" portrays universal themes of struggle and resilience, as the mother's words, "*Life for me ain't been no crystal stair*", vividly depict the painful journey faced by women in overcoming adversity. Similarly, Maya Angelou's autobiographical work "*I Know Why the Caged Bird Sings*" echoes the vibrant spirit of women. As she declares, "*I am the dream and the hope of the slave*", it symbolizes the enduring strength and resilience of women in the face of oppression and adversity. These relevant quotes from selected Indian and Afro-American literary works serve as powerful reminders of the nuanced portrayal of women's experiences and aspirations for a more equitable future. They capture the multifaceted challenges and triumphs encountered by women from diverse backgrounds, resonating with the overarching goals of women's reservation policies to address systemic inequalities and empower women in political and societal spheres. Through their reminiscent storytelling and insightful reflections, these authors shed light on the complexities of women's lives and advocate for social change in sync with the broader objectives of promoting gender equality and social justice.

Conclusion

The convergence of women's reservation policies with the profound insights from Afro-American and Indian literary landscapes presents a compelling narrative for societal transformation. By enacting measures that ensure women's representation in leadership roles and decision-making arenas, we embark on a journey towards dismantling age-old prejudices and fostering genuine inclusivity. Through the lens of literature, we are reminded of the resilience, strength, and wisdom inherent in women's narratives. From the powerful prose of Afro-American writers like Toni Morrison and Alice Walker to the evocative works of Indian authors such as Arundhati Roy and Anita Desai, we witness the multifaceted experiences of women navigating societal structures plagued with discrimination and oppression. Their stories serve as powerful reminders of the importance of amplifying women's voices and perspectives in shaping our collective future. Women's reservation policies stand as a beacon of hope, offering tangible pathways for breaking through the glass ceiling that has hindered women's progress for far too long. By providing equal opportunities for women to ascend to positions of power and influence, we not only challenge entrenched gender biases but also enrich decision-making processes with diverse viewpoints and insights. Moreover, the implementation of women's reservation policies sends a powerful message—that women's contributions are invaluable and deserving of recognition and respect. It signals a shift towards a society where meritocracy reigns supreme, and individuals are judged based on their abilities rather than their gender. As we embrace women's reservation as a potent instrument for social change, we sow the seeds for a future where all women are valued, respected, and empowered to lead. It is a future where barriers crumble, stereotypes dissolve, and inclusivity thrives. Let us heed the lessons of literature and the call for equity, and together, forge a path towards a more just and equitable society for generations to come.

REFERENCES

Angelou, M. (1969). *I Know Why the Caged Bird Sings*. Random House.

Butler, O. (1993). *Parable of the Sower*. Four Walls Eight Windows.

Das, K. (1973). *My Story*. Sterling Publishers.

Desai, A. (1980). *Clear Light of Day*. Houghton Mifflin Harcourt.

Deshpande, S. (1980). *The Dark Holds No Terrors*. Penguin Books.

Devi, M. (1985). *Draupadi*. Seagull Books.

Garg, M. (1994). *The Last Email*. Penguin Books.

Giovanni, N. (1968). *Black Feeling, Black Talk*. Morrow.

Gupta, S. & Williams, L. (2019). "Representation and Advocacy in Afro-American and Indian Literature: Insights for Women's Reservation Policies." *International Journal of Women's Studies*, *21*(3): 301-317. DOI: 10.1080/09589236.2017.1395689

Gupta, P. & Robinson, D. (2019). "Challenging Patriarchal Constructs: Afro-American and Indian Literary Narratives on Women's Reservation." *Gender & Society*, *28*(3): 301-317. DOI: 10.1177/0891243209350457

Hughes, L. (1922). *Mother to Son.* The Crisis.

Hurston, Z.N. (1935). *Mules and Men.* J.B. Lippincott & Co.

Hurston, Z.N. (1937). *Their Eyes Were Watching God.* J.B. Lippincott & Co.

Kumar, R. & Thompson, A. (2018). "The Role of Literature in Advocating for Women's Reservation: A Comparative Analysis of Afro-American and Indian Literary Works." *Journal of Women's Empowerment, 15*(2): 187-203. DOI: 10.1080/09589236.2017.1395689

Lahiri, J. (2003). *The Namesake.* Houghton Mifflin.

Lorde, A. (1984). *Sister Outsider: Essays and Speeches.* Crossing Press.

Morrison, T. (1987). *Beloved.* Alfred A. Knopf.

Patel, R. & Jones, M. (2020). "Exploring Intersectionality through Afro-American and Indian Literature: Implications for Women's Reservation Policies." *Journal of Comparative Literature, 35*(2): 201-218. DOI: 10.1177/0021989409350457

Patel, S. & Green, H. (2017). "Women's Reservation and Collaborative Leadership: Lessons from Afro-American and Indian Literature." *Journal of Political Leadership, 20*(2): 245-261. DOI: 10.1177/1354068814564383

Reddy, P. & Wilson, E. (2016). "Gender Stereotypes and Women's Reservation: Insights from Afro-American and Indian Literary Narratives." *Feminist Studies, 42*(1): 89-106. DOI: 10.2307/3178540

Roy, A. (1997). *The God of Small Things.* Random House.

Sahgal, N. (1985). *Rich Like Us.* Penguin Books.

Sahgal, N. (1989). *Mistaken Identity.* Penguin Books.

Sidhwa, B. (1991). *Cracking India.* Milkweed Editions.

Singh, M. & Harris, C. (2020). "Overcoming Social Prejudices: Insights from Afro-American and Indian Literary Perspectives on Women's Reservation." *Race & Class, 61*(4): 419-435. DOI: 10.1177/0306396804016001002

Sharma, A. & Davis, K. (2017). "Women's Reservation in Political Leadership: A Comparative Analysis of Afro-American and Indian Literary Perspectives." *Political Research Quarterly, 70*(2): 245-261. DOI: 10.1177/1065912907312530

Smith, J. (2018). "Women's Reservation in Political Leadership: Insights from Afro-American and Indian Literature." *Journal of Gender Studies, 25*(4): 419-435. DOI: 10.1080/09589236.2017.1395689

Tagore, R. (1912). *Gitanjali*. The Macmillan Company.

Walker, A. (1982). *The Colour Purple*. Harcourt Brace Jovanovich.

Williams, S. & Gupta, A. (2018). "Intersectionality and Women's Reservation: A Comparative Study of Afro-American and Indian Literary Perspectives." *Journal of Intersectionality Studies*, 5(1): 89-106. DOI: 10.1080/1554477X.2016.1148050

Section-II

Women's Reservation, Representation and Legal Regime

6

Woman's Reservation in Representations

A Sociological Consideration

M.C. Arunkumar

Introduction

Reservation has always provoked the minds of general peoples, intellectuals, leaders of various groups, and politicians. There have been different debates over the concept and necessity of reservation and its reasons and goals. The question of reservation is much more than statistical realities; the entire discourse on reservation is much deeper in history, social and cultural norms and politics. Historical experiences of different groups, communities within a group, social stratifications and cultural underpinnings are not similar. As society and state change from one phase to another, these historical experiences pose different questions at different times because the meanings of these experiences keep changing with new environments and political goals. Reservations for different castes, tribes, backward classes or women are based on one important notion of 'historically disadvantaged'. The notion is not well discussed;

rather, it is taken for granted. Any backwardness does not deserve reservation unless such backwardness is due to a particular definable 'historical disadvantage'. The notion cannot be equated with backwardness over periods; it is backwardness because the group was disadvantaged for various historical reasons, mainly exploitation by another group.

Considering the historical disadvantages of one group, post-Independent India, which adopts the principle of justice, inequality at any level among groups, communities or genders is taken as injustice. In order to deliver justice to those historically disadvantaged groups, reservation as an affirmative action is provided for equal opportunities for individuals from these groups to access education, employment and political representation. However, the debates and controversies over the reservation are becoming increasingly complex, hence, changes in reservation policy in India. The most visible controversy, sometimes more violent, is over the reservation of SC, ST and OBC; the issues that arise are reasons, proportion and related definitions. Even in the Constituent Assembly, there were two contrasting views on the reservation, though the majority of them agreed on affirmative action. Firstly, "Many members of the Assembly recognised the need for affirmative action policies to address the historical injustices and discrimination faced by particular communities... reservation policies were necessary to provide these communities with opportunities for social and economic mobility and to ensure they had a fair chance to compete in the education and job markets" (Imam, 2023: 677). Secondly, some members were concerned with the potential negative impacts of reservation policies on social cohesion and meritocracy. "Some members of the Assembly argued that reservation policies should be temporary and phased out once the disadvantaged communities had achieved a level of equality with other communities" (Imam, 2023: 677). The time frame of reservation and measurement of a level of equality has not yet been determined or objectively quantified; hence, no standard upper limit for defining a minimum level of equality has been set so far. Would members of Scheduled Tribes or Castes will be considered historically disadvantaged communities indefinitely? What would be the point of beginning equality if the reservation is considered a means to achieve equality? So far, the Republic of India has not debated when, how, or in which situation historically disadvantaged communities or groups or strata would be equal with the mainstream communities or groups or strata.

Reservation is given to the groups, though the basic principle of constitutional laws is individualism. Though rights are given to individuals in various Articles of the Constitution of India, terms for the groups are frequently used, such as caste, tribe, backward class, race, and women. In order to minimise group-related prejudices and to fill up the gender gaps in social and political spheres, reservations are given to the members of specified groups (considered to be backward). Legal thinkers, like M.P. Singh, consider equality in terms of group equality, as he says, "right to equality is always an individual right is not wholly true" … "group concept of equality is implicit in the very principle of proportional equality that equals are treated equally and unequal differently" (Singh, 1982: 53, 58). Group equality should be, however, adopted and formulated with complete knowledge in individualistic terms. Here, Agarwala (1990: 134) observes, "In fact, our Constitution is based on the political morality based on individualism, and hence these groups must be seen as permissible classifications to achieve legitimate state purpose retaining the individualistic understanding of equality." If we consider a reservation to bring equality among the groups, will individuals belonging to the particular 'preferred' group bring out the desired equality? Equality among the groups depends on various other social and political factors that are beyond the reservation given to individuals belonging to historically disadvantaged groups. Moreover, the argument of group equality as a legitimate state purpose behind reservation may not be good enough as all groups and castes, except the most advantageous one, should be given reservation benefits to achieve equality of groups (*ibid.*: 1990). One argument in favour of reservation is based on the impact of the reservation. Reservation in recruitment will not ensure group equality. However, it will help in reducing prejudice attached to the historically disadvantageous groups because "their very presence in these jobs and seats will help in reducing the caste prejudice" (*ibid.*: 136). The group prejudice may be reduced by the presence of group members against whom there is prejudice in roles incongruent with their social stereotypes.

In all the arguments for reserving a group, reservation is considered a means to achieve social equality, compensate the historically disadvantageous groups, or reduce associated prejudices with particular groups. The very mechanism of equalising the groups or compensating the historical injustice is a challenge, not only because of the problem's complexity but also because it depends on other factors like the government's political will and the nature of implementation.

Women: Is only Gender Stratification Enough?

In almost all known societies, there is gender stratification. Women are considered inferior and marginalised in comparison with their male counterparts. Strong sexual stereotypes are prevailing, and hence, gender discrimination. Their social and political positions are subordinate to their male counterparts. Many kinds of literature try to point out that, right from the socialization and value systems, societies give women inferior positions. Therefore, they are less represented in social and political forums. Often, in various literatures, fewer representatives in decision bodies of states are explained in terms of age-old cultural practices and patriarchalism.

In a society, there are three models of womanhood: *Imoinu-, Khamnu-* and *Panthoibi-models.* The terms are derived from Manipuri myths and legends. These three models and their dynamics can help us understand women in general and Manipuri women in particular. *Imoinu* model is of the ideal womanhood in a traditional system that obeys the existing social norms and values; on the other hand, *the Panthoibi* model is about free and independent womanhood. Between the two models, there is *the Khamnu* model, in which women take part in economics, trade, and commerce but are not as free as the *Panthoibi* model. Traditionally, individual Manipuri woman is part of her *Imoinu* model; collectively, they act in various social and political movements, such as *Panthoibi*. The collective *Panthoibi* should be transformed into individual personhood so that the woman can make an independent decision as a voluntary woman, free from traditionalism and patriarchalism (Moirangthem Cha, 1992). The democratization of womanhood can be defined as a transformation of *Imoinu* to *Panthoibi* at the individual level. In the social and political decision process, an individual woman should participate as a *Panthoibi*, having independent opinions and the capacity to make her own decisions. Women's reservation in the political sphere is a means to this transformation.

Ranjana Kumari (2013) argues in her "Women's Participation in Politics in India: Achieving Genuine Democracy" that India's social and cultural structure is hierarchical and discriminatory. Because of this, minority groups continue to be excluded from decision-making forums and experience widespread discrimination and disadvantage. Furthermore, she jumps to gender discrimination and inequality. Gender inequality is linked to the social and cultural structure of India. However, there is a question of women's homogeneity. Within women, there are classes, castes and tribes. In other words, within class, caste or tribe, there are women and respective gender stratification. When discussing gender inequality, we refer to the reality of genders. However, what about the reality found within women? There are other social stratifications besides gender stratification. Moreover, women cut all other social stratifications. Some women are in the upper strata, while many men are in the lower strata. In this direction, there is less discussion while debating women's reservations. The intersection between gender and other social stratification is critical to gender equality. In contemporary India, with the emergence of middle class in both caste and tribe, the problem of within-woman heterogeneity is becoming more complex. In the tribal middle class, too, the number of tribal women is increasing. Interestingly, in the reservation system of India, class (at least income) is recognised only in the case of OBC by introducing the 'creamy layer' and EWS by identifying a particular income slab in the general category. In the case of SC and ST, class or income is not considered a criterion for reservation benefits. In such a situation, women reservation cannot be considered only on gender stratification, as they do not belong to same caste, tribe or class.

For women's reservations, gender inequality in representation is the most commonly forwarded argument. Less representation in the legislature is well-reported across the globe. The following table shows how the numbers are compared; the percentage shown is calculated regarding the total number of MPs. As the percentage of female MPs is low, the percentage of male MPs is. These two tables show that there is a gender gap in the Lok Sabha; there is also a positive growth of female MPs from the first election to the fourteenth election. Women, on their own merit, can contest the election and win. On the other hand, the percentage of women representatives in Lok Sabha is still very small; the gender gap is too high. Of course, in India, Shrimati Indira Gandhi served the country as Prime Minister for more than one and half decades; women served as governors, Chief Ministers, Ministers in both Union and State Governments, many women are judges in different courts of India, Secretaries in the Governments. This does not meet the social and political expectations of equality in general and of gender equality in particular.

Statistically, the number and percentage of women elected are much below what should be in contemporary India. Though their percentages in Lok Sabha and Rajya Sabha are increasing every five years, the desired percentage is yet to be achieved. For reference only, the following two tables are reproduced from the Rajya Sabha Secretariat (2008), not for any analytical analysis.

Table 6.1: Number of Women Elected to Lok Sabha

General Election	No. of Women Elected	Percentage
First	22	4.4
Second	27	5.4
Third	34	6.7
Fourth	31	5.9
Fifth	22	4.2
Sixth	19	3.4
Seventh	28	5.1
Eighth	44	8.1
Ninth	28	5.29
Tenth	39	7.02
Eleventh	40	7.36
Twelfth	44	8.07
Thirteenth	49	9.02
Fourteenth	51	9.51

Source: Rajya Sabha Secretariat, 2008.

Table 6.2: Women Members of Rajya Sabha and their Percentage (1952-2008)

Year	Number	Percentage
1952	15	6.94
1954	17	7.79
1956	20	8.62
1958	22	9.52
1960	24	10.25
1962	18	7.62
1964	21	8.97
1966	23	9.82
1968	22	9.64
1970	14	5.85
1972	18	7.40
1974	18	7.53
1976	24	10.16
1978	25	10.24
1980	29	11.98
1982	24	10.16
1984	24	10.24
1986	28	11.98
1988	25	10.59
1990	24	10.34
1992	17	7.29
1994	20	8.36
1996	19	7.81
1998	19	7.75
2000	22	9.01
2002	25	10.20

(*Contd.*)

Year	Number	Percentage
2004	28	11.43
2006	25	10.41
2008	23	9.50

Source: Who's Who, Rajya Sabha (as reproduced in Rajya Sabha Secretariat, 2008).

Many countries today have fewer women representatives in legislation; unlike other countries, India's gender gap is linked with other social and political stratifications. This can be remembered by what Ngaire Niffine (1994) discussed about women. In her footnote, Ngaire Niffine observes that the problem with the idea that 'woman' is a coherent and unified category is that such insistence denies and suppresses "the multiplicity of cultural, social and political intersections in which the concrete array of 'women' are constructed" (Niffine, 1994: 11 fn 10). Women are not a single 'coherent and unified category'.

In the Indian context, gender inequality is not a mere social hierarchy between men and women regarding power, status and material resources. Beyond gender stratification, there is a deeper problem within the stratum of women; within this stratum, there is class stratification, caste stratification and tribe-caste stratification. Women are not of the same class, caste and tribe. In this complex social system, some women are more powerful than many men of other castes or tribes or classes. As the other two stratifications, class and caste, are still operative in society, while discussing women's reservation, these cross-cutting stratifications should also be considered. For this, quantitative data and qualitative information are required. On the other hand, besides inequality between genders, there is a large inequality within the women. Unlike castes and tribes, women were in different social strata throughout history. In these strata, women of higher strata were more powerful than men of lower strata; similarly, women of higher strata were more dominant than women of lower strata. Within the strata, women might be inferior to men. Combining the two or three stratification types, the question of injustice or historical disadvantage becomes more complex. Then, the two possibilities for the reservation strategy are: women's reservation in all strata or gender inequality being considered a type of inequality. Gender inequality cannot be taken without referring to the larger picture of social inequality. The question of equality is between both groups and individuals due to various social and cultural factors, historical reasons and/ or structural maladjustments. Each inequality between genders, among genders and women of different social strata (e.g., castes, tribes) cannot be considered independent of others.

The issue of low representation of women in the legislature may be addressed by women's reservation, no doubt. The number of elected or nominated women members will be increased. However, this will not address the issue of cross-group women's positions and their representations. Moreover, the success of these elected leaders may or may not link with other forms of social stratification. The presence and even longevity of elite female leadership do not necessarily guarantee or indicate an absolute improvement in women's political participation in the country (EPW Engage, 2024). While talking about women's reservations on the basis of gender gaps in representation, we should look at what we have learnt from the experiences in reservations and preferential treatment in castes and tribes. On the basis of caste hierarchy and the gap between tribes and non-tribal populations in the states, reservation and other means for uplifting these categories were adopted. With reservation and other welfare schemes, social change in tribal societies is obvious, no doubt. In almost all the indicators of change, tribal societies show remarkable progress. The gap between tribal and non-tribal communities in almost all the states has narrowed down over 75 years. However, the emergence of the tribal middle class shows that within the tribal societies, there is a new form of social stratification in the line of class. If same indicators used in comparison between tribal and non-tribal societies are used between tribal middle class and ordinary tribal peoples, the picture is quite different. New power brokers are coming up in the tribal societies. The situation is more complex in the case of women because women are not similar to other social categories like caste and tribe. The question remains: Who will be the elected women leaders—women of upper castes, middle class or newly emerged tribal middle class? Will it help to equalise the groups as desired?

The final touch on inequality is freeing each ordinary member from all forms of exploitation, whether gender, caste or tribe. If we cannot liberate women to become *Panthoibi*, the women's reservation will not serve the purpose. Mere filling up the gender gap may not bring the desired gender equality. Reservation is a means for equalisation, but how the reservation should be made is more important. Collective *Panthoibi* is a political force; it is not a mere participation in the election process, nor is it for gender equality. The voice of the Collective *Panthoibi* is of justice and against all forms of abuse. However, Individual *Panthoibi* is lagging behind.

Rudi Heredia (2012), in "Holding up Half the Sky: Reservation for Women in India", deals with the loss of individuality in the performance of elected women leaders, which discusses the common misconceptions that cloud our understanding of women's political participation. "When women do attain a national leadership role, it is often because they have inherited the mantle from their fathers or husbands, rather than as persons in their own right and are then projected as matriarchs, part of the joint family, complementary to the patriarchy rather than a challenge to it" (Heridia, 2012: 51). This image is because of the fact individual women are not fully liberated from the feudal patriarchalism and caste hierarchy. In concluding remarks, the author says, "Political representation is necessary for a liberal democracy. Political quotas are meant to address the absence of those who are excluded because of the inegalitarian social structures in which political processes are enacted. It is accepted as a legitimate justification for SC and ST quotas in legislatures and Parliament. Reserved quotas for women are a fair extension of that same principle" (*ibid.*, 2012: 60). Further, she cautions that such reservation should not serve the old hierarchies again. For this, according to her, structural and policy changes in a gender-biased society are needed. In a similar view, Sarvagya Sree and Aniruddh Ram (2023), focusing more on social and cultural norms, express that "Deeply rooted in cultural norms, patriarchal attitudes, socio-economic realities, and historical prejudices are these biases against women and their roles in society. To begin combating these obstacles and altering perceptions, multiple initiatives must be implemented simultaneously" (Sree & Ram, 2023: 514). Political representation in democracy, social or liberal, is, no doubt, the basis of the existence of democracy. Moreover, reservation is a necessary means for a while until equality is attained (though the measurement of this state of equality is not yet defined). However, gender bias or gender hierarchy is not the only hurdle to gender inequality, as women of some castes, tribes and classes are affected by many other social biases.

Two real challenges are now seen—the political women of *Panthoibi* who have merit and knowledge, not a 'proxy leader' (as many call it) and the political process of making women of *Panthoibi.* Society and state acknowledge the *Nari Shakti* in India, but the *Shakti* has not yet been channelised to flourish in social and political spaces. Women's reservation aims to improve the statistical figures; the real issue is much deeper than the statistical figures: *Nari Shakti* is there and used for individual woman, *Panthoibi*. After all, democracy is all about equality at all levels and at the individual levels.

REFERENCES

Agarwala, Binod Kumar (1990). "Philosophy of Reservation." *Indian Philosophical Quarterly, XVIII* (2).

EPW Engage (2024). "Women's Reservation Act of 2023: A Symbolic Geesture or a Significant towards Empowerment." *Economic and Political Weekly*, 20 March, https://www.epw.in/engage/article/womens-reservation-act-2023-symbolic-gesture-or-0

Heredia, Rudi (2012). "Holding Up Half the Sky: Reservation for Women in India." *Economic and Political Weekly, 47*(9).

Kumari, Ranjana (2013). "Women's Participation in Politics in India: Achieving Genuine Democracy", in Silke Franke, Susanne Schmid (eds.), *Ohne Frauen ist kein Staat zu machen: Gleichstellung als Motor für nachhaltige Entwicklung,* Hanns-Seidel-Stiftung e.V., Hausdruckerei, München.

Moirangthem Cha, Arunkumar (1992). unpublished thesis, *Women's Crime in Manipur,* Manipur University. Available at: https://shodhganga.inflibnet.ac.in/handle/10603/39386

Naffine, Ngaire (1994). "Possession: Erotic Love and the Law of Rape." *The Modern Law Review, 57*(3).

Rajya Sabha Secretariat (2008). *Reservation of Seats for Women in Legislative Bodies: Perspectives,* Rajya Sabha Secretariat, New Delhi.

Singh, M.P. (1982). "Jurisprudential Foundations of Affirmative Action: Some Aspects of Equality and Social Justice", *Delhi Law Review,* Vol. 10 & 11, 1981-82.

Sree, Sarvagya, and Ram, Aniruddh (2023). "Reservation for Indian Women as a means of Empowerment." *International Journal of Creative Research Thought, 11*(10).

7

Women's Political Participation and Representation

Manipur Experience

H. Sudhir and *Sylvia Yambem*

Introduction

The women representatives who constituted 15 out of 389 members of the Constituent Assembly of India in 1947 discussed reservation of seats for women[1]. However, reservation of seats for women, was perceived as impediment to their growth[2]. The women representatives believed that democracy, in its normal course of functioning, would ensure representation of all sections of Indian society. Ensuring women's political rights, the Constitution of India guaranteed women's political equality. Article 326 of the Constitution provides universal adult franchise[3], while Article 15 of the Fundamental Rights prohibits discrimination based on sex, religion, race, caste etc., thus confirming political equality for all citizens of India above the age of 18. The Constitution of India provides every woman citizen of India with a certain degree of political status or the "equality and freedom enjoyed by women in the shaping and sharing of power and in the value given by society to this role of women" (CSWI, 1974: 283).

I

The Women's Reservation Movement

The Constitutional guarantees, however, did not often translate into women's representation. The "Towards Equality Report"[4] submitted by the Committee on the Status of Women in India (CSWI, 1974), affirmed that women's participation as voters "understood in terms of the levels of acquisition and exercise of power and exercise of the political rights" had been increasing at a faster rate than men. Though however, women's representation as electoral candidates—irrespective of whether successful or unsuccessful—registered an opposite trend. During the nine years between the general Lok Sabha elections of 1962 and 1971, while the total voters' turnout increased by 0.95 per cent, the percentage of women voters increased by 2.52 per cent. Regarding direct participation as candidates in the electoral process, women's representation was much lower. As seen from Table 7.1, it was only in 1971 that women's representation reached 17 per cent of the total seats. Though compared to the total number of candidates, women's representation never exceeded 4 per cent.

Table 7.1: Women Contestants for the Lok Sabha

Year of General Election	Total number of seats contested	Total number of women contestants	% of women contestants	Number of women elected	% of winners
1962	491	65	13	33	50.6
1967	515	66	13	28	42.4
1971	518	86	17	21	25.9

Source: Towards Equality Report, 1974.

This data on women's political participation *versus* their representation significantly countered the correlation between political awareness and literacy. A striking argument on women's political participation is the role and impact of education on generating political consciousness and greater political participation. But, going against this relationship between education and political consciousness, the 1971 election showed that the most significant number of women candidates came from Bihar—increasing from 8 women candidates in 1962 to 18 in 1971. On the other hand, the number of women candidates, declined from 11 in 1962 and 1967 to 8 women in 1971 in the state of Madhya Pradesh. In states like Andhra, Tamil Nadu, Karnataka, Orissa, and Manipur, the Report noted the overall criticism that political parties supported very few women. These fewer women candidates represented not the political aspiration of women "but the indifference of political parties in giving them nominations". In Manipur, for the 1967 elections to the state legislative assembly, while there were 156 male candidates and many of them were supported by the national political parties such as the Indian National Congress (INC), Communist Party of India-Marxist (CPI-M), Communist Party of India (CPI), Praja Socialist Party and the Sanghata Socialist Party, there was no women representation[5]. Despite this lack of women's representation, yet women's political participation at 49.84 per cent constituted a sizeable percentage of the electorate.

The cause for women's reservation, however, did not gain much support even in the CSWI Report[6]. Though the Report, along with the Note of Dissent[7] did facilitate broader public discussion on women's participation in political bodies with a special focus on local bodies. The discourse beginning with the Ashok Mehta Committee in 1977, drew on discussions concerning the Panchayati Raj system and the principle of financial devolution to advance the principles of federalism. The

National Perspective Plan (NPP) 1988-2000 recommended 30 per cent reservation of seats for women at the panchayat and zilla parishad levels. Subsequently, states like Karnataka and Gujarat implemented some form of reservation for women in the Panchayati Raj Institutions (PRIs). This was followed by the 64th Constitutional Amendment Bill, 1989 to provide Constitutional status to the PRIs[8]. In 1993, the 73rd and 74th Constitution Amendments provided one-third reservation for women nationwide in the urban and rural bodies.

The demand for extension of women's reservations in the state assemblies and Parliament gained momentum ahead of the 1996 general elections. Under the leadership of the representatives of the All India Democratic Women's Association (AIDWA), All India Mahila Dakshata Samiti (AIMDS), All India Women's Conference (AIWC), Centre for Women's Development Studies (CWDS), Joint Women's Programme (JWP), National Federation of Indian Women (NFIW), Young Women's Christian Association (YWCA), and other organisations supporting the 1995 Declaration of the National Convention of Women in Beijing, put forth a demand for at least 33 per cent reservations of seats for women in the State Assemblies and Parliament. They appealed to the national political parties for inclusion in their manifestos a commitment to make the necessary amendments to the Constitution to ensure a minimum of one-third of seats in the Assemblies and Parliament for women. Despite the major political parties' support for the demands, less than 15 per cent of the total numbers of electoral tickets were given to women!

Following the women-led interventions, in 1996 the United Front Government led by Prime Minister Deve Gowda introduced the 81st Amendment Bill for 33 per cent reservation for women in legislative bodies. Despite numerous attempts in 1996, 1998, 1999, and 2008, it was only in 2023 that the Constitution (One Hundred and Twenty-Eighth Amendment)

Bill was introduced in Lok Sabha on September 19, 2023. The *Nari Shakti Vandan Adhiniyam*, 2023 provided reserving one-third or 33 per cent of seats for women in Lok Sabha, state legislative assemblies, and the Legislative Assembly of the National Capital Territory of Delhi. Women's reservation[9] was given for 15 years, but the delimitation of the reserved seats was to be made only after the Census (i.e. 2031). The Bill, while providing reservation of 33 per cent seats for women belonging to the SC/ST women within their respective quotas, does not mention reservations for the minority categories including the backward castes and others. The rotation of reserved seats after every delimitation, would further limit the effectiveness of women's political empowerment, as rotation of reserved seats implies that women leaders would have to give up their constituencies. They would have to seek re-election from new constituencies[10].

II

The Women in the Electoral Process of Manipur

The demand for women's reservation stems not only from the lack of women's political participation. But women's political participation does not translate into women's political representation. Women in India enjoy the Constitutional right of political participation but limited privilege of political representation. In the 2024 Lok Sabha elections, of the 8360 total number of candidates, women constituted around 10 per cent or only 800[11]. Of these, 74 women candidates or 14 per cent, were declared winners. Political party's support for women's representation is also disproportionally ranged. The national parties such as the Bharatiya Janata Party (BJP) supported 70 women candidates, of which 31 candidates were successful; the INC supported 41 women candidates with 13 women candidates winning, and all the 11 women candidates supported by the All

India Trinamool Congress (TMC) emerged successful. All the 38 women candidates supported by the Bahujan Samaj Party (BSP) and the 7 women candidates of the CPI(M) lost the election[12]. The other national political parties, such as the Samajwadi Party (SP), the Dravida Munnetra Kazhagam (DMK), Rashtriya Janata Dal (RJD), and Nationalist Congress Party (NCP) gave only minimal support to women's representation. Compared to the miserably low woman's political representation, women's political participation as voters at 65.78 per cent exceeded the 65.55 per cent of men voters[13].

Factors of social hierarchy, caste, literacy, political awareness or even economic empowerment do not necessarily impact women's political participation or representation. As seen, Manipur (13) has a dismally low proportion of women representation but very high political participation. The nature of the limited women's representation reveals that education or political awareness does not impact women's political representation, though they may contribute to their political activism as voters. In the last 2022 assembly elections, women's turnout was at 52 per cent, while only 17 women contested the elections. The challenges facing women's representation in electoral politics in Manipur thus go beyond the traditional factors of limited women's political participation. In the first electoral exercise conducted in Manipur, there were no women's political representation. Moreover, distinguished women personalities like Maharani Iswari Devi, wife of Maharaja Budhchandra who contested the 1951 parliamentary elections or even T. Sabi Devi a prominent woman leader of the 1939 second *nupi lan* and President of the Mahila Sanmelani lost the election of 1957. MK Binodini, the first woman graduate from Manipur and a celebrated literary figure, won her constituency in the election to the 30-member Electoral College for electing the members of the Rajya Sabha. Otherwise, women did not contest elections, and political parties did not support women candidates.[14]

In the first Manipur Legislative election in March 1972, of the 252 candidates, there were only 3 women candidates. The women representatives comprised 1 per cent of the total number of candidates. If we look at Table 7.2 below, we can see that from the first Manipur Legislative election up to the 12th Assembly election of 2022, within these 10 years, the total number of women representatives constituted around 3 per cent.

Table 7.2: Manipur Electoral Representation

Year	Total Number of Representations		Successful Women Representation	% of Electorate who Voted	
	Male	Female		Male	Female
1972	249	3	0	50	50
1974	262	3	0	49	51
1980	394	7	0	50	50
1984	359	5	0	49	51
1990	248	6	1	50	50
1991* (bye-election)	-	-	1	-	-
1995	332	11	0	50	50
2000	387	14	1	49	51
2002	361	7	1	49	51
2007	296	12	0	48	52
2009 (bye-election)	-	-	1	-	-
2012	264	15	3	48	52
2017	255	11	2	48	52
2022*	248	17	5	48	52
Total	**3655**	**111 (not including the bye-election)**	**15**		

*Excluding the third gender and postal ballots.

Source: Statistical Report on General Election to the Legislative Assembly of Manipur, relevant years.

From the assembly election of 1974, the percentage of women electorate voting increased to 51 per cent, which is even higher than the percentage of male voters of 49 per cent. Women's electoral participation markedly improved from 230857 voters to 307682, almost a 33 per cent increase. There is a discernible upward trend in the percentage of women's political participation, and from the 2000 elections, the percentage of women voters has continuously exceeded the percentage of male voters. Unfortunately, this trend in political participation is not reflected in the number of women's electoral representation, and more so in their successful candidacy.

Challenges to Women's Reservation and Representation

Women's reservation paves the way for increasing women's political representation and participation in the electoral process. The Nari Shakti Vandan Adhiniyam, 2023, aims to improve the political status of women, in the country. The Manipuri women play a vital role in the electoral process. However, while women's political participation as voters has surpassed men's electoral participation, women's political representation and successful candidacy is limited. From the first 1972 legislative assembly elections until the 12th Manipur Legislative Assembly of 2022, only 15 women have been elected to the state legislative assembly. To date, Manipur has two women cabinet ministers or members of the council of ministers.

The political space continues to be exclusively for men. For women to break into a public-political space is one of the most critical challenges to successful women's political participation. Like the globally accepted pattern of women in politics, factors determining women's success at the election were also tied to their political relationships, particularly from political families. Women from political families had more success in winning elections. In Manipur, of the 15 women legislators, 7 of them came from political families. While this relationship between women's successful representation and their political relationships reduces the women's agency, this causal relationship cannot be ignored in women's triumphant entry into politics. This factor of political families, or political support, has a tremendous impact on women's independence in electoral politics.

This same factor also deters women's entry into electoral politics. A comparative urban-rural women representation shows that of the 111 (excluding the bye-elections of 1991 and 2009) women contesting elections—there were only 19 women representing the urban constituencies (Table 7.3). No women from the urban constituency have been elected to the state legislative assembly despite women candidates contesting from the core urban constituencies of Keishamthong, Uripok, Thangmeiband, and Sagolband[15]. This provides critical insights into the behavioural patterns of the voters.

Table 7.3: Urban-Rural Women Representation

Year	Number of Women Candidates	Constituency		Successful Contestation	
		Urban	Rural	Urban	Rural
1972	3	1	2	-	-
1974	3	-	3	-	-
1980	7	3	4	-	-
1985	5	1	4	-	
1990	6	3	3	-	1
1991	-	-	-	-	-
1995	11	2	9	-	-
2000	14	1	13	-	1
2002	7		7	-	1
2007	12	1	11	-	-

(*Contd.*)

Year	Number of Women Candidates	Constituency		Successful Contestation	
		Urban	Rural	Urban	Rural
2009	-	-	-		-
2012	15	3	12	-	3
2017	11	2	9	-	2
2022	17	2	15	-	5
Total	**111***	**19**	**92**	**0**	**13 + 2 (from the bye-election)**

*Excluding the bye-elections.

Source: Statistical Report on General Election to the Legislative Assembly of Manipur, relevant years.

Conclusion

Reservation of seats for women is a critical topic of public discourse. No issue has polarised the Indian society as much as reservation of women—ranging from the patriarchal excuse that women cannot make public decision to even the issue of proxy candidates. Hence despite the widening political participation by women, women's political representation till date remains limited. According to the 2022 Global Gender Gap Report, India's Political Empowerment recorded a declining score of -0.010 "due to the diminishing share of years" or the reduced years of women's role as head of state in the past 50 years[16]. India's score of 0.267 on the political empowerment sub-index is even much lower than Bangladesh's 0.546 or even Uganda at 0.294. In terms of the political empowerment sub-index India is at 48th place, however overall, India is ranked 135 out of 146 countries on the global gender gap index. Reservation of seats for women would to an extent close the gender gap on political inequality, but the fact remains that inclusive political development is elusive. The study shows that women's political participation by only casting their votes does not ensure her political representation. While reservation would provide more women's political representation, the challenge would be to ensure women's political representation without the factors of monetary and muscle power, or even caste and class-based reservation. This is the real challenge to women's political empowerment and for a successful women's reservation policy.

NOTES

1. Reservation refers to the creation of statutory quotas. John, E. Mary. 2000. Alternate Modernities? Reservations and Women's Movement in twentieth century India. *Economic and Political Weekly*, Oct. 21 - Nov. 3, 2000, Vol. 35, No. 43/44 (Oct. 21 - Nov. 3, 2000), pp. 3822-3829.
2. Constitution Assembly Debates, Vol. 4, 18 July, 1947.
3. Article 326 of the Constitution of India declares that "The elections to the House of the People and to the Legislative Assembly of every State shall be on the basis of adult suffrage; that is to say, every person who is a citizen of India and who is not less than eighteen years of age on such date as may be fixed in that behalf by or under any law made by the appropriate Legislature and is not otherwise disqualified under this Constitution or any law made by the appropriate Legislature on the ground of non-residence, unsoundness of mind, crime or corrupt or illegal practice, shall be entitled to be registered as a voter at any such election."
4. The Committee, appointed by the Government of India in 1971, submitted its Report *towards Equality* on 1st January, 1975 to the Ministry of Education and Social Welfare. in 1974 the Committee on the Status of Women in India initiated a comprehensive review of the status of women in India since its independence.
5. Statistical Report on General Election, 1967 to The Legislative Assembly of Manipur, Election Commission of India.
6. The report though unanimously recommended the establishment of statutory women's panchayats and women's reservation in

municipalities. Before this, the Panchayat Acts of most states had reserved 1-2 seats for women, to be filled by nomination if no woman returned through the by-election process. But this remained a token gesture, and the CSWI recommended, instead, that the reserved seats be occupied by elected office-bearers of the proposed women's panchayat.

7. Against the CSWI's majority suggestion, Lotika Sarkar and Vina Mazumdar (also the committee's member secretary) submitted their dissent note. This Note of Dissent pointed out that despite never having been supporters of exceptional representation or class representation in any form, they were compelled to confront the question and disagree with the majority view in the Committee because "a political system cannot be based on ideology alone but must keep in touch with the actualities of the social situation and so adjust its operation as to achieve the desired goals of the society."
8. The amendment has been criticised on various grounds such as that the Bill transgressed the powers of the state government, or that the Bill provided access for the centre to the panchayats using direct financing of panchayats, and (c) that the Bill, in its earlier version, had empowered the governor rather than the state government to dissolve the panchayats, See, B. K. Chandrashekar, Panchayati Raj Bill: The Real Flaw, *Economic and Political Weekly*, Vol. 24, No. 26 (July 1, 1989), pp. 1433-1435.
9. The Act reserves one-third of all seats for women in the Lok Sabha, State Legislative Assemblies, and the Legislative Assembly of the National Capital Territory of Delhi. However, the Act would be effective once the Census and the delimitation of seats are completed. after every delimitation exercise, the reserved seats were also to be allotted by rotation.
10. The policy of rotation of constituencies, according to a study by the Ministry of Panchayati Raj should be discontinued at the panchayat level because almost 85 per cent women leaders were first-timers and only 15 per cent women could get re-elected as the seats they were elected from were de-reserved. See, prsindia. org
11. Number of Candidates per Constituency, Election Commission of India, Elections 2024 (18 Lok Sabha).

12. Participation of Women in National Parties, Election Commission of India, Elections 2024 (18 Lok Sabha).
13. P.C. Wise Voters Turnout (excluding data of Surat), Election Commission of India, Elections 2024 (18 Lok Sabha).
14. Manipur is celebrated for the two women's wars, the iconic women's market and women organisations like the Meira Paibis and the Nisha Bandhis. Even colonial administrators like E.W. Dun in his 1886 '*Gazetteer of Manipur*' observed that "The women of Manipur, married or unmarried, are not confined in Zenanas, as they are in Bengal or Hindustan; all classes are alike in this respect; neither do they cover their faces before strangers." Manjusri Chaki-Sircar, writing in 1984, almost 98 years after Dun's account, notes that 'in spite of the strong ideological impact of Hindu Brahmans, Meitei women have retained their vital roles in the public sphere, the dissonance with Brahmanism being particularly evident in their unaffected contact and interaction with Meitei men.' See, E.W. Dun, *Gazetteer of Manipur*, 1886, Manas Publications: New Delhi, Reprinted 1992. Manjusri Chaki-Sircar, *Feminism in a Traditional Society: Women of the Manipur Valley*, Shakti Books, 1984. Sudhir, H. 2013. *Market and State: Women's Political Participation in Historical Perspective*, New Delhi: Sunmarg Publishers & Distributors.
15. Some notable women candidates include R.K. Mukhra Devi from Keishamthong, M. Punyabati from Thangmeiband, Wahengbam Joymati from Sagolband, Ph. Iswori Devi from Wangkhei, R.K. Sorojini Devi (INC) from Sagolband, Y. Sakhitombi Devi from Singjamei, Yumnam Romola Devi from Keishamthong, G. Satyabati Devi from Sagolband, or Brinda Thounaojam from Yaiskul. Irom Sharmila, 'Iron Lady of Manipur,' contesting from Thoubal forfeited her electoral deposit.
16. World Economic Forum, 2022. Global Gender Gap Report 2022, Insight Report July 2022.

8

A Discourse on Legal Regime and Political Reservations for Women in India

N. Bangkim Singh

Introduction

Reservation is a term that evolved along with modernism as a disguised blessing to justify democracy and social justice. Tharu, S., Prasad, *et al.* (2007) wrote that reservation is more of social and political representation than social justice. Reservation serves more as a means for the expression of class/caste interests. The current politics of reservation need not be assumed to be an unquestionably progressive development. This benevolent approach, which provides reservation to the womenfolk, is the least affirmative action that the state is considering. Women as a category fall under the purview of reservation as recognised by modern civilised nations. The circumstances that led to the implementation of reservation for women are more compelling than the legitimacy that serves the cause. According to William Hurst, legal regime is a system or framework of rules governing some physical territory or discrete realm of action that is, at least in principle, rooted in some sort of law. He added that politics shape legal regimes, but once in place legal regimes, structure political and social relationships and contestation. In simple words, it is the law-state-society relations. Legal regimes can be defined as sets of rules, policies, and norms that surround political reservations for women in India. The circumstances enabling the sequence of events that led to the reservation policy and political reservation of women in India. In this context, the present study aims to analyse and untangle the circumstances that shaped the reservation policy in India, especially the political reservation of seats for women in India.

Reservation Policy in India: A Legal Inspection

Let us revisit the reservation policy in India, which is rife with controversy due to its demographic and socio-cultural dynamics. The Constitution of India included many provisions for extending reservations to different groups of population. The most exclusive reservation laid down was for the Scheduled Tribes (ST) and Scheduled Castes (SC) in terms of education and employment. The Constitution, through Article 334 provides reservations in the Upper House and Lower House to Scheduled Castes, Scheduled Tribes and the Anglo-Indian community subjected for a period of 10 years. Through many amendments[1], it has been extending without diluting the criteria of reservation, thereby referring that their political participation is still due, failing to provide favourable circumstances even after 77 years of independence. The criteria remain the same without any alteration, but the judiciary interprets them differently based on different cases.

Shortly after adoption of the Constitution of India, in the *State of Madras* v. *Champakam Dorairajan*[2], the Supreme Court of India struck down caste-based reservations in educational institutions, ruling that they violated Article 15(1) of the

Constitution and were *ultra vires* under Article 29(2). This landmark decision emphasized equality but led to the first constitutional amendment enabling reservations, and Clause 15(4)[3] has been added. Regarding the maximum limit to reservation, the Apex Court in *M.R. Balaji* v. *State of Mysore*,[4] established the principle that reservations in educational institutions and public employment should not exceed 50 per cent. to ensure fairness and prevent excessive reservations from undermining equality. The decision is diluted by asserting that the 50 per cent limit on reservations is not absolute, as decided in *State of Kerala* v. *N.M. Thomas*[5]. The Court recognized the state's power to exceed this limit in special circumstances to promote social justice and equality for historically disadvantaged groups. After the Mandal Commission recommendation, due to the federal structure, especially reservation is subjected to the State Executive, many states have passed laws exceeding 50 per cent cap. The discrete categories of providing reservation Other Backward Classes are left to the discretion of the state governments. Sheth (1987) asserted that reservation policy has been wavering in several of its aspects and has been diluted in its implementation, and it requires reorientation to equality and social justice enshrined in the Constitution.

In *Indra Sawhney* v. *Union of India*,[6] the Supreme Court of India upheld the 50 per cent ceiling on reservations and provided guidelines for determining backwardness. This landmark judgment balanced social justice with equality, ensuring reservations do not undermine the rights of the general population. Since then, exclusion of creamy layer among the group identified as OBC (Other Backward Class) has been an important issue. The Supreme Court of India in *M. Nagaraj* v. *Union of India*,[7] held that before implementing a reservation provision, a state must demonstrate compelling factors such as backwardness, lack of participation and overall administrative efficacy in each case. In *A.K. Thakur* v. *Union of India & Others*[8], the validity of reservation extended through 93rd Amendment was challenged. Additional ruling in this case was the exclusion of creamy layer to the socially and educationally backward classes from the purview of reservation but not applicable to SCs/STs as they are separate class by themselves. In *Janhit Abhiyan* v. *Union of India*,[9] the Supreme Court upheld the 103rd Constitutional Amendment, which introduced a 10 per cent reservation for Economically Weaker Sections (EWS) in education and public employment. This judgment affirmed the validity of economic criteria for reservations without breaching the 50 per cent limit and said that it is mere enabling in nature rather than mandatory on the part of the state to render reservation. Regarding the identification of socially and educationally backward class, Article 342A has been inserted through 102nd Amendment empowering the President to notify the said class.

Regarding single post reservation it was decided that the apex court decided that there shall be violation of equality[10] but overturned with an observation that reservation could be provided.[11] It was overturned again and held that where there is a single post in a cadre, the same cannot be reserved either directly or by the device of rotation of roster.[12] It would amount to a 100 per cent ratio and violate the equality principle in the Constitution. The Constitutional Bench in the *Indra Sawney case* formulated vertical reservation and horizontal reservation. Vertical reservation are social reservation and higher form of special provision that are intended exclusively for members of the backward classes SC, ST, and OBC thereby mean that positions secured by the members of these categories on the basis of their own merit are not counted against vertically reserved positions. Horizontal reservation is of lower form of special provisions that are intended for other disadvantaged groups of citizens like children, women, disabled etc. and adjustment with the number of positions cannot be shifted even through merit. Due to the lack of explicit process of implementation of this classification renders defective although in many subsequent cases it has been followed. Reservation of women is a horizontal reservation providing equal opportunities for women, veterans, transgender community, and individuals with disabilities.[13] In *Saurav Yadav* v. *State of Utter Pradesh*,[14] the Apex Court ruled that a candidate from an intersection of the vertical-horizontal reserved category qualified without the vertical reservation, the candidate shall be considered as qualifying.

The above discussion shows the intricate process involved in extending reservations to different sections of society. It may be in terms of deciding criteria or proportion to be met by a specific population and all to contain the overall. The criteria and limit of reservation change from time to time according to the merit of the judicial interpretation. There is a possibility that these unresolving issues can percolate down to reservation policy initiated by the state for the amelioration of certain sections of the population. Nevertheless, 'reservation' has the legitimacy and legal validity, we cannot wish that reservation policy shall also change with the same pace and pattern of change happening in the society. Many times, this has been undermined by the policymakers.

Reservation Policy and Women in India

It was during the social reform movement sweeping across India during British colonial period, in 1881 Mahatma Jyotirba Phule in his statement to Sir William Wilson Hunter, a civil servant of British government conceived the idea of a reservation system for the backward class in the country. Reservation remains one of the most contentious issues in India since its inception during British colonial rule. Chhatrapati Sahu, the ruler of the princely state of Kolhapur passed an administrative order in the *Kolhapur State Gazette* on 26th July, 1902 that

> "His Highness is please to direct that from the date of this order, 50 per cent of the vacancies that may occur shall be fixed by recruits from among the backward classes. In all offices in which the proportion of officers of the backward classes is at present less than 50 per cent, the next appointment shall be given to a member of those classes."[15]

At that time, populations of 'Backward Classes' are non-Brahmins and the reservation was extended in a rudimentary form.

The British governance included special representation under the Indian Councils Act of 1892 and followed by the communal electorates, 1909 which was reversed post-Independence.[16] Between this, Ms. Margaret Cousins along with Smt. Sarojini Naidu led the movement for the inclusion of women in Indian legislature resulted in opening door in 1927 by the Madras State Provincial Legislature for the women. Women's movement have been merged with the Indian political independence movement thus, no considerable fruit is resulted till Independence for the faith of women regarding political reservation. At the time of the Indian independence, women representatives in the Constituent Assembly differed to the reservation of women, including political reservation. On consensus, it was acknowledged by the Constituent Assembly including women members that women do not require any special privileges in any form including reservation with the hope that welfare policies will bring gender justice. Nevertheless, Articles 325[17] & 326[18] has been added providing political equality to all including women which yet to be capitalised by women till date. This has not happened in the coming decades after independence which women folk could not undo their faith and hope to the welfare policy. But it failed to translate into political empowerment of women.

Till two decades after Independence women have been left out from the process of development. The government did not realise that half of its populations are toiling under the traditional patriarchy. The gendered hierarchy in the society reduced non-contribution of the half of the population which is detrimental to the growth and development of the country. All stakeholders need to realise and resort to untangle these gendered barriers to political participation to bring an effective society.

India ratified to Convention on the Political Rights of Women in 1961, although India was a signatory member in 1953. But the situation changed, when in early 70s United Nations advised all countries to submit a report including the status of women. In response to this request from the United Nations (UN) for a report on the status of women ahead of the International Women's Year, 1975, the Committee on the Status of Women in India was appointed by the Ministry of Education and Social Welfare, Government of India in 1971 with a primary purpose was to study the status of women in India, the Committee comes out with a report titled 'Towards Equality' in 1974-75 highlighting discriminatory socio-cultural practices, political and economic process based on constitutional, administrative and legal provisions; and also women's education and employment apparatus. From 1975-1985 UN declared as the 'Decade for Women' and reviewed the status report of the 'Decade for Women' in 1985 Nairobi Conference.[19] Between this, Convention on the Elimination of All Forms of Discrimination against Women (CEDAW) was adopted in 1979 emphasizing that all nations shall bring changes in the legal provisions to protect women from all forms of discrimination and uphold women's right to participate in public life. In 1990, the United Nation's Economic and Social Council endorsed the implementation of measures to reach a target of 30 per cent women in national legislatures by 1995. Following this, many countries have implemented political reservation of seats for women. Tinker (2009) stated that even in countries with significant women's representation, policy change is even. Since most parties are male dominated, political parties often rig the outcome by putting women at the end.

These chains of actions at the international front obligated many countries to come up with concrete plan and positive outcome with the status of women. The compulsions from the international bodies and subsequent compliance of many rules and regulations compelled the government to come up with a concrete plan and action for the amelioration of the status of women in the country. In addition to this, the intensity of crimes against women were also rising which became a concern for the law making and implementing agencies of the state. 73rd and 74th Amendments, 1992 through which one-third proportion of seats reservation at Panchayati Raj System and Municipality System can be envisioned as results of the mounted pressure of compliance with the international bodies but not with regards to the commitment to political empowerment of women. Structural impediments, mainly the patriarchal control within political institutions perpetuate gender disparity in representation. Kamala (2024) mentioned that inadequate implementation of legal frameworks, such as reservation quotas for women in local bodies, undermines their effective participation.

> "Although token legislation has been passed from time to time and various special programmes have been created to empower women and diminish their social disadvantage, there is a justified feeling that as the economy has expanded, the lot of ordinary women has worsened, atrocities towards women have increased and their chances for a real equality of opportunity and a fair share of distributive justice have diminished."[20]

He commented that lack of economic independence as one of the recipe of electoral success and women are left out at the early stage.

Women's Reservation Bill, 2023 (*Nari Shakti Vandan Adhiniyam*)

As per the UNDP rankings, India ranked 151st in terms of the proportion of female members of Parliament.[21] After 27 years finally the 106th Amendment Act, 2023 reserves one-third, i.e. 33 per cent (181 seats out of 543 seats of Parliament) of the total seats for women in Lok Sabha, State Legislative Assemblies, and the Legislative Assembly of the National Capital Territory of Delhi, including those reserved for SCs & STs. The aggregation of reserved seats for women, overarching the male domain, is a positive step towards gender equality and social justice. The final calculation comes out to be 137 seats out of 412 seats in the unreserved category; 28 out of 84 seats reserved for SCs will be reserved for women and 16 out of 47 seats reserved for STs will be reserved for women. To serve the purpose, Article 330A has been inserted, providing reservations for women in Lok Sabha; Article 332A has been inserted, providing reservations for women in State Legislative Assemblies; Article 239AA has been inserted providing reservations for women in NCT of Delhi. No changes in the Bill for 15 years from the day of commencement once it becomes an Act but can be extended. Regarding the smooth passage of the Women's Reservation Bill, 2023, Tabassum (2023) cited two reasons,

> "women in India emerged as a significant constituency with increasing participation as voters in the elections, which no political parties can ignore; and the dominance and relevance of social

> justice or mandal politics, political parties have declined at present, in comparison with the past."

Nevertheless, without much opposition the Bill is passed unanimously, the implementation of the Bill will be delayed because of the Constitutional requirements. The Bill will be implemented in the electoral process once the first consensus is taken after 2026 as per Article 82 of the Constitution of India.[22] And, also the newly inserted Article 334A mentioned that reservations for women to become effective after delimitation are undertaken and Census is conducted. As regard to the implementation in the State Assemblies, ratification of the States by 50 per cent is required as per Article 368 of the Constitution. After the Home Ministry notifies CAA (Citizenship Amendment Act, 2019) rules then the census will be conducted followed by the constitution of the delimitation panel. The whole process will not be possible to complete till 2029, but the challenge is whether the changes occurred in the society within this ambit of said period can be compatible with the Bill. Another requirement is that the seats reserved for women will be rotated after each delimitation is exercised.

It is also assured that the adaptation of the Bill will follow the triple test. In *K. Krishna Murthy v. Union of India*,[23] Honourable Apex Court outlines the triple test or conditions for deciding the proportion basis for providing reservation. Upholding this judgement, the Apex Court in *Kishanrao Gawali* v. *State of Maharashtra and others*[24], the Apex Court held that the proportion basis for providing reservation cannot be a static arrangement; rather, it must be subjected to review from time to time so as not to violate the principle of over-breadth of such reservation. In, *it was held that backwardness with relation to local bodies must be political and it may differ from other categories of reservation for adhering. It has been made mandatory for States to implement the triple test before the OBC reservation in Local Body elections but not applicable to political reservation for SC's & STs, since the reservation in election applies under Article 334. The modality of triple test to activate the process of reservation of seats for the women is not compatible with the OBC.*

The Bill does not mention reservation in either Rajya Sabha or State Legislative Council. The reason may be because some members of these bodies are indirectly elected and can lead to constitutional constraint to bring them under the ambit of the Bill. Along with the delay on implementation of the Bill, arguments are there that categories like Other Backward Classes and Muslim community are not included in the Bill. The Bill seems to target women only confining to specificity accommodating 50 per cent cap imposed by the Supreme Court. Being a member of the group makes one eligible for the quota, which is against the spirit of the relevant requirements embedded in the Constitution. The less competent person can take the advantages denying the others if being membership is enough to avail the quota. To have a more egalitarian society, affirmative actions are directed towards 'group' not 'individual'. Unfortunately, enabling provisions, where it does not mention the criteria for identification will not fulfil the equality principle provided under Article 14 of the Constitution of India.

The conditions that led to the reservation of women in India are not a transient and calculative process but emanated from compulsion with a presumption that all members of the categorised will be benefited without discrimination. After all these years, the reservation policy extended to ST & SC is still far from achieving the desired outcome since it has not yet been identified who are uplifted and who are not within the group. To make the procedure easier for the people who are not benefited within the group by this policy, this identification is necessary. Many times, judicial interventions are there to address issues arising from and within reservation policy. It is an evolving domain where many more groups are accommodating to realise the objectives of social justice. There are possibilities for such flows to be infiltrated the present reservation policy extended to women in India. Any reservation must guarantee that the terms are fair and workable. Targeted population must be benefited through devolution from the quota available exclusively to the group. Time-bound structure and well-planned eligibility will enhance the fairness principle enshrined in the Constitution.

Suggestions

Based on the analysis of legal regimes and political reservations for women in India, below are few recommendations:

1. The Bill requires accelerate the process of implementation engaging with all relevant stakeholders to execute and achieve the goal.
2. The Bill must ensure strict adherence to reservation laws to guarantee the effective implementation of women's reservations. This includes preventing proxy representation, where male family members unduly influence or control the decisions of elected women representatives, thereby undermining the purpose of reservation.
3. Reinforce legal protections for women in politics against violence, harassment, and discrimination. This can be achieved by establishing fast-track courts and enforcing stricter penalties for violations of gender equality laws within political contexts. Such measures will provide a safer and more congenial environment for women in politics.
4. Develop comprehensive training programmes for women candidates and elected representatives to enhance their leadership, governance, and policy-making skills.

Partnering with non-governmental organizations, international agencies and academic institutions will ensure continuous growth and development, equipping women with the necessary skills to succeed in political participations.

5. Implementing mentorship programmes that pair experienced women politicians with newcomers. These programmes along with networks and platforms for sharing experiences, challenges, and best practices will support new female politicians in navigating the political landscape and overcoming obstacles.
6. Fostering gender sensitivity and equality within all political institution is required. Emphasizing the importance of women's participation in politics and actively working to address the gender inequality will create more inclusive and supportive environment for women in politics.
7. Meaningful reservation requires political party and electoral reforms. Political parties should implement internal quotas for women candidates and ensure their active participation in decision-making processes. Additionally, introducing proportional representation or mixed electoral system can facilitate better representation of women in political parties' decision-making bodies, thereby enhancing their influence and impact.
8. Establish independent bodies to monitor the implementation of reservations, ensuring transparency and accountability. These bodies should regularly publish reports and statistics on women's political participation and the effectiveness of reservation policies at the local level. This will help tract progress, identify challenges, and make necessary adjustments to improve the system.

By adoption and adhering to these recommendations, India

can move towards greater gender equality in political reservations for women. This will enhance the overall effectiveness and inclusiveness of its democratic institutions, ensuring that women's voices are heard and represented in the political arena, in turn can achieved gender equality.

Conclusion

The legality of the reservation, although defined contextually in the Constitution of India, often raises question of the criteria and reason for extending the reservation to any category of the population. The evolution of reservation policy is surrounded by issues, and affects many more people within and beyond the targeted population. Controversies revolving within reservation policy of the Indian constitution percolated to other spheres and the prominent is the reservation of women in political bodies. Reservation is a process through which the principle of social justice shall be achieved. Even after the adoption of the Constitution till date there have been no such evidently achieved-changes happening among the communities enjoying reservation policy, if then there must also be changes in the criteria among the communities between those who have been uplifted and those who have not. We never try to tap parallelly reservation policy to the needy population in turn resulted far distance from achieving the goal.

Women constitute a major chunk of the population but shall not be treated as a homogenous group, consisting of sub-categories by their caste, religion, economy, region etc. This has been denied recognition while making affirmative action for the women resulted backlog in the implementation of upliftment of women in the society. Legal regime is not only the law making and interpretation process but also the socio-economic circumstances that give meaning to the people underlying that shapes the reservation policy for the women. Reservation of seats in the political sphere is significant process to achieve gender equality, which we can envision through the success of 73rd and 74th Amendments. The celebration of 73rd and 74th amendments may be the limitation of the local population where people are concentrated in a small area and known to each other. This facilitated the success story which may not be possible at the macro-level where population are diverse. Politics and party politics are strictly patriarchal and any kind of gender-based leverages may not be successfully conducted at the macro-level.

The Women's Reservation Bill, 2023 which extended 33 per cent reservation of women, may have required certain checks and balances mechanisms beforehand implementation so that through 33 per cent it can bring gender equality in the society. The identification of the truly deserved women leaders is important so that the benefits can percolate down to the rest of the women. Political reservation for women has been extended with the belief that a proportion of women legislators will pass subsequent legislation that addresses gender inequality.

NOTES

1. 8th Amendment (1969), 23rd Amendment (1969), 45th Amendment (1980), 62th Amendment (1989), 79th Amendment (1999), 95th Amendment (2019), and 104th Amendment (2020).
2. AIR 1951, SC 226.
3. Nothing in this article or in Clause (2) of Article 29 shall prevent the state from making any special provision for the advancement of any socially and educationally backward classes of citizens or for the Scheduled Castes and Scheduled Tribes.
4. 1963 Supp (1) SCR 439.
5. (1976) 2 SCC 310.
6. 1992 Supp (3) SCC 217.
7. (2006) 8 SCC 212.

8. AIR SC 2008. It provides reservation to other backward classes (OBC) Scheduled Castes and Scheduled Tribes in the private and unaided educational institutions as well as central institutions.
9. 2022 SCC online SC 1540.
10. Supreme Court in Dr. Chakradhar Paswan v. State, AIR 1988 SC 959.
11. *Madhav* v. *Union of India*, (1997) 2 SCC.
12. Supreme Court in *Post-graduate Institute of Medical Education and Research, Chandigarh* v. *Faculty Association*, AIR 1998 SC 1767.
13. Vertical reservation refers to the reservation for Scheduled Castes, Scheduled Tribes, and Other Backward Classes. Each of these groups has its own separate reservation under the law, as mentioned in Article 16(A) of the Constitution of India and, horizontal reservation provides equal opportunities to other beneficiary categories such as women, veterans, the transgender community, and individuals with disabilities. These reservations cut across the vertical categories and are mentioned under Article 15(3) of the Constitution of India.
14. (2021) 4. SCC 542.
15. Akshay Chavan (2019). *The First Reservation in India.* Available at https://www.peepultree.world/livehistoryindia/story/people/the-first-reservations-in-india accessed on 23th April, 2024.
16. The Indian Councils Act, 1892.
17. Article 325 says that No person to be ineligible for inclusion in, or to claim to be included in a special electoral roll on ground of religion, race, caste or sex.
18. Elections to the Lok Sabha and Legislative Assemblies of States to be on the basis of adult suffrage.
19. CEDAW (Convention on the Elimination of All Forms of Discrimination against Women), 1979 emphasised the changes in the legal provisions to protect women from all forms of discrimination and women's right to participate in public life
20. Dhavan, R. (2008). "Reservations for Women: The Way Forward." *Nat'l L. Sch. India Rev., 20*(1): 1-45.
21. United Nations Development Programme, Human Development Reports, Table 5: Gender Inequality Index (2017).

22. Article 82 mentions the process of Delimitation. Due to the delimitation process, the number of Lok Sabha seats allotted to various states as well as the total number of seats in a state's Legislative Assembly may change.
23. In *K. Krishna Murthy* v. *Union of India*, (2010) 7 SCC 202, it was observed that "The identification of backward classes for the purpose of reservations is an executive function and as per the mandate of Article 340, dedicated commissions need to be appointed to conduct a rigorous empirical inquiry into the nature and implications of backwardness. It is also incumbent upon the executive to ensure that reservation policies are reviewed from time to time so as to guard against over breadth."
24. (2021) 6 SCC 73.

REFERENCES

Ahmad, S.W., Nilofer & Parveen, G. (2008). "Women's Political Participation and Changing Pattern of Leadership in Rural Areas of UP." *The Indian Journal of Political Science*, 69(3): 661-672.

Basavaraju, C. (2009). "Reservation under the Constitution of India: Issues and perspectives." *Journal of the Indian Law Institute, 51*(2): 267-274.

Bose, P. (2010). "Women's Reservation in Legislatures: A Defence." *Economic and Political Weekly, 45*(14), 10-12.

Buch, N. (2009). "Reservation for Women in Panchayats: A sop in Disguise?" *Economic and Political Weekly, 44*(40): 8-10.

Chary, M.R. (2012). "Women and Political Participation in India: A Historical Perspective." *The Indian Journal of Political Science, 73*(1): 119-132.

Das, B. (2000). "Moments in a History of Reservations." *Economic and Political Weekly, 35*(43/44): 3831-3834.

Dhavan, R. (2008). "Reservations for Women: The Way Forward." *Nat'l L. Sch. India Rev., 20*(1): 1-45.

Hurst, W. (2018). *Ruling before the Law: The Politics of Legal Regimes in China and Indonesia.* Cambridge: Cambridge University Press.

Panda, S. (2021). "Political Participation of Women in India: Problems and Prospects." *NAM today, Dr. Manas Chakrabarty, CIII*(4): 16-24.

Hegde, S. (2015). "The Many 'Truths' of Reservation Quotas in India: Extending the Engagement." *Social Scientist, 43*(3/4): 61-104.

Heredia, R. (2012). "Holding Up Half the Sky: Reservations for Women in India." *Economic and Political Weekly, 47*(9): 51-60.

Imam, M.A. (2023). "Evolution of Reservation System in India: An Overview." *International Journal of Trend in Scientific Research and Development (IJTSRD)*, 7(2): 674-681.

Kamala, K. (2024). "Shaping the Future: Women's Empowerment Through Political Participation in India." *Journal of Indian School of Political Economy, 36*(2): 28-34.

Khanna, M. (2023). "Political Participation of Women in Politics of Uttar Pradesh." In *Women in State Politics in India* (pp. 101-115). Routledge India.

Khanna, M. (2009). "Political Participation of Women in India." *The Indian Journal of Political Science, 70*(1): 55-64.

Kumar, J.P. (1997). "Policy of Reservation: Its Envisioned Perspective." *Journal of the Indian Law Institute, 39*(2/4): 330-337.

Kunovich, S. & Paxton, P. (2005). "Pathways to Power: The Role of Political Parties in Women's National Political Representation." *American Journal of Sociology, 111*(2): 505-552.

Minch, M.I. (2012). "Women and Politics." *The Indian Journal of Political Science, 73*(3): 489-492.

Mori, Y. & Kurosaki, T. (2016). "Does Political Reservation Affect Voting Behaviour? Empirical evidence from India." *Economic and Political Weekly, 51*(20): 37-46.

Ojha, S. (2009). "Reservation of Women in the Indian Parliament: Lessons from Other Countries." *The Indian Journal of Political Science, 70*(2): 471-479.

Palshikar, S. (2008). "Challenges before the Reservation Discourse." *Economic and Political Weekly, 43*(17): 8-11.

Pandit, L.A. (2010). "Political Leadership of Women: Constraints and Challenges." *The Indian Journal of Political Science, 71*(4), 1139-1148.

Rai, P. (2011). "Electoral Participation of Women in India: Key Determinants and Barriers." *Economic and Political Weekly, 46*(3): 47-55.

Sheth, D.L. (1987). "Reservations Policy Revisited." *Economic and Political Weekly, 22*(46): 1957-1962.

Singh, R.K. & Mishra, A. (2015). "Electoral Participation of Women in India and The Role of Political Parties." *The Indian Journal of Political Science, 76*(2): 209-217.

Tharu, S., Prasad, M.M., Pappu, R. & Satyanarayana, K. (2007). "Reservations and the Return to Politics." *Economic and Political Weekly, 42*(49): 39-45.

Tinker, I. (2009). Assumptions and Realities: Electoral Quotas for Women. *Geo. J. Int'l Aff.*, 10(1): 7-16.

Tabassum, S. (2023). "Women's Reservation Law in India: A New Journey towards Political Empowerment." *Third Concept, 37*(442): 45-48.

Yoganandham, G., Kareem, M.A.A., Khan, M.E.M.I. & Elanchezhian, M.G. (2023). An Evaluation of the Reservation System in India. *International Journal of all Research Education and Scientific Methods, 11*(3): 218-229.

9

Limits of 'Gender' as a Political Category

Reflections on Women Reservation Debate in India

Suraj Beri

Introduction

The concept of gender has been a central category in feminist politics and scholarship. However, in the Indian context, the use of gender as a unidimensional political category has been contested, particularly in the debate around women's reservation. This chapter argues that an unqualified ahistorical 'abstract' notion of gender has fundamental limits in terms of its representational claims as well as political meanings and practices (Chakravarti, 2003). The debate around women's reservation in India highlights the need for a more nuanced understanding of gender, one that takes into account the intersectionality of caste, class, and religion. Nineteenth century movements for autonomy and independence in India played a significant role in shaping the discourse around gender as a crucial aspect of social, economic, and political emancipation. As noted by sociologist Gail Omvedt (1993), these movements, including the Indian

National Congress and the All India Women's Conference, brought to the forefront the need to address gender-based discrimination and inequality as part of the broader struggle for freedom and democracy. The different waves of feminist and women's movements in India, as discussed by Uma Chakravarti (2003) and Nivedita Menon (2012), further deepened the notion that modern debates on liberal democracy and freedom must investigate the gendered dimensions of domination, discrimination, and exclusion. However, in recent years, there has been a growing recognition and deliberation on the internal heterogeneous layers within the gender category. The debate around women's reservation in India has been a contentious one, with arguments for and against the policy. Supporters of women's reservation, such as Rajeshwari Deshpande (2002) and Zoya Hasan (2000), argue that it is a necessary step towards ensuring greater political representation and empowerment of women. They contend that in a patriarchal society like India, where women face multiple barriers to political participation, reservations can help level the playing field and provide a space for women's voices to be heard.

This chapter argues that a nuanced understanding of gender, one that is sensitive to the intricacies of caste, class, and religion in the Indian context, is essential if the concept of gender is to retain its radical potential for democratic values and progressive politics. The notion of intersectionality of gender with caste, class, and religion in the Indian context, argues that a unidimensional understanding of gender fails to capture the complexities of women's lived experiences and struggles. This chapter aims to juxtapose gender as a differentiated category *vis-à-vis* the women's reservation discourses in contemporary India and makes a point that an unqualified ahistorical 'abstract' notion of gender politics has fundamental limits in terms of its representational claims as well as political meanings and practices. It is important to recognize the internal heterogeneity of the gender politics. The debate around women's reservation in India highlights the need for a more nuanced understanding of gender politics well beyond the recognitional claims and acknowledging the intersectionality of caste, class, and religion and addressing the redistributive aspects, i.e. land rights, property rights and labour question as well. Only by embracing such a contextualized and historically grounded notion of gender politics can we hope to realize its full potential for democratic values and progressive politics in India.

Methodology

The chapter is based upon the critical review of the debates on gender politics and the challenges of gender politics solely based on demand for women reservation. It draws upon the analytical insights of scholars who argue for representational politics and those who argue for redistribution politics. The chapter then takes a case of Nagaland and Naga women's to analyse the issues of gender politics. The discursive dimension of the chapter provides a comprehensive framework for analysing the complex interplay of representation and redistribution in gender politics in Nagaland. By integrating theoretical debates and specific issue in Indian context on women reservation, the chapter aims to offer a nuanced understanding of the challenges and opportunities for advancing gender politics as a substantive contribution to democratic politics.

Gender Politics: Questions of Representation

Gender politics refers to the ways in which gender identities and relations influence political structures, processes, and policies. It encompasses the struggle for gender equality and justice, addressing issues such as representation, rights, and resource distribution. Gender politics interrogates the power dynamics between different genders and seeks to transform the socio-political landscape to achieve a more equitable society. This section discusses the key dimensions of gender politics in terms of representational claims. It would draw upon the insights from the writings of two well known frameworks suggested by Anne Phillips and Drude Dahlerup and makes an attempt to understand how gender politics with its focus on representation questions gets over determined by it and ignores the redistribution politics of gender politics. Ensuring that women and other marginalized genders have equal representation in political institutions and decision-making bodies. This includes advocating for gender quotas and reservations in parliaments, state assemblies, and local governance.

Anne Phillips' work, *The Politics of Presence* (1995), is centred around the concept of the "politics of presence of women in political institutions". She argues that the mere presence of women and other marginalized groups in political institutions is crucial for achieving genuine democratic representation. This presence ensures that the perspectives and experiences of these groups are brought into the decision-making process. Phillips distinguishes between "descriptive" and "substantive" representation. Descriptive representation refers to representatives who physically resemble the demographic characteristics of the population, while substantive representation concerns the advocacy of policies that benefit the represented groups. She argues that without descriptive representation, substantive representation is often inadequate, as those who do not share the lived experiences of marginalized groups may lack the necessary insight to advocate effectively on their behalf. Phillips provides a strong defence of gender quotas as a means to achieve the politics of presence. She argues that quotas are necessary to overcome historical injustices and systemic barriers that prevent women from entering politics. Quotas can ensure a critical mass of women in political institutions, which is essential for changing the dynamics and priorities of these institutions. She addresses common criticisms of quotas, such as the argument that they undermine meritocracy or lead to tokenism. Phillips contends that the concept of merit is often biased against marginalized groups and that quotas can help to level the playing field.

Drude Dahlerup (2006), in her work, *Women, Quotas and Politics*, begins by discussing the concept of gender quotas, defining them as measures designed to ensure that women constitute a significant proportion of candidates or elected representatives. She introduces the notion of "critical mass," arguing that a certain threshold of women's representation (often cited as around 30%) is necessary to bring about substantial changes in legislative priorities and policy outcomes. This concept is crucial for understanding the rationale behind gender quotas and their intended effects. Dahlerup delves into the challenges of implementing gender quotas, discussing both formal and informal barriers. She highlights issues such as resistance from political elites, cultural opposition, and legal obstacles. Despite these challenges, Dahlerup presents evidence that gender quotas have been effective in increasing women's representation in many countries. She emphasizes that the impact of quotas goes beyond numbers, contributing to changes in political agendas, legislative priorities, and the broader political culture. Dahlerup counters these arguments by pointing out that political recruitment is often biased against women, and quotas can help level the playing field. She also discusses concerns about tokenism, where women elected through quotas may lack real power or influence.

Homogeneous Conception of 'Woman' Category: Significance of Intersectionality for Gender Politics

Embracing intersectionality in gender politics has significant implications for feminist praxis. It calls for a shift from a singular focus on gender to a more comprehensive understanding of how multiple forms of oppression intersect and shape women's lives. This shift requires building solidarities across differences and centring the experiences and voices of marginalized women, such as Dalit women and Muslim women, in feminist movements (Rege, 1998; Hasan, 2010). Nivedita Menon (2000) challenges the notion of a homogeneous "woman" category, arguing that it is not a pre-given or natural category but is constituted differently in various historical and cultural contexts. This argument highlights the need to recognize the internal heterogeneity within the gender category and the diverse experiences of women in India. Several problems emerging from politics based on a homogeneous category of women also limit the gender politics and the uproar and controversy on women reseration in India refletcs this lack of intersectional understanding of women in India. Mary E. John (2000) and Satish Deshpande (2006), argue that the women reservation policy fails to take into account the heterogeneity within the category of 'women' and may end up privileging upper-caste, upper-class women at the expense of more marginalized groups. They point out that in a society deeply divided along the lines of caste, class, and religion, a blanket reservation for women may not necessarily translate into greater representation for all women. Carole Pateman in her book, *The Sexual Contract* (1988), presents a gendered approach to citizenship by analyzing Mary Wollstonecraft's dilemma between the principles of equality and difference. Pateman's analysis sheds light on the complex challenges faced by women in modern democracies as they navigate the tension between being recognized as 'equal citizens' and having their specific experiences and needs as women acknowledged.

The Equality Strategy

One approach to women's citizenship emphasizes the importance of equality and inclusion. This strategy focuses on ensuring that women are treated as 'equal citizens' and have access to the same rights, opportunities, and responsibilities as men. The equality strategy is rooted in the idea that women should be judged based on their individual merits and abilities, rather than their gender. However, Pateman argues that the equality strategy has a significant limitation. By emphasizing sameness and downplaying gender differences, this approach tends to deny women's particularity 'as women'. It overlooks the unique experiences, perspectives, and challenges that women face due to their gender, such as reproductive rights, caregiving responsibilities, and gender-based violence. In striving for equality, the specific needs and concerns of women may be overlooked or marginalized.

The Difference Strategy

The alternative approach to women's citizenship focuses on recognizing and including women's differences and particularities. This strategy acknowledges that women have distinct experiences and needs that should be considered and accommodated within the framework of citizenship. It emphasizes the importance of valuing and representing women's voices, perspectives, and contributions as women. However, Pateman points out that the difference strategy also has its pitfalls. By emphasizing women's differences and particularities, this approach risks reproducing inequality. It may reinforce gender stereotypes and perpetuate the notion that women are inherently different from and inferior to men. The focus on difference can also lead to the marginalization of women's voices and the exclusion of women from certain spheres of citizenship, such as politics and the workplace.

Pateman's Solution: Differentiated Citizenship Model

To address the dilemma between equality and difference, Pateman proposes a 'differentiated citizenship model'. This model seeks to reconcile the principles of equality and difference by recognizing women both as equal citizens and as individuals with specific experiences and needs. The differentiated citizenship model acknowledges that women's experiences and perspectives are shaped by their gender, but it does not treat gender as a basis for exclusion or inequality. Instead, it advocates for the inclusion and representation of women's voices and concerns within the framework of citizenship. This model calls for policies and practices that take into account women's specific needs and experiences, such as reproductive rights, caregiving support, and measures to address gender-based violence.

The Missing Redistributive Politics

Redistribution scholars argue that focusing on cultural recognition can divert attention from addressing economic inequalities. They contend that material conditions and economic structures fundamentally shape individuals' lives, and thus, efforts to achieve justice should prioritize redistributive measures. Nancy Fraser (2003) herself acknowledges that while recognition is important, it should not overshadow the need for economic redistribution, which addresses fundamental issues of poverty and inequality. Let us discuss some of the key critiques of one-sided representational reduction of gender politics.

- *Fragmentation of Social Movements:* Another critique is that recognition-based approaches can lead to the fragmentation of social movements. Redistribution scholars argue that emphasizing identity politics can create divisions among marginalized groups, weakening the collective struggle against systemic economic inequalities. They assert that a focus on class-based solidarity and collective action is essential for achieving substantial and lasting social change (Fraser, 2003).

- *Risk of Essentialism:* Recognition-based approaches often rely on fixed notions of identity, which can lead to essentialism. Redistribution scholars criticize this tendency to treat identities as static and unchanging, arguing that it can reinforce stereotypes and limit the potential for social transformation. They advocate for a more fluid and dynamic understanding of identity, which recognizes the interplay between economic conditions and cultural identities.
- *Interconnection of Capitalism and Patriarchy:* Marxist feminists argue that capitalism and patriarchy are interconnected systems of oppression that must be addressed together. Economic exploitation and gender inequality are mutually reinforcing, and any attempt to achieve social justice must tackle both simultaneously.
- *Significance of Redistribution of Resources in Society to address Gender Inequality:* Redistribution of wealth and resources is seen as the foundation for achieving gender equality. Marxist feminists advocate for policies such as progressive taxation, universal healthcare, affordable housing, and education, which can address the material conditions of women's lives. Material redistribution for substantive equality: Proponents argue that formal equality (e.g., equal rights under law) is insufficient without material resources to exercise those rights. For example, the right to education means little if women cannot afford schooling or are burdened with unpaid care work.
- *Emphasis on Collective Action:* Feminists emphasize the importance of collective action and solidarity among

marginalized groups. They argue that united struggles against capitalism and patriarchy are more effective in achieving social justice than fragmented movements focused solely on identity recognition.

- *Integration of Intersectionality:* Marxist feminists integrate intersectionality into their analysis, recognizing that women's experiences of oppression are shaped by multiple, intersecting factors such as race, class, sexuality, and ability. However, they argue that economic redistribution is crucial for addressing these compounded inequalities.

The Case of Naga Women and Weak Gender Politics

Naga society is heavily ingrained with patriarchal systems that systematically exclude women from positions of power and economic influence. Nagaland has a lamentable track record in terms of women's political representation. Since gaining independence in 1963, Nagaland has not elected any women to its State Assembly till 2023. In 2023 Legislative elections, first time in the history of Nagaland, two women, Hekani Jakhalu and Salhoutuonuo Kruse became MLA. Furthermore, one woman, named Rano M. Shazia, was elected to the Lok Sabha in 1977. And the second, woman to become Rajya Sabha MP was Phangnon Konyak, only in 2022. The presence of women in traditional village councils, established under the Nagaland Village Councils Act of 1978, is extremely limited, resulting in negligible female engagement in government. Although rules have been passed to ensure that 33 per cent of seats in municipal and town councils be reserved for women, their enforcement has been delayed, resulting in a complete absence of women's participation in these bodies.

Opposition to Women's Reservation

The opposition to women's reservation is based on the intention to uphold customary customs and traditional government institutions, which fundamentally embody male dominance. Skeptics contend that the implementation of gender quotas will weaken these systems and disturb societal cohesion. In 2012, the Nagaland Legislative Assembly passed a resolution opposing the implementation of women's reservation in Urban Local Bodies (ULBs). The assembly argued that such a reservation would violate Article 371(A) of the Constitution of India, which provides special protections for Naga customary laws and social practices. This decision reflects the ongoing tension between constitutional provisions for women's representation and the preservation of traditional Naga customs and governance structures.

This resolution highlights the complex interplay between national policies aimed at increasing women's political participation and the special constitutional provisions granted to Nagaland to protect its unique cultural practices. It underscores the challenges in reconciling gender equality initiatives with the preservation of customary laws and traditional social structures in Nagaland. The Nagaland Municipal (First Amendment) Act, 2006, which requires a 33 per cent quota for women in municipal councils, has encountered substantial resistance. Legal disputes arose when the state administration declined to conduct local elections, citing customary laws. The Supreme Court ultimately decided to enforce the reservation, however, the state administration has not yet taken any action in response to this urban local body (ULB) elections in Nagaland, held for the first time in 20 years. The elections were significant for including a 33 per cent reservation for women, marking a historic milestone for women's representation in the state.

The first ULB (Urban Local Bodies) Elections were conducted on 26th June, 2024 in Nagaland after 20 years of the Municipal Act was enacted in 2004 (*The Hindu*, 2024). Out of 523 total candidates, 198 were women candidates, out of which 102 were victorious, including eight in unreserved wards. This marked a significant achievement in the history of elections in Nagaland, reflecting the impact of the 33 per cent reservation for women. The elections were the first since the enactment of the Municipal Act in 2004, which initially did not include reservations for women. The subsequent attempts to hold elections with women's reservations in 2012 and 2017 faced significant opposition, resulting in violence and political upheaval.

Hurdles to Property Rights and Inheritance

Women from the Naga community have substantial obstacles when it comes to property rights and inheritance according to traditional legal practices. Historically, the inheritance of property has been passed down exclusively through the male lineage, resulting in women having restricted or non-existent entitlements to ancestral property. The situation of Naga women in terms of land and property rights presents a complex interplay of traditional customs, modern legal frameworks, and evolving gender norms. Despite constitutional provisions and efforts to implement gender equality, Naga women continue to face significant barriers in achieving equitable treatment in these domains. Jelle J.P. Wouters (2017) highlights the resistance to women's reservation and the entrenched nature of customary practices. He argues that Naga customary law, deeply rooted in the community's cultural and social fabric, prioritizes male lineage for property inheritance and land ownership. This traditional system systematically excludes women from these rights, limiting their economic independence and reinforcing their dependency on male relatives. Customary practices are not static; they have evolved over time, influenced by colonialism, Christianity, and interactions with the Indian state. However, the core patriarchal structures remain resilient, significantly affecting women's status and opportunities. Customary law dictates that land and property are inherited through the male line, effectively barring women from owning ancestral property. This exclusion restricts women's economic autonomy and their ability to accumulate and control wealth, perpetuating gender-based economic disparities. Women's participation in political processes and decision-making bodies is minimal. Despite constitutional provisions for women's reservation, the implementation of these policies faces strong resistance rooted in the preservation of traditional gender roles. As a result, women are significantly underrepresented in political institutions and leadership positions. The lack of property rights directly impacts women's economic status, limiting their opportunities for entrepreneurship and financial independence. This economic dependence on male relatives further entrenches gender inequality within the household and the community.

Gender Politics *via* both Representation and Redistribution

Fraser argues that redistribution and recognition should be seen in different perspectives on justice, rather than separate spheres. Fraser's argument is the dual-aspect theory of justice, which posits that a comprehensive approach to social justice must address both economic inequalities (redistribution) and cultural injustices (recognition). She contends that these two dimensions are interrelated and mutually reinforcing, and therefore, cannot be effectively addressed in isolation. She talks about 'participatory parity', this concept suggests that justice requires social arrangements that allow all members of society to interact as peers. This requires both economic resources and cultural recognition. critics from a recognition perspective argue that simply reserving seats for women does not address the deeper cultural and social norms that marginalize women. They emphasize the need for policies that recognize and value women's contributions across all spheres of society, beyond just political representation. This includes challenging patriarchal norms and ensuring that women from diverse backgrounds are included and represented.

Drawing on Fraser's dual approach, the debate on women's reservation in India can benefit from integrating both redistribution and recognition. While ensuring reserved seats for women is a crucial step towards addressing political and economic inequalities, it should be complemented by efforts to challenge and transform cultural norms that perpetuate gender discrimination. This includes educational reforms, public awareness campaigns, and policies that promote gender equality in all areas of life. The critiques of recognition-based approaches by redistribution scholars highlight important considerations in the pursuit of social justice. While recognition of diverse identities is essential, it should not overshadow the need for economic redistribution and structural change.

Conclusion

The discourse on gender politics, particularly in the context of Nagaland, underscores the necessity of integrating both representational and redistribution dimensions to achieve substantive gender equality. The historic urban local body elections in Nagaland, with the implementation of a 33 per cent reservation for women, marked a significant milestone. However, this progress highlights the broader struggle: gender politics must not be confined solely to demands for political representation. To fortify gender politics, it is imperative to extend the struggle beyond mere representation. While ensuring that women have seats in political institutions is crucial, it is equally important to address the underlying socio-economic inequalities that persist. Redistribution of resources, including land and property rights, economic opportunities, and access to education and healthcare, are essential components of a comprehensive approach to gender equality.

In Nagaland, the resistance to women's reservation is deeply rooted in the preservation of customary laws and traditional gender roles, which often exclude women from property inheritance and decision-making processes. Addressing these issues requires a dual approach that encompasses both the symbolic inclusion of women in political spaces and the substantive redistribution of resources that empower them economically and socially. The case of Nagaland illustrates that gender politics, if reduced solely to the demand for women's reservation, risks becoming superficial and tokenistic. Without parallel efforts to dismantle the patriarchal structures that control social, economic, and political resources, the impact of representational gains will be limited. For gender politics to be effective and transformative, it must integrate the demands for both representation and redistribution, ensuring that women not only have a seat at the table but also the resources and power to effect meaningful change.

In conclusion, strengthening gender politics in India, and particularly in regions like Nagaland, requires a holistic approach that addresses both the representational and redistributional dimensions of justice. Only by combining these efforts can we achieve true gender equality and empower women to fully participate in all aspects of society.

REFERENCES

Baruah, S. (2003). *Ethnonationalism in India: A Reader*. Oxford University Press.

Kikon, D. (2019). *Living with Oil and Coal: Resource Politics and*

Militarization in Northeast India. University of Washington Press.

Chakravarti, U. (2003). *Gendering caste through a Feminist Lens*. Popular Prakashan.

Crenshaw, K. (1989). *Demarginalizing the Intersection of Race and Sex: A Black Feminist Critique of Antidiscrimination Doctrine, Feminist Theory and Antiracist Politics*. University of Chicago Legal forum, *1*: 139-167.

Dahlerup, D. (2006). *Women, Quotas, and Politics*. London: Routledge.

Deshpande, R. (2002). Increasing Women's Political Representation and Participation in India. *Feminist Review*, (71), 95-98.

Deshpande, S. (2006). "Exclusive Inequalities: Merit, Caste and Discrimination in Indian Higher Education today." *Economic and Political Weekly*, pp. 2438-2444.

Fraser, Nancy (2003). *Redistribution or Recognition? A Philosophical Exchange*. Verso Books.

John, M.E. (2000). "Alternate Modernities? Reservations and Women's Movement in Twentieth Century India." *Economic and Political Weekly*, pp. 3822-3829.

Hasan, Z. (2010). "Gender, Religion and Democratic Politics in India." *Third World Quarterly, 31*(6): 939-954.

Hasan, Z. (2000). *Politics and the State in India*. Sage Publications India.

Menon, N. (2012). *Seeing like a Feminist*. Penguin, UK.

Menon, N. (2000). "Introduction" in N. Menon (Ed.), *Gender and Politics in Indi*a (pp. 1-36). Oxford University Press.

Omvedt, G. (1993). *Reinventing Revolution: New Social Movements and the Socialist Tradition in India* (Vol. 27). ME Sharpe.

Phillips, A. (1995). *The Politics of Presence*. London: Oxford University Press.

Rai, S. (2002). Class, Caste and Gender: Women in Parliament in India. International IDEA, Women in Parliament, Stockholm.

Rege, S. (1998). "Dalit Women Talk Differently: A Critique of 'Difference' and towards a Dalit Feminist Standpoint Position." *Economic and Political Weekly*, 33(44): WS39-WS46.

Rege, S. (2006). *Writing Caste, Writing Gender: Reading Dalit Women's Testimonies*. Zubaan.

The Hindu, (2024). "NDPP Sweeps Historic Civic Polls in Nagaland, Wins All 3 Municipal Councils, Most town Councils", 30th June,

2024, URL: https://www.thehindu.com/news/national/ndpp-sweeps-historic-civic-polls-in-nagaland-wins-all-3-municipal-councils-most-town-councils/article68351457.ece, accessed on 19th July, 2024.

Wouters, J.J.P. (2017). "Land Tax, Reservation for Women and Customary Law in Nagaland", *Economic and Political Weekly*, *52*(9): 20-23.

10

Women's Representation in Indian Judiciary

A Case for Women Reservation

Kaustav Choudhoury

Introduction

The Indian Judiciary, often hailed as the bedrock of democracy, stands as a beacon of justice and fairness in the nation's legal landscape. Its solemn duty to uphold the rule of law and its performance since its inception in 1951, safeguarding the rights of citizens has earned it widespread admiration and respect among all the foundational pillars of Indian democracy. Yet, beneath its august facade, lurks a glaring gender disparity that has long plagued its halls of justice. Despite its noble mandate, the Indian Judiciary has grappled with the stark underrepresentation of women in judicial roles, casting a shadow over its purported commitment to equality and inclusivity. The recent remarks by present Chief Justice D.Y. Chandrachud's on gender diversity within Indian courts bring to light this critical and ongoing issue. Despite significant strides in various professional fields over the years, the Indian judiciary continues to be predominantly male.

Women judges make up only a small fraction of the total number of judges in both the Supreme Court and the various High Courts and this study provides a comprehensive examination of the historical context, current statistics, and far-reaching implications of gender disparity in the Indian judiciary, along with potential measures to address this systemic imbalance.

Historical Context of Women Reservation in Indian Judiciary

The Indian judiciary, much like other institutions in India, has been shaped by societal norms and cultural expectations. Historically, the legal profession in India has been a male bastion, with women facing significant barriers to entry and advancement. In Colonial India, Justice Anna Chandy's appointment as a judge in 1937 was a groundbreaking moment. As the first woman judge in colonial India, and indeed one of the first in the world, Justice Chandy faced immense challenges. Her appointment was not only a personal triumph but also a significant milestone for women in the judiciary. However, her experience also highlighted the deep-seated gender biases within the legal system and society at large (Rao, 2018).

In post-colonial India, the pioneering efforts of trailblazers like Cornelia Sorabji further stand as shining beacons of courage and resilience. In 1892, Sorabji defied societal conventions and shattered barriers to become the first woman admitted to the legal profession in India. Her historic achievement marked a watershed moment in the annals of Indian legal history, challenging entrenched prejudices and paving the way for subsequent generations of women to chart their course in the legal landscape (Chandrachud, 2015). Sorabji's journey was fraught with obstacles and adversities, as she navigated a male-dominated profession with tenacity and determination. Despite facing widespread skepticism and opposition, she persevered, carving out a niche for herself in a realm traditionally reserved for men. Her trailblazing efforts not only challenged the *status quo* but also inspired countless women to follow in her footsteps, emboldening them to defy societal expectations and pursue careers in law (Menon, 2009). Sorabji's legacy serves as a poignant reminder of the transformative power of courage and conviction in the face of adversity. Through her pioneering efforts, Sorabji laid the groundwork for a more inclusive and equitable legal landscape, where women could assert their rights and claim their rightful place at the table of justice (NCW, 2017). Further, Justice Leila Seth's appointment as the first woman Chief Justice of a High Court in 1991 marked another significant achievement in the same narrative. Her autobiography, "*On Balance*", offers a poignant narrative of her experiences, shedding light on the additional burdens carried by women in the judiciary (World Bank, 2019). Justice Seth's career as auto biographed by her was marked by instances of gender bias, from colleagues who found it difficult to work with a woman to societal expectations that pigeon holed her into traditional gender roles, such as making tea arrangements at social gatherings. Her story underscores the broader challenges faced by women in breaking through the glass ceiling of the judiciary (Baxi, 1982).

Challenges Faced by Women Judges in Indian Judiciary

As of June 2023, women constitute only 13 per cent of the judges in all High Courts. None of the 25 High Courts have a woman Chief Justice. The Punjab & Haryana and Madras High Courts lead with 13 women judges each, while five High Courts (Manipur, Meghalaya, Patna, Tripura, and Uttarakhand) have no women judges at all. The situation in the Supreme Court is similarly bleak. In the 73 years since its establishment, the SC has had 268 judges, of whom only 11 have been women. The first woman appointed to the SC was Justice Fathima Beevi in October 1989. For the first 39 years of the SC's history, no woman served on the Bench. The year 2010 saw some improvement, with the appointment of five women justices, including Justices Gyan Sudha Misra, Ranjana Prakash Desai, R. Banumathi, Indu Malhotra, and Indira Banerjee. The year 2021 was particularly notable with the appointment of Justices Hima Kohli, B.V. Nagarathna, and B.M. Trivedi, bringing the total number of women judges to four—the highest ever. Despite this, women constitute only 12 per cent of the 33 sitting judges. Despite the incremental progress witnessed in recent years, women navigating the terrain of the legal profession in India still find themselves ensnared by systemic barriers and deeply entrenched biases. These obstacles, both overt and covert, cast a long shadow over their professional journey, impeding their progress and limiting their opportunities for advancement. Discrimination, ingrained within the fabric of the legal ecosystem, permeates every facet of their experience, leaving women lawyers grappling with a myriad of challenges as they strive to carve out their place within the legal fraternity (Planning Commission of India, 2013).

One of the most pervasive forms of discrimination faced by women lawyers is the subtle yet pervasive exclusion they encounter within legal circles. Despite their qualifications and expertise, women often find themselves sidelined and overlooked, denied access to critical cases and decision-making processes. This exclusion not only undermines their professional growth but also perpetuates a cycle of marginalization that stifles their potential within the legal profession. The path to judicial appointments, often perceived as the pinnacle of success within the legal realm, is fraught with hurdles for women aspiring to ascend the judicial ladder. Cultural stigmas and societal expectations surrounding gender roles serve as formidable barriers, imposing rigid constraints on women's professional aspirations and limiting their opportunities for advancement. Moreover, the dearth of support structures and mentorship opportunities further exacerbates these challenges, leaving women to navigate the complexities of the judicial landscape largely on their own. Gender biases, deeply entrenched within the legal system, pose yet another formidable obstacle to women's advancement in the judiciary. From implicit biases embedded within hiring practices to overt discrimination within courtroom dynamics, women encounter a multitude of barriers that impede their progress and perpetuate inequalities. These biases not only undermine women's credibility and competence but also erode trust in their ability to dispense impartial justice, further marginalizing them within the legal fraternity. Through their resilience and determination, they serve as beacons of hope, inspiring others to challenge the *status quo* and strive for a more just and inclusive society.

Implications of Gender Disparity in the Judiciary

The underrepresentation of women in the judiciary has significant and multifaceted implications. The primary pool for appointing SC judges comes from HC judges, and the lack of women in HCs directly impacts gender diversity in the SC. The other pool for SC appointments is the Bar, from which only one woman, Justice Indu Malhotra, has been elevated directly to the SC. This scarcity of women in both pools makes it challenging for the SC collegium to enhance gender diversity. The lack of women in judicial positions affects the judiciary's ability to reflect the diverse perspectives and experiences of the population it serves. Women judges bring unique insights into issues such as gender-based violence, discrimination, and family law. Their presence is essential for a judiciary that aims to be fair and representative of the society it governs. Their lived experiences provide them with a nuanced understanding of such cases, which is often lacking in their male counterparts. This perspective is crucial in ensuring that the judiciary not only upholds the law but also delivers justice in a manner that is sensitive to the complexities of gender.

The landmark the case of *Vishaka* vs. *State of Rajasthan*, which popularly known for laying down specific guidelines for 'Prevention of Sexual Harassment at Workplace' was delivered by J.S. Verma (then C.J.I.), Sujata Manohar and B.N. Kirpal. It is pertinent to note that had not been Justice Sujata Manohar in the bench, the judgment would have been different from what it is today. The tenure of women judges also plays a crucial role in their impact on the judiciary. The average tenure of women judges in the SC is 4.3 years, compared to the overall average of 5.25 years for all judges. Short tenures limit their ability to sit on Constitution Benches, which handle the most significant constitutional cases. For instance, Justice B.V. Nagarathna, despite being on track to become India's first woman Chief Justice, will serve in that capacity for only 36 days, far below the average tenure of 18 months for Chief Justices. This short tenure will limit her ability to implement significant changes.

The Collegium system, which involves the Chief Justice and the four senior-most judges making key judicial appointments, has not favoured gender diversity. Of the 11 women appointed to the SC, only two have served on the Collegium: Justices Banumathi and Ruma Pal. Their relatively long tenures (over six years) facilitated their inclusion in the Collegium. However, the average tenure of women judges remains short, hindering their chances of being included in this crucial decision-making body. The process of judicial appointments in India is governed by a combination of Constitutional provisions and judicial pronouncements. Article 124 of the Constitution of India, 1950 establishes the Supreme Court and regulates the procedure to appoint the justices. In addition to this constitutional provision, four critical Supreme Court judgments further delineate the process of appointment. *The First Judges Case* held that the President must consult the Chief Justice substantially before appointing judges. *The Second Judges Case* (1993) declared that the Chief Justice would have primacy over judicial appointments. *The Third Judges Case* (1998) explicated that the Chief Justice, in consultation with four senior-most judges, would decide on appointments. *The Fourth Judges Case* (2015) held the National Judicial Appointments Commission (NJAC) Act unconstitutional, reaffirming the Collegium system and preventing overarching legislative interference with judicial appointments.

Currently, the Chief Justice and four senior-most judges form the Collegium, making crucial decisions around appointing judges to the Supreme Court and High Courts. However, the seniority-based system has often been unfavourable to women, who typically have shorter tenures due to later appointments or earlier retirements.

The Case for Reservation of Women Judges in Indian Judiciary

Women judges play a pivotal role in shaping the landscape of justice within the Indian Judiciary, bringing to the bench a unique perspective informed by their lived experiences of gender discrimination and bias. Their presence not only enhances the diversity of viewpoints within the judiciary but also fosters a more empathetic and equitable dispensation of justice. Drawing upon their personal experiences, women judges offer insights into the nuanced complexities of gender dynamics, shedding light on issues that may have previously gone unnoticed or overlooked. Their firsthand understanding of the challenges faced by women in society enables them to empathize with litigants and victims, ensuring that their voices are heard and their rights protected within the judicial process.

Moreover, women judges serve as stalwart advocates for gender justice, championing the cause of equality and fairness within the legal system. Armed with a deep-seated commitment to justice, they challenge systemic inequalities and advocate for victim-centric approaches to dispensing justice. By centering the needs and rights of the marginalized and disenfranchised, women judges help to rectify historical injustices and pave the way for a more inclusive and equitable society. The impact of women judges is perhaps most evident in the landmark judgments they deliver, which serve as beacons of progress and catalysts for change within the legal landscape. For instance, Justice Fathima Beevi's historic appointment as the first woman judge to the Supreme Court of India in 1989 shattered barriers and inspired generations of women to pursue careers in law. Her groundbreaking achievement not only marked a significant milestone in the journey towards gender equality but also signalled a broader shift towards greater inclusivity within the judiciary.

Similarly, Justice Sujata Manohar's pivotal ruling in the *Vishakha case*, which recognized sexual harassment at the workplace as a violation of fundamental rights, underscored the transformative impact of women judges in shaping the trajectory of justice in India. By upholding the rights of women and challenging entrenched patriarchal norms, Justice Manohar's judgment set a precedent for addressing gender-based violence and discrimination within the legal framework.

Initiatives undertaken by Indian Judiciary to Encourage Women Participation

Numerous initiatives have been championed to encourage

women to pursue careers in law and the judiciary, recognizing the pivotal role of gender diversity in fostering a more inclusive and representative legal system. These initiatives encompass a wide array of programmes and support mechanisms aimed at dismantling barriers and empowering women to thrive in the legal profession. Mentorship programmes stand as a cornerstone of these initiatives, providing aspiring women lawyers with invaluable guidance and support from seasoned legal professionals. Through mentorship, women receive personalized advice, career guidance, and insights into navigating the complexities of the legal landscape. Mentors serve as role models and advocates, offering encouragement and wisdom as women chart their course in the legal profession. Formal training modules also play a crucial role in equipping women with the requisite skills and knowledge needed to excel in the legal arena. These training programmes cover a range of topics, from legal research and writing to courtroom advocacy and case management. By honing their skills through structured training modules, women gain confidence and proficiency in their legal practice, enhancing their prospects for success in the judiciary. Financial aid programmes further bolster women's participation in the legal profession by providing assistance with tuition fees, living expenses, and other educational costs. These programmes alleviate financial barriers that may deter women from pursuing legal education, ensuring equitable access to opportunities within the legal field.

Support networks serve as a vital source of encouragement and camaraderie for women navigating the challenges of the legal profession. These networks provide a platform for networking, mentorship, and professional development, fostering a sense of community and solidarity among women lawyers. By connecting women with like-minded peers and mentors, support networks create a supportive ecosystem conducive to their growth and success. For women aspiring to ascend to the bench, a multifaceted approach is indispensable in preparing for the rigours of judicial office. Emphasizing the pivotal role of education, aspiring judges must pursue legal education from esteemed institutions, cultivating a robust foundation of knowledge and expertise in the law. Practical experience gained through internships and apprenticeships under seasoned legal practitioners is invaluable in providing aspiring judges with firsthand insights into the intricacies of legal practice and courtroom dynamics. By immersing themselves in real-world legal settings, women gain practical skills and develop a nuanced understanding of the judicial process. Diligent preparation for competitive examinations is essential for aspiring judges, as judicial appointments are often contingent upon successful performance in rigorous selection processes. This entails thorough study of legal principles, case law, and procedural rules, coupled with diligent practice and preparation. Building robust networks within the legal fraternity is paramount for aspiring judges, as connections and relationships within the legal community can open doors to opportunities and supports their professional growth. Actively engaging in legal discourse, participating in professional associations, and attending legal conferences and seminars are effective ways to expand one's network and forge meaningful connections.

Exhibiting resilience in the face of adversity is a hallmark of successful judges, as the journey to judicial office is often fraught with challenges and setbacks. By maintaining a steadfast commitment to their goals and persevering in the face of obstacles, aspiring judges demonstrate their readiness to uphold the tenets of justice with unwavering integrity and diligence. Staying abreast of evolving legal paradigms and embracing a lifelong commitment to learning are essential attributes for aspiring judges. By remaining curious, adaptable, and receptive to new ideas, women judges ensure their readiness to confront the complex legal issues of the day and deliver reasoned and principled judgments that uphold the rule of law.

Conclusion

The journey of women in the Indian Judiciary stands as a testament to their resilience, determination, and unwavering commitment to justice. Despite facing formidable challenges and systemic barriers, women have forged ahead, carving out a path towards greater gender diversity and inclusivity within the legal profession. While significant strides have been made the road to equality remains fraught with obstacles. It is requiring continued efforts and collective action to overcome. The journey of women in the Indian Judiciary is marked by moments of triumph and progress, as well as moments of setback and adversity. From the pioneering efforts of trailblazers like Cornelia Sorabji, who defied societal norms to become the first woman admitted to the legal profession in India, to the landmark appointments of women judges to the highest echelons of the judiciary, the journey has been characterized by resilience and perseverance in the face of adversity. While progress has been made, persistent challenges continue to hinder the full realization of gender equality within the Indian Judiciary. Discrimination, bias, and cultural stereotypes pose significant barriers to women's advancement, impeding their access to opportunities and recognition within the legal profession. Moreover, the underrepresentation of women in leadership positions and decision-making roles further exacerbates inequalities, perpetuating a culture of exclusivity and marginalization. However, amidst these challenges, the trajectory of women in the Indian Judiciary signals a promising future characterized by increased representation, equitable opportunities, and a steadfast commitment to justice. Initiatives aimed at promoting gender diversity and inclusivity, such as mentorship programmes, formal training modules, and support networks, are paving the way for greater participation of women in the legal profession. Moreover, landmark judgments delivered by women judges on issues of gender justice and equality are reshaping the contours of legal discourse and challenging entrenched norms and practices. By fostering a culture of inclusivity and empowerment, dismantling systemic barriers, and amplifying women's voices, India can realize the vision of a judiciary that truly mirrors the diversity and aspirations of its populace. Through concerted efforts and unwavering commitment, we can create a legal system that upholds the principles of equality, fairness, and justice for generations to come.

REFERENCES

Bagri, N. (2016). "Women in the Indian Judiciary: Breaking through the Glass Ceiling." *International Journal of Law and Social Sciences, 5*(2): 45-60.

Bandyopadhyay, S. (2023). "Breaking the Glass Ceiling: Women in the Indian Judiciary." *Legal Perspectives, 15*(3): 45-62.

Baxi, U. (1982). *The Crisis of the Indian Legal System*. Vikas Publishing House.

Chandrachud, A. (2015). *An Independent, Colonial Judiciary: A History of the Bombay High Court during the British Raj, 1862–1947*. Oxford University Press.

Chatterjee, P. (2022). "Gender Disparity in the Indian Judiciary: Challenges and Opportunities." *Indian Legal Journal, 8*(2): 78-91.

Chaudhry, S. (2014). 'The Supreme Court of India and the Right to Health: Concretizing Social Rights in a Developing Constitutional Democracy." *South Asian Law Review, 2*(3): 210-228.

Das, A. (2024). A Tale of Resilience: Women's Journey in the Indian Judiciary." *Law Review, 20*(1): 112-130.

Deshpande, S. (2004). "Mapping the 'Middle': Issues in the Analysis of the Non-poor Classes in India." *Economic and Political Weekly, 39*(46): 5001-5009.

Government of India. (1974). *Report of the Committee on the Status of Women in India*. Ministry of Education and Social Welfare.

Gupta, N. (2021). "Promoting Gender Diversity in the Indian Judiciary: Initiatives and Progress'. *Journal of Legal Studies, 12*(4): 205-220.

Jain, P. (2023). "Women Judges in India: Challenges and Achievements." *Legal Gazette, 7*(3): 32-48.

Kumar, R. (2022). "Empowering Women in the Legal Profession: Strategies for Success." *Law and Society Review, 25*(2): 155-170.

Menon, N.R.M. (2009). *A Handbook of Human Rights and Criminal Justice in India: The System and Procedure*. Oxford University Press.

Ministry of Law and Justice, Government of India. (2022). *Judicial Appointments and Diversity*. Law and Justice in India. Retrieved from www.lawandjustice.in/judicialappointments

Mukherjee, A. (2012). "Gender Justice and the Indian Judiciary: Progress and Challenges." *Journal of Gender Studies, 15*(1): 23-38.

National Commission for Women. (2017). *Gender Justice in the Judiciary: A Report*. National Commission for Women.

Parliament of India. (1946-1950). *Debates of the Constituent Assembly of India*. Lok Sabha Secretariat.

Patel, S. (2024). "Towards Gender Equality in the Indian Judiciary: A Vision for the Future." *Indian Legal Review, 14*(1): 88-105.

Planning Commission of India. (2013). *Twelfth Five Year Plan (2012–2017): Social Sectors*. Sage Publications.

Rao, B.S. (1968). *The Framing of India's Constitution: Select Documents*. Indian Institute of Public Administration.

Rao, N. (2018). "The Role of Women Judges in the Indian Judiciary." *Indian Journal of Legal Studies*, 10(2): 112-128.

Sen, A. (2008). "Justice and Gender: Reflections on the Indian Experience." *Journal of Human Development and Capabilities, 9*(3): 257-276.

Sharma, M. (2021). "The Role of Women Judges in Promoting Gender Justice: Insights from the Indian Judiciary." *Legal Insights, 9*(4): 75-90.

Singh, A. (2023). "Charting the Course: Suggestions for Aspiring Women Judges in India." *Legal Mentorship Quarterly, 6*(2): 115-130.

Subramanian, K.S. (2009). "Judicial Activism and Social Change: A Study of Selected Decisions of the Supreme Court of India." *International Journal of Law and Policy*, 7(4): 350-370.

Supreme Court of India. (2022). *Judgments and Orders*. Retrieved from www.sci.gov.in/judgments

Supreme Court of India. (2022). *Annual Report*. Supreme Court of India Publications.

Verma, P. (2022). "Women's Representation in the Indian Judiciary: Progress and challenges." *Legal Dynamics*, 11(3): 67-82.

World Bank. (2019). *Gender and Justice in India. World Bank Reports*. Retrieved from www.worldbank.org/en/country/india/publication/gender-justice

11

Feminist Perspectives on Media Representation of Women in Politics

Lucy Mishra

Introduction

Women in politics encounter biased, sexist, and discriminatory media coverage. Studies over the last several decades show that female politicians remain at a disadvantage regarding media attention. Journalists frequently highlight women's traditional roles and concentrate on their appearance when reporting on women in politics. They reinforce stereotypes of female politicians as weak, indecisive, and emotional. As countries globally aim for democratic progress, it becomes increasingly crucial to incorporate marginalized groups and diverse perspectives into each nation's political framework. Despite significant advancements in voting rights and the reduction of direct obstacles to holding office, most societies are still far from achieving governance bodies that truly represent their populations. Research indicates that in many developed nations, the gap in political participation between men and women is not about the quantity of involvement but rather the different ways they engage in the political process.

Feminism Waves, Women in Politics and Views towards Unequal Representation

The second wave of feminism, which began in the 1960s in the United States and spread to Europe in the late 1960s and 1970s, heightened interest in media and their relationship to gender. Feminists questioned the role of media in creating gender stereotypes and upholding patriarchal values, suggesting that media perpetuate a distorted, male-centric worldview. These inquiries led to the development of specific fields of study for feminist scholars, such as stereotypes and social roles, ideology, and pornography (Van Zoonen, 1994), which are now explored in three academic disciplines: psychoanalysis, social psychology, and cultural studies. Moreover, feminist scholars scrutinized academic knowledge itself. They critiqued the androcentric nature of Western knowledge, aligning feminist political views with academic inquiry. This critique gave rise to three feminist epistemologies: feminist empiricism, feminist standpoint theory, and feminist post-modernism (also known as post-modern feminism). These traditions share the belief that Western knowledge is androcentric and overly emphasizes rationality (Hawkesworth, 1989). However, they differ significantly on how to change this androcentric character and develop alternative conceptions of knowledge (Smith, 1998).

Exploring Gender Inequality in both Politics and Media

Some works categorically focus on female political leaders, offering diverse perspectives on how they are portrayed. Campus (2013) attributes women's lack of political leadership to issues of power and masculinity. Drawing on gender studies and supported by leadership and management studies, Campus discusses the historical male dominance in leadership roles. Leadership is traditionally associated with masculinity, implying that power is inherently a male domain. Campus examines these traditional views of power, noting the psychosexual associations with masculinity—strength, force, and authority. The persistence of stereotypical imagery and text in the coverage of women in politics has been internalized to such an extent that it often overshadows the capabilities of women. Although women's entry into politics marks a positive social change, their media depictions remain contentious. Female political leaders face heightened media scrutiny due to gender stereotypes favouring men in power. Often, their clothing, hairstyle, and emotional demeanor overshadow their policy positions and arguments. Further, author reveals that newspaper articles are more likely to comment on a female candidate's appearance than a male's. While male politicians are not immune to such trivial mentions, they receive less coverage of this nature. The limited research on media framing of women in politics is partly due to their recent participation in politics and the small number of women in this field.

Political Participation, Feminist Organisation and the Creation of Inclusive Democratic Spaces

The recent context of women's political participation has been framed as "women asking for seats at the table where public policy is discussed." Given the slow increase in the number of women in politics, many countries use quotas as their preferred method to promote greater gender balance in political institutions. According to the Institute for Democracy and Electoral Assistance (IDEA) Database, more than half of the countries worldwide employ electoral quotas for their parliaments (IDEA, 2020). While these quota systems signify a significant shift towards policies with precise goals and means, the discussion on gender-balanced political processes and the inclusion of women must go beyond merely increasing numbers or bringing women into parliaments (Ballington *et al.*, 2005). The assumption that formal or numeric participation in state institutions will automatically lead to the representation of women's interests and the enhancement of democracy has proven insufficient. Consequently, quotas have not effectively addressed the underlying factors that restrict women's participation in concrete terms.

Feminist scholars investigate women's presence, as exemplified by Cynthia Enloe in her book "*Bananas, Beaches, and Bases*" (Enloe, 2000). Enloe explores women's histories, highlighting their activities, actions, silences, and protests. Her work reveals that women are visible when their presence is acknowledged in ways that lead to tangible outcomes. It is important to recognize the limitations of relying heavily on quotas to address women's marginalization in the public sphere, especially in decision-making roles. This urgency is underscored by Rottenberg's concept of "Neoliberal Feminism" (Rottenberg, 2018). Women also organize in various other domains beyond political spaces. To address the imbalance and marginalization of women in society, it is essential to understand the sites of participation and the roles women play in these areas. Visible presence should be coupled with influence that transforms mere formal representation into substantial presence. This shift is more sustainable and can make decision-making spaces more democratic, inclusive, and gender-fair.

From Formal to Substantive Representation

Paxton and Hughes (2007) outlined women's equal representation using three criteria: formal, descriptive, and substantive representation.

Formal representation: The primary form of representation, formal equality, is typically established through legal means. It assumes that individuals elect representatives based on political ideologies or competencies. However, in many developing democracies, this assumption has not translated into reality. Globally, women often face barriers to elective positions unrelated to their political views or abilities. During the 1980s and 1990s, the women's movement and activists took steps to address gender imbalances, highlighted by the Beijing Platform for Action advocating for 30 per cent affirmative action for women's political participation. During this period, many African constitutions incorporated affirmative action as a temporary measure to address the historical gaps in women's political involvement. For instance, Uganda's 1995 constitution introduced a gender quota to rectify the longstanding inequalities faced by women in the country, as did the constitutions of Eritrea and Rwanda. Additionally, several other countries have clauses in political party charters mandating the formal inclusion of women.

Descriptive representation, the second type, establishes a connection between representation and constituency. Here, the quantity of women is contextualized within interests and constituency dynamics. Consequently, electoral systems that promote the election of women include party lists, proportional representation (PR), and large district magnitudes. These systems are less competitive compared to majority-based systems relying on single-member districts. In a single-member setup, a woman is often positioned as the primary choice for her party's participation in the election. Moreover, in proportional representation systems with extensive district magnitudes, a woman may secure a seat even if placed further down on the party list (Matland & Brown, 1992). Arnesen and Peters (2017) expanded on the benefits of descriptive representation and its legitimacy concerns. However, it is noted that proportional representation tends to favour party systems with numerous parties, opening doors for new parties to enter the parliamentary landscape. Despite these advantages, various analyses suggest that even when descriptive representation is implemented, it does not always translate into improved conditions or significant benefits for women (Lena Wangnerud, 2009).

Substantive representation, as posited by Paxton and Hughes, constitutes women's direct engagement rather than representation by others, asserting that true equality hinges on women speaking and acting autonomously in decision-making processes. This form of representation, surpassing formal and descriptive models in legitimacy, has shown notably favourable outcomes. Recognizing the importance of substantive representation in feminist organizing and policy inclusivity, it underscores the necessity for women's participation beyond mere numerical representation. This involves amplifying diverse women's voices across various social strata and intersecting identities within institutional frameworks fostering inclusive democratic principles. However, feminist movements face a pivotal question: how can alternative women's organizing fundamentally reshape male-dominated political spaces?

Societal Norms, Gender Roles and their Impact on Political Representation of Women

The exclusion of women from leadership roles can be traced back to the pre-capitalist era, particularly when crop production became established. As human societies transitioned from nomadic lifestyles to settled agricultural communities, surplus production began. Recognizing women's significant role in reproduction, early societies instinctively excluded them from crop production and hunting. This exclusion gradually became a societal norm. Friedrich Engels, in his book "*The Origin of the Family, Private Property and the State*", describes how women's biological roles in reproduction were acknowledged in the early division of labour (Engels, 1884). Overtime, this recognition was transformed into a myth that supported claims of male superiority, a notion that Eleanor Leacock, in her work "*Myths of Male Dominance: Collected Articles on Women Cross-Culturally*", argues lacks factual, historical or anthropological evidence.

Political Economy of Power and Party Politics

Political parties are often seen as exclusive entities with little inclusivity. Party politics revolve around competition and access to benefits. As a result, political parties are not appealing to potential female activists who seek to promote collective goals. Most parties lack a clear agenda for gender equality, and women's involvement is limited to the women's wing, where they are expected to act as cheerleaders, manipulating the political landscape. Occasionally, men will promote certain women who can further their own interests.

The urgent necessity lies in fostering critical awareness among female parliamentarians through feminist advocacy and lobbying efforts. This is crucial for challenging entrenched conservative, anti-women, and hetero-normative norms and structures. Establishing women—only spaces facilitates dialogue among female parliamentarians and between them and women citizens, serving as a potent tool to dismantle patriarchal dominance in personal and political realms (Tripp, 2003).

Neoliberal Politics and Women's Rights

Neoliberal politics have fallen short in advancing the agenda for women's rights. While gender policies are implemented, they often only scratch the surface, failing to challenge the existing power dynamics or resource distribution. Real progress in enhancing women's participation and representation can only occur by breaking away from the capitalist-driven logic of the neoliberal state. Decision-making processes must involve negotiation among the state, market forces, and civil society. It is argued that the political arena has historically been dominated by men, with a masculine model of governance prevailing, where men set the rules and lead the political game. This male-centric model either dissuades women from engaging in politics altogether or pushes them to reject the prevailing masculine norms, as highlighted by Okeke (2003).

A More Holistic Understanding of Participation

Political participation involves involving individuals in the crucial decisions of society. If participation occurs without representing every segment of society—encompassing women across various demographics (whether rich, poor, heterosexual, LGBTQ+, with or without children, young, old, with or without academic backgrounds, with disabilities, or without)—the aim is to ensure all voices are heard in decision-making processes, fostering inclusivity and fairness. It proposes a radical notion that democratic institutions should prioritise equality, equity, and justice, enabling people to reshape the political system for the collective good, particularly benefiting the marginalized.

Feminism, within this broader framework of participation and transformation, can contribute in diverse ways. In the political sphere, a feminist perspective aids in dismantling gender-based discrimination and expanding political dialogue. The endeavour to enhance women's involvement and representation in decision-making roles seeks not only numerical parity but also to reform decision-making structures for greater inclusivity. Women's political engagement and progressive consciousness can hold political entities accountable and alter decision-making dynamics. Feminists engage in substantive discussions about real issues, eschewing bureaucratic or overly cautious language.

Negotiating and Redefining the Democratic Space

The abstract concept of space illustrates how it is influenced by gender and politics across societies. Various spaces have been culturally, religiously, and politically categorized as either "male" or "female" throughout human history. Female spaces have typically been associated with roles related to reproduction and nurturing in all societies. Meanwhile, public spaces have traditionally been seen as male-dominated, excluding women from the critical decision-making processes related to power for centuries.

To challenge the dominance of patriarchal systems in both politics and everyday life, women need to actively occupy public spaces with the aim of advocating for gender equality and transformative change. It is essential to recognize that the division between public and private spaces is artificial, and patriarchal influence persists across all spaces, including those shaped by colonial legacies. Therefore, addressing the exclusion of women from political participation requires mobilization at the grassroots level. This involves empowering women in local communities and neighbourhood groups, where they are most accessible and effective. Achieving true gender inclusion in public spheres, encompassing both political and economic realms, necessitates challenging existing power dynamics and advocating for societal change. While the acceptance of state-sanctioned spaces should not be discouraged, genuine feminists should prioritise and promote grassroots-driven initiatives, referred to as "invented spaces". These spaces derive legitimacy from grassroots invention and occupation, enabling collective action to directly confront established power structures.

Feminizing Legislatures: Advancing Gender Equality

If the goal is to integrate gender equality into politics and public policy, simply increasing the number of women in public spaces is ineffective unless accompanied by efforts to address gender issues in various other areas where political interests are developed. In fact, this approach might even hinder progress towards gender equality. For example, the 31 per cent female representation in Iraq's assembly does not protect against the conservative Islamist push to overturn the secular family law from the Ba'ath era. Many female assembly members are from the Islamist Shia faction and advocate for Sharia law in personal matters. Iraq's Minister of Women's Affairs, Sunni Kurd Narmeen Othman, expresses frustration: "It's very hard to counter this when female politicians themselves support Sharia. The men say: 'Even these women agree with us.'"

Increasing female representation in legislative bodies can have negative consequences. It might reduce the quality of democracy and public debate if reserved seats are used to bolster the ruling party with loyal female members who do not challenge authoritarian leadership, as seen in Rwanda and South Africa. Women often lack experience in public debate, opposition, or negotiation due to limited political training, making them ineffective or easily manipulated legislators. Denise Walsh highlights how gender differences in debating styles and inadequate preparation hinder women's effectiveness in the South African legislature. Mahau Phekoe of the Women's National Coalition notes that during a budget speech, one woman struggled to read a prepared speech in English and was criticized for her delivery, while two others failed to research their comments, discrediting them.

The push for more women in public office is part of a broader effort to deepen democracy. Feminists aim to build a political community focused on gender-based injustices, advocating for broader female representation in politics and the democratization of other areas, including the private sphere.

However, this feminist project faces challenges, as many women in public office serve as role models but struggle to survive in formal politics or influence policy-making significantly.

Expanding Democratic Space: New Possibilities for Women?

Liberalization and governance reforms have disrupted traditional political institutions and encouraged the emergence of new democratic spaces for public participation. This shift in governance potentially enhances the representation of historically marginalized political actors. Previously, pathways into politics were well-defined and predominantly excluded women. New democratic spaces provide various opportunities for learning and networking, potentially creating new leaders and alternative political entry points. In this discussion, we first explore the benefits and drawbacks of donor enthusiasm for promoting 'democracy' through civil society support. We then examine the newly created democratic spaces, particularly at the local government level, to assess their impact on women's representation. Specifically, we question whether influence and access to one set of deliberative spaces can facilitate leverage in others.

The 1990s good governance agenda's focus on 'strengthening civil society' aimed to expand the public sphere by fostering social actors who would represent diverse interest groups and hold the state accountable. The significant growth of 'civil society organizations' and the new political spaces resulting from democratization waves have allowed women's organizations and movements to influence policy processes outside formal political institutions. However, the positive portrayal of 'civil society' in donor discourse contrasts with the complex reality of the diverse organizations it encompasses, some of which may suppress marginalized interests rather than champion them.

Within this diversity, women's movements are promising candidates for advancing the 'engendering democracy' project. However, they are varied in composition and motivation across different cultures and political contexts. While women's movements can incubate political leaders, this role is scrutinized because success in grassroots mobilization, service provision, and fighting social issues often does not translate into leadership in formal governance institutions. Questions arise about whether these institutional forms provide alternative democratic spaces for women's participation and political apprenticeship to content with the masculinism of formal political arenas. Nonetheless, feminist NGOs continue to play crucial roles in creating 'subaltern counterpublics,' as termed by Nancy Fraser, which are 'parallel discursive arenas' where marginalized groups can find a voice and foster political learning outside formal political settings. An example is a project by a consortium of north-eastern Brazilian feminist NGOs, which established 'feminist schools' to address women's political apprenticeship through popular education, creating spaces for potential political candidates and women in public office to discuss feminist theory and share engagement tactics. External support to feminist NGOs and movements has been instrumental in these efforts.

Conclusion

How can we advance the feminist agenda in political participation? What insights have we gained from increasing women's formal engagement in politics? What barriers hinder significant representation and feminist priorities in the political sphere? And how can we transform male-dominated and patriarchal environments in political decision-making? One key takeaway from various feminist development approaches is the necessity of addressing structural hurdles within the state to promote redistributive agendas. Establishing "safe spaces" is crucial for fostering effective analysis and strategies in collective advocacy. It is imperative to reconstruct feminist platforms within movements and political parties, providing venues where women can connect and collaboratively shape common agendas. Despite efforts to create political spaces for women, male politicians often maintain dominance through structural and institutional measures. Hassim (2002) pointed out that women advocating feminist perspectives and navigating patriarchal institutional changes may face challenges, risking political marginalization or exacerbating divisions among women due to differing political affiliations and alliances.

REFERENCES

Arnesen, S. & Peters, Y. (2018). "The Legitimacy of Representation: How Descriptive, Formal, and Responsiveness Representation Affect the Acceptability of Political Decisions." Sage, *Comparative Political Studies, 51*(7): 868-899.

Ballington, J. & Karam, A. (Eds.) (2005). *Women in Parliament: Beyond Numbers.* International IDEA, Stockholm.

Campus, Donatella. (2013). *Women Political Leaders and the Media.* New York: Palgrave Macmillan.

Engels, F. (1884). *The Origin of the Family, Private Property and the State.* New York: International.

Enloe, C.H. (2000). *Bananas, Beaches and Bases: Making Feminist Sense of International Politics.* Berkeley, University of California Press.

Hawkesworth, M.E. (1989). "Knowers, Knowing, Known: Feminist Theory and Claims of Truth." *Signs, 14*(3): 533-557. doi: 10.1086/494523

Hassim, S. (2002). "A Conspiracy of Women: The Women's Movement in South Africa's Transition to Democracy." *Social Research, 69*(3): 693-732.

Inglehart, R. & Norris, P. (2003). "Leacock, E. Myths of Male Dominance: Collected Articles on Women Cross-culturally."

Monthly Review. Retrieved from https://monthlyreview.org/product/myths_of_male_dominance/

Institute for Democracy and Electoral Assistance (IDEA) (2020). Gender Quotas Database. Retrieved from https://www.idea.int/data-tools/data/gender-quotas/quotas

Okeke, A. (2003). "Women and Politics in Nigeria's Fourth Republic." *The Constitution: A Journal of Constitutional Development, Centre for Constitutionalism and Demilitarisation*, (CENCOD). Panaf Press, Lagos, p. 71.

Paxton, P. & Hughes, M.M. (Eds.) (2007). *Women, Politics and Power: A Global Perspective*. London: Pine Forge Press.

Rottenberg, C. (2018). *The Rise of Neoliberal Feminism*. Oxford University Press, Oxford.

Shireen Hassim. (2003). "Representation, Participation and Democratic Effectiveness: Feminist Challenges to Representative Democracy in South Africa", in Anne Marie Goetz and Shireen Hassim (eds.), *No Shortcuts to Power: African Women in Politics and Policy-Making*. London: Zed Books.

Smith, M.J. (1998). *Social Science in Question*. Thousand Oaks, CA: Sage.

Tripp, A.M. (2003). "Women in Movement: Transformations in African Political Landscapes". *International Feminist Journal of Politics*, *5*(2): 233-255.

Van Zoonen, L. (1994). *Feminist Media Studies*. Thousand Oaks, CA: Sage.

Wängnerud, L. (June 2009). "Women in Parliaments: Descriptive and Substantive Representation." *Annual Review of Political Science, 12*: 51-69. Retrieved from https://ssrn.com/abstract=1600551 or http://dx.doi.org/10.1146/annurev.polisci.11.053106.123839

12

Pioneering Equality

Media Narratives and the Progressive Representation of Women in Indian Politics

Bhavana Devi Tekcham and *Hidam Ajit Meetei*

Introduction

The media portrayal of Indian women in politics represents a blend of historical trends, contemporary phenomena and the impact of legal measures designed to promote gender equality. It highlights the progress made and obstacles still facing women in power fighting for gender equality. The Role of Progressive Media Narratives and Legislative Measures to Ensure Gender Equality in Indian Politics by addressing the problems surrounding a lack of representation, sensationalism and cyberbullying, there perhaps can be an overall better political environment using social media for its strengths. The purpose of this article is to increase the clout and agency of women, push for their substantive participation, and eventually overhaul India's democratic system. This examination assesses these dimensions in detail.

Historical Patterns and Trends

In the history of Indian politics, men have always come or, with a small number of places, women entered their names by following in line and ready to make invisible. The 1952 general elections saw the first instance of women being allowed to vote, but their representation in legislative bodies has been pathetic, hovering between five and ten per cent until 2004—touching approximately 14 per cent in the current Lok Sabha (R.R., 2024, July 17). This is despite the fact that women really have a right to vote. Over a period of years, the image projected by women entering media was often sensationalistic and not oriented towards serious politics, thereby contributing to perpetuated stereotypes in which on-screen women are almost always seen as secondary characters in governmental platforms.

Transitions in the Modern Era

Due to increasing awareness and movements advocating for women's rights, the portrayal of female politicians in media is finally changing after many years. Issues around gender and women's empowerment have become more prominent in the media. Landmark cases such as the *Nirbhaya case* and movements against Triple Talaq were given more attention, ultimately initiating broader conversations around women's rights and representation. The coverage of these instances and movements has provoked a few discussions. However, the media still tends to emphasise women in roles that are domesticated and focus on their possibilities as human persons despite all of this progress. Female politicians are objectified in this way repeatedly, reflecting underlying sexism; circulating memes like these diminishes their clout and trivialises all they have achieved (Ghosh, A.K., 2023: 1).

Legislative Measures and the Effects

The role of legislation in promoting gender equality is clearly evident from the cause of Indian Politics. Women also reserved one-third of the positions in local administration through constitutional amendments 73rd and 74th, respectively, in 1992. Resultantly, it has bolstered their engagement at the grassroots level. However, the representation in Lok Sabha and State Assemblies is not up to that mark as the women's reservation bill (Women's Quota Bill) intended to seek 33 per cent of seats both at national and state levels could not be enacted. Adopted by Parliament in September 2023, the One Hundred and Sixth Amendment of the Constitution. The Amendment is introduced with the goal of ensuring that elected representatives to one-third of seats in the Lok Sabha and State Assemblies will be women. But this is subject to the delimitation that follows after a census tally. The reform in law is expected to enhance women's representation and influence on the political process, thus shaping policies that are gender sensitive (*Ibid.*, 4). Media portrayal of women in Indian politics has undoubtedly improved, but there is a long way to go because our culture itself carries along with the legacy and conception unvaryingly entrenched from yet another era. While legislative actions have made inroads towards improving the representation of women, the media remains a robust political actor and continues to wield influence on public perceptions and attitudes regarding women in politics. New research shows that efforts to increase the number of women in Parliament must continue but also focus on how they are represented and seen as leaders.

Historical Roles of Women in Ancient India

Indian women occupied various roles in ancient and medieval India, which reveals a complex web of leadership unknown to us by looking into how they are presented in modern media. These figures of Pravabati Gupta, Gargi, and Maitreyi have been known from history till now aged 35 years) as an authentic look at women's leadership in historical times. In ancient India during the Vedic period (approximately 1500-600 BCE), women occupy a marginal status. They were educated and knowledge-filled women, participating in religious rituals and making their own choice of spouses using the *Swayamwara* method. Female philosophers and intellectuals like Gargi and Maitreyi were respected personalities in ancient times, exemplifying the intellectual independence of women during that era. Still, in the later Vedic interval, we see a stoop within the progressive viewpoint. Ladies were having fun years before this time due to add-ons like *Manusmriti* (establishing more strategies to control women's independence). With ascending patriarchal structures, ridiculous practices child marriages and the *devadasi* system were implemented to impede women from enjoying their basic rights.

India during the Medieval Period

Women in the Middle Ages (8th to 18th century, women as historians)—The Medieval period witnessed significant continuity and change for women. Apart from queens like Razia Sultana, who became the Sultan of Delhi and Rani Durgavati- a warrior queen who ruled in Gondwana displaying some extraordinary leadership qualities they were effectively patrilineal; consequently, Pati-Parmeshwar tradition regarded women as inferior human beings designed to serve men. Yet, even within these constraints the women of this family exhibit impressive political ingenuity and military acumen (Roy, Kumkum, 1999: 7-14).

Women often held positions of power, especially in royal households, which allowed them to influence the administration.

An example of women's involvement in political matters very well relates to the case of Pravabati Gupta, who served as a regent for her son. The presence of female monarchs and chief ministers like Queen Rudrama Devi from the Kakatiya Dynasty illustrates that in a male-dominated culture, women had the freedom to pass their young days away at dances.

Modern Portrayals in the Media

Media representation of women politicians in the contemporary era, in contrast to how they were seen traditionally, now focuses on their personality traits rather than any political capabilities. Female politicians repeatedly remain cased in a kind of hype that focuses on their outlooks and personal lives more reasonably than what they stand for or have the ability to choose. This portrayal serves both to weaken the sustained impact of history's powerful women and to sustain established perceptions about what political functions should be reserved for women today.

Comparing with Historical Figures

The historical figures that are eluded to, such as Gargi, Maitreyi, Razia Sultana, Rani Durgavati, and Pravabati Gupta, offer a rich lineage of exceptional leadership and intellectual acumen that often goes overlooked in present-day narratives. While women in politics were still celebrated for their credentials and abilities in the media of the era, current mass media relegates women in politics to their gender, dramatising their role just within the context of womanhood. The evolution from past to recent representations of women in governmental roles indicates not merely change over time but a shift in cultures of origin's perception of women in authority. The concept of some level of this history that must be understood to depict women in political offices with fair narrative applies significantly to present-day issues. Understanding the significance of women's contribution to India's governance would enhance current comprehension of this continuous battle (Alfred D'Souza, 1975: 27). A study of contemporary figures such as Indira Gandhi, Sushma Swaraj, and Mayawati reveals the nuances involved in media representation of women in Indian politics. These leaders are also uniquely portrayed, highlighting the politics of their role as well as society's prejudices against women in power.

The only woman ever to be prime minister of India, Indira Gandhi (the name alone is iconic), and the epithet was made famous by Henry Kissinger as he wielded it in reference to her: "the Iron Lady". The appellation highlights her steadfast, unyielding political method. It is notable to say that the media has painted varying pictures of Gandhi as an iron lady through her fearless decisions, like during Operation Blue Star, while some others have portrayed a contradicting figure due to her dictatorial rule in the Emergency, 1975–77 (Ayaz, S., 2019: 2). While she is richly remembered for her exceptional contributions domestically, where memories of the Green Revolution and the 1971 war leading to the birth of Bangladesh are still vivid in popular memory, she has also been accused of being a power-hungry despot indulging in human rights abuses. She has such a layered personality that, for example, many films or documentaries about her cannot quite capture it all.

The undulating encomium-and-smash-text rhythm they strike mirrors the both/and nature of assessments over her leadership. External Affairs Minister and senior BJP leader Sushma Swaraj, who was one of the most accessible politicians, is known for connecting directly with people over social media. She was good at using social media to connect with people and responding quickly when calls for help came in, especially during crises that affected Indians living outside the country.

Most media accounts focused on her effectiveness and ability to connect with individuals—primarily representing her as the type of contemporary party leader who had managed to square traditional values with twenty-first-century government. Meanwhile, however—brought into focus by the occasional note in media coverage reminding her that she was a woman rather than an elected official with considerable heft of legislative accomplishment (a pattern reminiscent at large of reporting sisterly head-of-government antics)—Brewer found herself running up against some impediments to being cast as Wonder Woman (*Ibid.*, 5).

A more exaggerated and flamboyant representation by the media has been seen of Mayawati, ex-Chief Minister of Uttar Pradesh, a leader in the Bahujan Samaj Party (BSP). The media attention Mayawati has received over the years focuses on her personal life and clothes and more on political symbols of statutes than policies or performance in governance. Such reporting often frames her as the antagonist of various political dramas and a self-made woman who has risen to wield enormous power. The public follows sensationalist stories. The sensationalist narrative may, however, trivialise her significant role in the fight for oppressed populations and how she worked hard to empower Dalits, rickshaw pullers and women on the political front for state elections in 2014. The media's fixation on the fronts of her parts and the controversies concerning her commission history often act as a red herring from primitive transformations in deep alfresco reps, revealing many women naturalise at last having their presence cared for during democracy converse.

Illustrations of Indira Gandhi, Sushma Swaraj and Mayawati have established that women in Indian politics are always caught between the devil and the deep sea. For Indira Gandhi, it was more a case of extraordinary political feats, and for Swaraj, the admiration lay in her personable nature and approachability.

At the same time, Mayawati is often sensationalised by the media. These common representations reflect broader cultural understandings of female executive behaviour and reveal the critical need for more sensitive, balanced media portrayals. This is the subject of this study, which looks at persistent barriers among Indian lawmakers and highlights their underrepresentation in Parliament through themes such as sensationalisation and cyber harassment. It further underscores the potential of social media for public direct mobilisation and narrative control, as well as delving into some legislative proposals like the 73rd Constitutional Amendment Act or the Women Reservation Bill proposed by the year 2023, which serves as an integral mechanism to achieve gender parity over political representation.

Major Obstacles Encountered by Women in Politics

1. Insufficient Representation

Despite progress, women remain grossly underrepresented in Indian politics. In 2023, women account for only about 15 per cent of the Parliament, which is an increase from previous years but still far below reflecting gender parity. Not only that, they are confined to home and hearth because of various socio-cultural barriers placed before them by the male-dominated society whose stereotyped views on gender politics often stop women from embracing a political vocation. Second, women often have less access to party resources and backing in political parties, which increases the challenges of winning nominations and advancing through party hierarchies.

2. Media Hype, Clickbait and Exaggeration

Women politicians are more likely to be portrayed in the media as sensational set pieces—where their personal attributes take precedence over their political acumen. Media coverage disproportionately focuses on a female candidate's physical beauty or personal life, ignoring her qualifications and policy achievements. Such depictions are likely to damage both a general perception of women as competent, impactful political actors and to the extent they promote gender stereotypes that undermine their authority and credibility.

3. Cyberbullying

Violent threats can be particularly virulent for Indian female politicians, who are among the women most targeted worldwide with gender-based insults and death or rape threats. The report finds that women in politics receive a substantially higher proportion of online abuse than their male counterparts, much of which is not related to professional behaviour but based on physical appearance and personal history. This type of treatment will turn women off to careers in policy and create a toxic political environment where would-be candidates are loathing to step forward. Female politicians encounter obstacles and opportunities in social media. While yes, it can be an avenue for bullying, on the other hand, it can offer a direct way in which the public becomes involved in narrative shaping. However, women can use social media and, by extension, public opinion to make contact with their electorate, express themselves and challenge bad narrations. She said direct contact might empower female politicians to be more visible, as well as gain support and attention that traditional media outlets can sometimes keep from them.

Legislative Measures

It is also known as the 73rd Constitutional Amendment Act or Amendment 73, as executed in 1992, reserved one-third of seats for women only in Panchayati Raj Institutions over time; however, it has given a significant boost to their participation at local level governance. As an integral part of this legal legislation, giving women a say in established gender norms or behaviour and the opportunity to be part of the decision-making at the local level made way. However, there remain some challenges that need to be addressed, including the need for more training and support in anticipation of women who would like to play a crucial role in politics (Asmat, S. & Chanda Devi, 2012: 335-337).

The Women's Reservation Bill, 2023

The 2023 Women Reservation Bill, passed on 26 September, 2023, stipulates the reservation of one-third of seats in the Lok Sabha and state legislative assemblies exclusively for women. While this is a monumental step in female representation, the Act still needs to be enforced after the next delimitation. Admirers and sceptics of the law abound; some see it as a potential catalyst for substantial change, while others view it to be little more than an act that will barely make waves in altering women's status in Romanian politics—"it is fake like any other" (*Ibid.*: 336). Challenges faced by women in politics: The case of India—Needs structural change and societal support. While social media can enable, one must not forget the legislative measures to break through, such as the 73rd Amendment (Panchayats) and the Women's Reservation Bill for 33 per cent reservation in all elected posts set to be passed in early-2023 at least with respect of Parliamentary seats. Overcoming the challenges faced by women in politics and ensuring an appreciation of their viewpoints require sustained support and involvement from every sector.

Essential Elements of the Strategy

The article suggests an interdisciplinary method in order to improve the representation and portrayal of women in Indian politics with the help proposed through media literacy campaigns, development supported for female leadership among journalists, and public awareness programmes. To this end, it is essential to engage in and ramp up these activities for women politicians to pursue a more accurate representation of gender equity than before, challenge patriarchal biases, and sustain their participation by playing a much more significant role in defining India's political landscape (Deepanjali Mishra, 2015: 2-4).

1. Initiatives Designed to Educate on the Various Skills and Knowledge Required in Order to Comprehend and Evaluate Media Default State

Media literacy programmes are important to help people critically analyse media messages and how women are portrayed in the political arena. These efforts all play a role in the battle against stereotypes and work to create a better understanding of the portrayals of female politicians by informing them of how media operation affects their images.

Critical Analysis Skills: Media literacy stimulates critical thinking and encourages people to question media messaging by asking who creates these messages, why they make them this way, and how it affects our perceptions about gender roles. This approach can lead to an electorate that is more knowledgeable of an appreciative of the role played by women in political life.

Increasing Knowledge and Awareness of Information to Strengthen Capacity and Power: When women are equipped with principles that they can use in media, this will increase their self-esteem, allowing them to more openly partake in political discussion so as to play a role towards better politics.

2. Empowering Female Leaders in Media Industry

If more women are in media leadership roles, a variety of perspectives can be represented during the news process and storytelling. Men and women journalists in influential positions, particularly within the media establishment, are using their authority to question go-along storylines—they point out stories that deserve rethinking even before other parties can seize upon them (Deepanjali Mishra, 2015: 2-4). Female leaders in the media can also serve as exemplars inspiring potential women journalists and media experts, leading more ladies to enter this industry and changing how female politicians are portrayed.

The storytelling of differences: Female representation offers a richer story, celebrating women's roles and successes in politics instead of demonstrating salacious or simplistic stereotypes.

3. Consumer-oriented Marketing Campaigns

Public awareness can take a toll and change society's perception towards women in politics, and these campaigns can remind the electorate of how important it is to have more women in political office and generate a general movement towards gender parity. Challenging traditional male hegemonic societal structures: resist/reject campaigns can challenge and question the ever-present patriarchal beliefs in society, which say that women are unsuitable to be fitted for leadership/administrative roles.

Engagement and Mobilisation: By creating awareness about the challenges that woman face in politics, these campaigns can help garner the community support required to sustain initiatives directed at increasing political leadership among women. Such a comprehensive approach, which includes media literacy programmes and promotion of leadership and sex representation among women in these areas with public awareness campaigns, is imperative to ensure more gender-equal images emerge around Indian female leaders. The endeavour seeks to provide a conducive environment in India's political space by assuaging issues pertaining to absenteeism, sensationalisation, and cyberbullying. Elaborate crosscutting analysis of media narratives in the context and changing representation regarding women in Indian politics through its past accomplishments, ongoing impediments and dynamics for potential change. This research highlights that women in India have become significantly more politically engaged following universal suffrage. And yet, for all these substantial laws brought through—including the 73rd and 74th Constitutional Amendments in India and recently The Woman Reservation Bill of the year 2023 that pushes one-third quota single-seat allotment to woman member representation at Lok Sabha to State Assemblies—here remains a complex set of challenges along the way towards full gendering equality.

Conclusion

The role of media narratives is important in shaping public opinion as well as making a political environment feel its presence. While there is a movement towards depicting strong portrayals for women leaders, they continue to be sensationalised and framed in gendered ways that undercut the legitimacy of their claims—even when it is an actual fact on the record. The portrayal of women in politics often swings between flattering and deploring, reflecting long-standing cultural biases that the media promotes. If we want to see positive images of women in political discourse, then there must be more excellent advocacy for outstanding female leadership both in the media and through literacy programmes against these stereotypes.

In addition, the advent of social media creates a lot of opportunities and challenges. As new technology allows women to reach the public more directly and tell their stories, it also reveals them to a tide of online harassment. Ensuring that women can use these digital spaces effectively is a key to increase their political engagement and influence. A three-pronged strategy of legislative changes, along with media responsibility and societal transformation, is required to achieve the goal of gender parity in Indian politics. It is bad enough that such a Western country can indulge in the Most Toxic Frat Boy fantasy Rhetoric when it comes to clearly Female presidential character. But India should do better to move closer towards democracy and representation by convincing itself that male-dominated ways are worth the interrogation: our stories too must be woven with women taking part in Sustainable Political Processes. A commitment to be at the forefront of advancing equal media narratives and political representation would empower women but also strengthen democracy in a way that benefits all citizens by contributing towards ensuring greater infrastructure spending is more likely.

REFERENCES

Alfred D'Souza. (1975). *Women in Contemporary India: Traditional Images and Changing Roles*. Manohar Book Service.

Algor Cards. (n.d.). *The Evolution of Women's Rights in Ancient and Medieval India*. Retrieved from https://cards.algoreducation.com/en/content/V4kGlVod/evolution-womens-roles-india.

Altekar, A.S. (1938). *The Position of Women in Hindu Civilization.* The Cultural Publication House, Benares Hindu University.

Asmat, S., & Chanda Devi. (2012). *Women Empowerment in India.* Mittal Publications.

Ayaz, S. (2019). "Indira Gandhi's 102nd Birth Anniversary: The Iron Lady is Still Missing from Bollywood Scripts." *The Indian Express.* Retrieved from https://indianexpress.com/article/entertainment/bollywood/indira-gandhi-as-seen-through-the-eyes-of-bollywood-5448084/#google_vignette

Chary, M.R. (2012). "Women and Political Participation in India: A Historical Perspective." *The Indian Journal of Political Science*, *73*(1): 119-132. Retrieved from https://www.jstor.org/stable/41856567

Di Meco, L., & Brechenmacher, S. (30 C.E.). *Tackling Online Abuse and Disinformation Targeting Women in Politics.* Carnegie Endowment for International Peace. Retrieved from https://carnegieendowment.org/research/2020/11/tackling-online-abuse-and-disinformation-targeting-women-in-politics?lang=en

Deepanjali Mishra (2015). "Media JHERSS Portrayal of Women in Media." *Journal of Higher Education and Research Society: A Refereed International*, *3*(2).

Drishti IAS. (2023, March 14). *Women's Underrepresentation in Politics.* Retrieved from https://www.drishtiias.com/daily-updates/daily-news-editorials/women-underrepresentation-in-politics

Drishti IAS. (2024, July 19). *Political Representation of Women.* Retrieved from https://www.drishtiias.com/daily-updates/daily-news-analysis/political-representation-of-women

Drishti IAS. (n.d.). *Political Representation of Women.* Retrieved from https://www.drishtiias.com/daily-updates/daily-news-analysis/political-representation-of-women

EPW (2024, May 13). "Women's Reservation Act of 2023: A Symbolic Gesture or a Significant Stride towards Empowerment? "*Economic and Political Weekly*. Retrieved from https://www.epw.in/engage/article/womens-reservation-act-2023-symbolic-gesture-or-0

EPW (2025, February 4). "Women's Reservation Act of 2023: A Symbolic Gesture or a Significant Stride towards Empowerment?." *Economic and Political Weekly.* Retrieved from https://www.epw.in/engage/article/womens-reservation-act-2023-symbolic-gesture-or-0

Ghosh, A.K. (2023). Women's Representation in India's Parliament: Measuring Progress, Analysing Obstacles. Observer Research Foundation. Retrieved from https://www.orfonline.org/research/women-s-representation-in-india-s-parliament-measuring-progress-analysing-obstacles

Misra, Rekha (1967). *Women Mughal India (1526-1749).* Munshiram Manoharlal, New Delhi.

Moser, O.N.C. (1993). *Gender Planning and Development Theory, Practice and Training.* London; New York: Routledge.

Naman (n.d.). *Representation of Women in Indian Media*—SK Children Foundation: NGO in Delhi. S.K. Children Foundation: NGO in Delhi. Retrieved from https://skchildrenfoundation.org/representation-of-women-in-indian-media/

R.R. (2024, July 17). "On Political Representation of Women: Explained". *The Hindu*. Retrieved from https://www.thehindu.com/news/national/on-political-representation-of-women-explained/article68415532.ece#

Roy Kumkum (1999). *Women in Early Indian Societies*. Manohar Publishing House.

Saxena Kiran (2000). *Women and Politics*. New Delhi: Gyan Books.

Sen Anima (1999). *Problems and Potentials of Women Professionals*. New Delhi: Gyan Books.

Seth Mira (2008). *Women and Development: The Indian Economy*. Sage Publication.

Sinha, Niroj (2000). *Women in Indian Politics—Empowerment of Women through Political Participation*. Gyan Books.

Souza, Alfred de (1975). *Women in Contemporary India: Traditional Images and Changing Roles*. Manohar Book Service.

The Evolution of Women's Rights in Ancient and Medieval India (n.d.). Algor Cards. Retrieved from https://cards.algoreducation.com/en/content/V4kGlVod/evolution-womens-roles-india

Section-III
Reservation Act, Politics and Empowerment

13

Women's Empowerment and Dwindling Fertility in Sikkim*

Komol Singha, Kh. Jitenkumar Singh and
Swati Akshay Sachdeva

Introduction

Sikkim is one of India's most peaceful states, with the second-lowest crime rate and negligible corruption in 2017-18 (Singha & Singh, 2022). In terms of economic dimension, Sikkim was ranked as the second richest state in the country, with per capita Net State Domestic Product (per capita NSDP) estimated at Rs. 2,59,938 in 2022-23 (at 2011-12 constant prices), next to Goa with Rs. 3,33,709?[1]. The state was declared the cleanest in rural sanitation, with 100 per cent of individuals using household toilets and 98.2 per cent of homes having

* This paper is part of an ongoing research project titled, "Reproductive conundrum: An assessment of Sikkim's dwindling fertility rate", funded by the National Commission for Women, Govt. of India, New Delhi, Reference No. NCW/1202112309580/RS/2023-2024/4416, dated 16/08/2023. The authors thank NCW for their support.

sanitary toilets (Shah, 2019). Sikkim is also well-known for women's safety, and it places the highest priority on women's empowerment. The Sikkim Panchayat (Amendment) Bill, 2011, provides 50 per cent reservation to women in grassroots-level administration, and the Sikkim Succession Bill, 2008 is another such initiative by the state to empower women socially and economically (Subba, 2014). These are all signs of development, gender equality, and women's empowerment. Even though Sikkim joined the Indian Union in 1975, the state is fast flourishing, with women's empowerment at an all-time high, and the Government of Sikkim (GoS) has done its best to improve women's empowerment (Subba, 2024).

On the other hand, Sikkim is the least populous state in the country, with 6.9 lakh people in 2024 (*Statistics Times*, 2025). Migration has been one of the main dangers, which appears to be outnumbering the indigenous population and traditions (Vandenhelsken, 2021; Rai, 2003). Aside from the large-scale migration, the fertility rate of the state has been rapidly dropping in recent decades. For example, the National Family Health Survey's fifth round (NFHS-5) report published in 2019-21 indicates that Sikkim had the lowest Total Fertility Rate (TFR) with 1.1 childbirths per woman. It is less than the population replacement rate of 2.1 and significantly lower than Bihar and the national rates of 3 and 2.8 children per woman, respectively (World Population Dashboard, 2024; IIPS & ICF, 2021). However, a separate study report by the GoS in 2023 revealed that the TFR in the state stands at 0.89 (GoS, 2023; Rai, 2023), which is more or less the same rates as Hong Kong and South Korea, the world's lowest TFR by 2024 (World Population Dashboard, 2024). This extraordinarily falling fertility rate is a pressing concern in Sikkim today. Many civil society groups are worried that the indigenous population of the state will soon become extinct, overtaken by migrants (Rai, 2003). It is hypothesised that increases in women's empowerment are connected with lower fertility levels, while patriarchal cultural factors and a preference for sons are associated with higher fertility (Phan, 2023).

Realising the seriousness of dwindling fertility, the GoS invited demographers, fertility experts/doctors, policymakers, and academia from across the country on July 10, 2023, to discuss, identify and advise them on the causes of the rapidly declining fertility rates in Sikkim (GoS, 2023). As an immediate initiative, the Government of Sikkim started providing cash to childless women of reproductive age for *in vitro* fertilisation treatment. It also provides a monthly stipend of roughly Rs 7,000 ($80) to couples with one child who wish to have more. Civil servants and state government employees are also being offered salary increments, yearlong maternity leave, and even a babysitter if they expand their families (Yasir, 2023). It is generally understood that as the health sector improves and wealth and educational levels rise (which are some of the basic indicators of women's empowerment), population growth and fertility/birth rates will be slow. Though the correlations between women's education and fertility are typically negative, the relationships between wealth and fertility vary across the population (Colleran & Snopkowski, 2018). Nevertheless, it is undesirable to have a very low fertility rate, below the replacement rate (the fertility rate required to maintain a society's population size). Sikkim's current fertility rate (1.1 as per the estimation of NFHS-5 or 0.89 by the GoS) is extremely low and worrisome. Understanding the paradox of improved women's empowerment and low fertility rate in Sikkim, the present study attempts to answer three basic research questions:

1. Is the hypothesis of a negative association between women's empowerment (mainly education and income) and fertility rates valid in Sikkim? Is this association an indefinite process?

2. What are the most likely causes of Sikkim's extraordinarily low fertility rate in recent years?
3. Are the Sikkim government's efforts to empower women inappropriate in light of the state's rapidly declining fertility rate?

Literature Review

Women's empowerment and autonomy, as well as the improvement of their political, social, economic, and health status, are all critical issues that have been debated, discussed, and taken up in policy initiatives for a long time around the world. Furthermore, it is necessary for the attainment of sustainable development (UNFPA, 1994). According to Kabeer (2001), a woman's ability to make choices/decisions is synonymous with her empowerment. A review paper by Upadhyay *et al.* (2014), which included 60 research papers on women's empowerment, revealed that the most common measures were women's participation in household decision-making, which included decisions about personal healthcare, buying children's clothes, visiting relatives, and acquiring land. Further, their review work found that some papers utilised socio-demographic indicators (like education, employment, age, gender, place of residence like rural or urban etc.) as control variables, whereas others used them as indicators of women's status/empowerment. However, Woldemicael (2009) used educational achievement, employment, household economic status, and rural/urban location as indicators of women's empowerment.

At the same time, some of the important elements that influence women's empowerment, such as education, health, income, and employment/occupational structure, also have an impact on their fertility rates. By employing 221 surveys over 75 countries (both developed and developing countries) for the periods from 1985 to 2014, Kim (2016) found a substantial negative relationship between female education and fertility, meaning that as a woman's education level increases, her fertility level decreases. Nonetheless, this association differs across nations and depends on women's education level, health status, and the stage of development of the country. Norberg & Pantano (2016) discovered that maternal choice, most likely influenced by economic factors, a desire for more children, access to health care, and so on, has significant negative relationships between caesarean section and future fertility in the United States of America, despite the fact that women who have caesarean sections have fewer offspring. In a slightly different vein, Chen (2023) investigated how rising marriage postponement is driving China's rapid fertility decline. It has been principally caused by an increase in women's years of schooling and a rise in the proportion of women in higher education. A recent paper by Dioikitopoulos & Varvarigos (2023) has also highlighted the postponement of childbearing/parenthood in Nordic countries mainly due to economic-related and preference-related factors. In Sweden, Björklund (2006) investigated how public policy influenced the fertility rate in Swedish women compared to other neighbouring countries where government incentives were not as generous as in Sweden. The study results suggest that the expansion of the policy enhanced the level of fertility, decreased the spacing of births, and caused oscillations in the period fertility rates, but it did not modify the negative association between women's educational level and fertility rate. The scenario is similar in Canada, where women are more likely to have at least one kid, and less likely to have more children, owing to the direct impact of education on earnings and marriage age (DeCicca & Krashinsky, 2023).

In the present study area, in Sikkim, a study by Chauhan & Bhutia (2022) on the decreasing fertility rate demonstrates that factors such as higher education levels in women, women's participation in the workforce, ease of access to contraception, their socio-economic status, and family planning all contribute to lower fertility rates. Similarly, Lepcha & Mondal (2022) investigated the relationship between socio-economic conditions and their impact on the fertility and mortality rates of the Lepcha community, Mangan district of Sikkim (formerly North Sikkim district), and their findings revealed a positive relationship between socio-economic conditions and Lepcha community fertility rates. However, the existing literature appears to be unable to provide a comprehensive and scientific study at the state level. The majority of studies on the topic (women's empowerment and fertility) in Sikkim have focused on perception and social factors, with no statistical or scientific approaches used to establish the influencing determinants of fertility in Sikkim.

Methodology

The present study is based on both primary and secondary data. The secondary data were obtained from the four rounds of the National Family Health Survey rounds 2 to 5 (NFHS-2 to NFHS-5), and descriptive statistics were used to analyse the NFHS data. The Total Fertility Rate (TFR) is used interchangeably with 'fertility rate' and is also an important metric to ascertain typical childbirth rates for women of different age groups (Roser, 2014). Since the present study tries to estimate the causes and effects of individual married women's fertility level, the standard technique/method of measuring TFR (number of births per 1000 women) is not applicable in this chapter. As a result, a functional definition of fertility rate or the proxy of the individual married woman fertility rate, known as the *Individual Marital Fertility Rate* (IMFR), is developed. This concept is a slightly modified version of the conventional

Marital Fertility Rate (MFR), in which the marital version of the measure includes births to married women in the numerator and all married women in the denominator (Census Bureau & USAID, 2003). Unlike TFR and MFR, which measure children born per 1000 women using primary data, IMFR is designed to examine each married woman's fertility level and analyse the probable factors that influence her fertility level. The formula of IMFR is framed as follows:

$$\text{IMFR} = \text{NC/YML} \quad \dots (1)$$

where IMFR implies Individual Marital Fertility Rate, NC implies Number of Childbirth, and YML implies Years of Married Life.

For this purpose, altogether 2400 samples were collected from Sikkim's six districts, and the respondents were only married women aged 15-49. By administering a well-structured schedule a stratified random sampling method was used to represent the various sections of the heterogeneous society and different geographical locations of the state. To achieve the research questions/objectives set above, apart from the descriptive statistics, including cross-tabulation, correlations, and graphs, the Ordinary Least Square (OLS) regression technique was used, which was carried out using Stata software. The OLS regression model is given as:

$$\text{IMFR} = \beta_0 + \beta_1\text{OCC} + \beta_2\text{INC} + \beta_3\text{EDN} + \beta_4\text{AGE} + \beta_5\text{PLA} + \beta_6\text{GIR} + u \quad \dots (2)$$

where IMFR is the individual marital fertility rate (dependent variable), β_0 is a constant term, *OCC* stands for the occupational status of the woman (working or not working), *INC* implies income level, *EDN* demotes educational level (years of schooling), *AGE* and *PLA* indicate the age at the time of marriage and the place of residence (rural or urban), respectively, *GIR* implies the number of girl children (son preference), and u is the error term. Based on the pieces of literature reviewed above, the variables *income and education* were used as proxies or the determinants of individual women's empowerment level. This is done mainly to enable us to measure the causes and effects of empowerment on her fertility rate/level individually.

State's Policy on Women Empowerment

As mentioned in the previous sections, Sikkim is one of the first states in the country to provide 50 per cent reservation for women in grassroots administration (Panchayati Raj Institutions). The state government has a 30 per cent job reservation for women, which will be filled by direct recruitment in the government and public sector units. Women in Sikkim have a higher involvement rate in decision-making than in most other Indian states. This is undoubtedly a sign of empowerment and gender equality (Rai, 2019). Apart from these, free education for women till the college level is effectively implemented by the Government of Sikkim (*Sikkim Today*, 2018). The Small Family Scheme encouraged women to postpone marriage and pursue their studies. However, the government of Sikkim grants an incentive of Rs. 2,000 if she marries after the completion of 21 years, an additional incentive of Rs. 5,000 if she marries at the age of 22, and an additional incentive of Rs. 1,000 if she marries at the age of 23 (Lama, 2001 as cited by Rai, 2019). In terms of property inheritance, the Sikkim Succession Act, 2008 says:

> As per the Sikkim Succession Act, 2008, wherever there is no Will left behind by the land owner, the wife, sons (including minors), and unmarried daughters (including minors) would be eligible for an equal share in the property left behind by the land owner. In case the property is being shared only among the sons, then the NOC of the wife and

> unmarried daughters of the land owner, countersigned by the Ward Panchayat, is mandatory, as per the Act. If a son/unmarried daughter is a minor, then he/she shall also be given an equal share of the property or the partition of property shall be done only after the minor attains majority (Revenue Section, 2008).

In 2023, the Government of Sikkim introduced a scheme to empower mothers in the state by opening savings bank accounts. The scheme provides Rs. 20,000 annually to every mother in the state who is not working, single or divorced, a victim of child sexual abuse, an unwed mother, or a widowed mother, mainly to empower women socially and economically (NDTV, 2023). Currently (as of June 26, 2024), the Women and Child Welfare Department, Government of Sikkim is open with online registration, apart from other 5 (five) welfare schemes, two of the important schemes for women, the Unmarried Women Pension Scheme, which provides Rs. 2,000 per month to the unmarried (above 45 years of age), from the state government and the Indira Gandhi National Widow Pension Scheme, which provides Rs. 2,000 per month to the widows, from the state and central shares[2]. These demonstrate the significance placed on women in Sikkim, as well as the government's attempts to promote gender equality and women's empowerment.

Results and Discussion

As highlighted in the introduction section, the fertility rate of Sikkim is recorded as the lowest in the country and even in the world. In terms of TFR by residence, even Sikkim's urban areas have never been comparable with the population replacement rate (2.1). Although the TFR in urban Sikkim was 1.9 in NFHS-2 (1998-99), it fell consistently to 1.3, 1.1, and 0.7 in

NFHS-3 (2005-06), NFHS-4 (2015-16), and NFHS-5 (2019-21), respectively. As a result, the state's TFR fell from 2.75 in NFHS-2 to 2.02 in NFHS-3, and further dropped to 1.17 and 1.05 in NFHS-4 and NFHS-5, respectively. Of course, in rural Sikkim, the TFR was somewhat above the replacement rate until the NFHS-3, at 2.9 in NFHS-2 and 2.2 in NFHS-3, before falling significantly below the replacement rate in succeeding rounds (Fig. 13.1). Since the rounds of NFHS-4 and NFHS-5, the pattern and trend of fertility rates have been more or less identical, with no discernible difference between rural and urban populations (Table 13.1).

Table 13.1: Total Fertility Rates (TFR) in Sikkim and India

State/Nation	NFHS-2 (1998-99)	NFHS-3 (2005-06)	NFHS-4 (2015-16)	NFHS-5 (2019-21)
India	2.9	2.7	2.2	2.0
Sikkim	2.8	2.0	1.2	1.1

Source: Authors' compilation from NFHS-2 to NFHS-5.

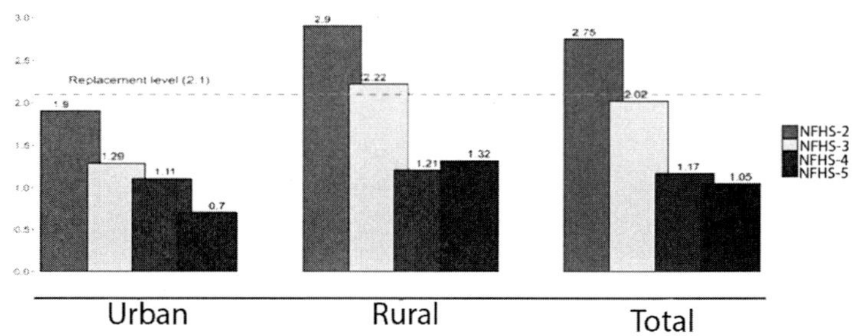

Source: Authors' compilation from NFHS-2 to NFHS-5.

Fig. 13.1: Trends of TFR by residence in Sikkim.

In terms of the age-specific fertility rate, Figure 13.2 clearly shows that the NFHS-5 trend differs from the three prior rounds of NFHS. For all three rounds of NFHS (NFHS-2 to

NFHS-4), the age range 20-24 turned out to be the peak/prime reproductive age group, as high as 171 children born per 1000 women in NFHS-2. However, in NFHS-5, the age range of 25-29 turned out to be the prime reproductive age group, despite being the lowest (68 children born per 1000 women) of any other NFHS rounds. Nonetheless, the pattern of age-specific fertility rates is more or less consistent over all rounds of NFHS, from 1998-99 to 2019-21, with fertility rates decreasing after the age cohort of 20-30.

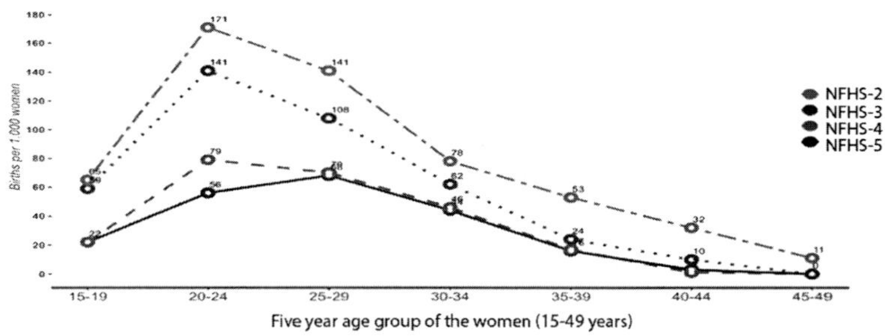

Source: Authors' compilation from NFHS-2 to NFHS-5.

Fig. 13.2: Age-specific fertility rates in Sikkim.

The pattern of fertility rate across the different income categories is also more or less identical in the first two NFHS rounds (Fig. 13.3). In NFHS-4, the associations between income ladders and fertility rates were negative, meaning that fertility rates declined moderately as income ladders rose. However, in NFHS-5, the trend of fertility rates was discovered to be uneven. For example, the fertility rates of the "rich" and "richest" income categories were found to be identical, though somewhat lower than that of the poorer income quintiles, while the poorer income category women had higher fertility rates than those of the poorest income sections. This further disproves the premise that as empowerment increases, fertility rates decrease.

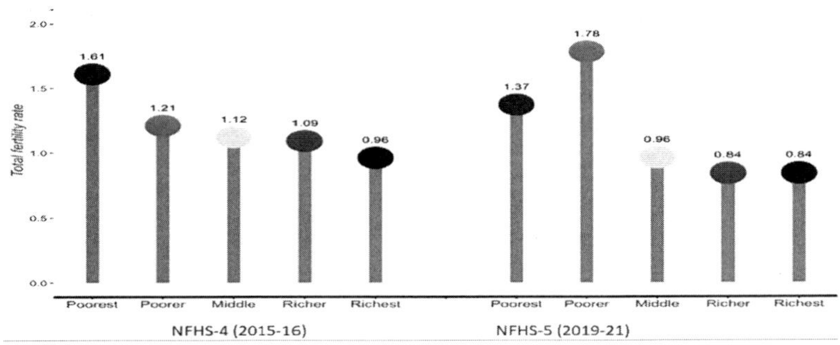

Source: Authors' compilation from NFHS-4 and NFHS-5.

Fig. 13.3: Fertility rate by income category in Sikkim.

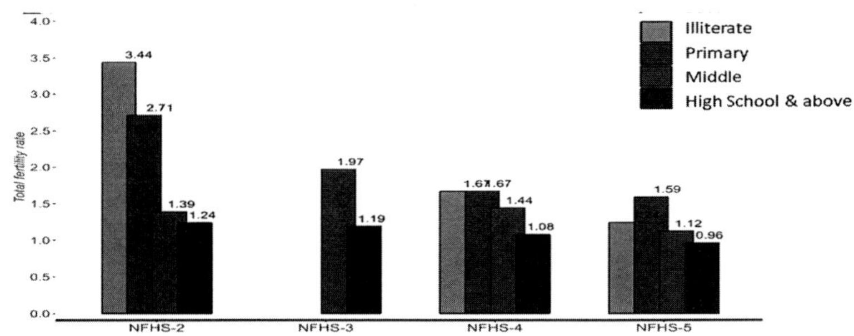

Source: Authors' compilation from NFHS-2 to NFHS-5.

Fig. 13.4: Fertility rate by educational level in Sikkim.

Similarly, the fertility rates across different education levels have been quite uneven in NFHS-4 and NFHS-5. Though the hypothesis (negative link between education and fertility rate) appears to be clearer in the NFHS-2, the relationship appears to be quite ambiguous in the NFHS-4 and NFHS-5. In NFHS-4, the primary and illiterate education categories have roughly equal fertility rates; however, in NFHS-5, the primary level education category has a greater fertility rate than the illiterate level category. Overall, after the NFHS-2, the fertility rate does not appear to be uniformly associated with the education level in the last three rounds of NFHS in Sikkim (Fig. 13.4). It also disproves the hypothesis of a negative relationship between women's empowerment and fertility rates, suggesting that fertility rates do not fall as women's empowerment increases, albeit there have been slightly lower fertility rates when education and income levels rise.

As described in the methodology section, the Ordinary Least Squares (OLS) regression analysis is performed after establishing the data set's normal distribution to investigate the relationship between fertility and women's empowerment (Table 13.2). Although the R^2 value is slightly low[3] (the value is not presented here), significant coefficient values allow us to proceed with the model. While estimating the regression analysis, necessary diagnostic tests (heteroscedasticity, multicollinearity etc.) have been done, and the mean Variance Inflation Factor (VIF) value is within a reasonable range (value is not presented here). Based on the statistics given in Table 13.2, it is unclear whether women's empowerment has a negative association with Sikkim's fertility rate. Some of the primary indicators of women's empowerment, such as the respondent/woman's employment status (employed or unemployed), income level/slab (low, medium and high-income categories), and age at marriage, all have a negative influence on the fertility rate. For instance, employed woman seems to have fewer children *vis-à-vis* unemployed women. Similarly, income earners have fewer children than non-income earners or housewives, and women who marry later have fewer children than those who marry younger.

However, one of the most crucial markers of women's empowerment, education, appears to have little effect on the fertility rate in Sikkim. It is not true that women with higher education have fewer children than their counterparts with lower education. Women with lesser educational levels also had fewer children in Sikkim. This suggests that some unexplained

Table 13.2: OLS regression result

IMFR	Coefficient	Std. Err.	t	P>t	[95% conf.	interval]
OCC →						
• Employed	-0.0299187***	0.008391	-3.57	0	-0.04637	-0.01346
INC →						
• 10-20K	-0.0277509***	0.009289	-2.99	0.003	-0.04597	-0.00953
• 20-50K	-0.0301493**	0.011398	-2.65	0.008	-0.0525	-0.0078
• >50K	-0.0698718***	0.023949	-2.92	0.004	-0.11684	-0.02291
EDN →						
• < 5 Years	-0.0117104	0.017904	-0.65	0.513	-0.04682	0.023401
• 5-9 Years	0.0087465	0.013392	0.65	0.514	-0.01752	0.035009
• 10-11 Years	0.0092795	0.015589	0.6	0.552	-0.02129	0.039851
• >12 Years	0.0342489	0.015987	2.14	0.032	0.002898	0.0656
AGE →	-0.0099608***	0.000895	-11.13	0	-0.008205	-0.011716
PLA →						
• Rural	0.0076534	0.010152	0.75	0.451	-0.01225	0.027562
GIR →	0.0067144	0.004177	1.61	0.108	-0.00148	0.014907
_Cons.	-0.0196751	0.023917	-0.82	0.411	-0.06658	0.027228

Notes: ** and *** imply significance at 5 % and 1%, respectively.

sociological and cultural elements influence fertility (low) rates in Sikkim that cannot be captured by statistical and quantitative analysis. Over-beauty obsession and body consciousness seem to be an important factor for dwindling fertility in Sikkim (not statistically estimated. However, this does not invalidate the Sikkim government's initiatives to empower women and implement policies to improve women's status in the state. This is an effort of a developed society and political system.

Summary and Conclusion

A falling fertility rate as women gain empowerment is a reality in any advanced society, but there must be a limit. It cannot continue to fall continuously and indefinitely; it will come to an end when society develops and the economy stabilises. One may argue that developed/high-income countries like Hong Kong and South Korea have extraordinarily low fertility rates, and Japan is no different. Have not their economies and women's empowerment levels been developed? Are we waiting for Sikkim's economy or women's empowerment level to surpass above mentioned advanced nations' (e.g., Japan, Hong Kong, South Korea) current level? As Sikkim is developing at a very fast rate, its fertility rate will undoubtedly improve in the coming years. People in the state are maturing, and the state's economy is becoming more stable.

In totality, according to secondary information and primary data analysis, women's empowerment levels, as measured by education, income, location of residence, employment, and other social indicators, have increased significantly in Sikkim, far beyond many of the states in the country. At the same time, the state's women's fertility rate has dropped to an all-time low, much below that of any other state. As indicated by the data analysed above, no clear and logical relationships between the two (empowerment and fertility rate) were discovered. Fertility rates do not vary greatly between rural and urban residents. A similar result can be seen among married women who have obtained varying degrees of education/schooling and different income levels (in the secondary data analysis). Of course, there is evidence that when a woman marries late in order to complete her education and find a suitable job, her fertility rate naturally decreases. It reflects the woman's maturity, society's maturity, and her level of empowerment. As a result, Sikkim's present low fertility rate will undoubtedly improve shortly. The current study results show a negative association between women's empowerment and fertility (though not uniformly across different sections of society), however, this is not an infinite process. The government's efforts to promote women's status in society are an indication of a mature administration system. The Sikkim government's recent incentives for improving the fertility rate, such as cash incentives for the second child, year-long leave for female employees, and free education for girls, are all commendable efforts.

NOTES

1. https://mospi.gov.in/sites/default/files/press_releases_statements/State_wise_SDP_as_on_15032024.xls
2. Women and Child Welfare Department, Government of Sikkim. for more details on the benefits, please refer to the link: https://pensionscheme.sikkim.gov.in/#
3. Some fields of research have an inherently higher level of unexplained variance. in such cases, R^2 values of the regression will undoubtedly be low.

REFERENCES

Björklund, A. (2006). "Does Family Policy affect Fertility? Lessons from Sweden." *Journal of Population Economics, 19*(1): 3-24.

Census Bureau & USAID (2003). "Demographic Analysis: Fertility-concepts and Measures." *United States Census Bureau and USAID from the American People* [Accessed on June 18, 2024. https://aitrs.org/sites/default/files/Fertility%20Concepts%20and%20Measures.pdf].

Chauhan, B.K. & Bhutia, D.T. (2022). "Decreasing Fertility Trend in Sikkim: An Area of Concern." *BLDE University Journal of Health Sciences, 7*(2): 262-265.

Chen, W. (2023). "Changing Fertility Patterns in China." *Chinese Journal of Sociology, 9*(4): 497-521.

Colleran, H. & Snopkowski, K. (2018). "Variation in Wealth and Educational Drivers of Fertility Decline Across 45 Countries." *Population Ecology, 60*: 155-169.

DeCicca, P. & Krashinsky, H. (2023). "The Effect of Education on Overall Fertility." *Journal of Population Economics, 36*(1): 471-503.

Dioikitopoulos, E. & Varvarigos, D. (2023). "Delay in Childbearing and the Evolution of Fertility Rates." *Journal of Population Economics, 36*(3): 1545-1571.

Gietel-Basten, S. & Scherbov, S. (2020). "Exploring the 'True Value' of Replacement Rate Fertility." *Population Research and Policy Review, 39*(4): 763-772.

GoS (2023). *Identifying Research Priority and Roadmap for Understanding The Declining Fertility Rates in Sikkim, Report on Expert Panel Meeting,* July 10, 2023, Gangtok: Government of Sikkim.

GoS (2008). Revenue Section, *Gangtok District, Government of Sikkim* [Accessed June 26, 2024 https://gangtokdistrict.nic.in/revenue-section/#:~:text=As%20per%20the%20Sikkim%20Succession,behind%20by%20the%20land%20owner.]

IIPS & ICF (2021). *National Family Health Survey (NFHS-5), 2019-21*, India, Volume I. Mumbai: International Institute for Population Sciences.

Kabeer, N. (2001). "Reflections on the Measurement of Women's Empowerment", in Sisask, A. (Ed.), *Discussing Women's Empowerment—Theory and Practice*, Stockholm: Sida studies, pp. 17-57.

Kim, J. (2016). *Female Education and Its Impact on Fertility*, Ajou University, Republic of Korea and IZA World of Labour [Accessed on June 9, 2023. https://wol.iza.org/uploads/articles/228/pdfs/female-education-and-its-impact-on-fertility.pdf]

Lama, M.P. (2001). *Sikkim Human Development Report 2001,* Government of Sikkim and Social Science Press, Delhi.

Lepcha, M. & Mondal, N. (2022). "Association of Socio-economic Factors with Fertility and Mortality among Lepchas of North Sikkim, India." *Online Journal of Health Allied Sciences, 21*(1): 2. Available at URL: https://www.ojhas.org/issue81/2022-1-2.html

NDTV (2023). "In a First, Scheme to 'Empower Mothers' in Sikkim Who Are Homemakers." *NDTV March 05, 2023* [Accessed on June 26, 2024 https://www.ndtv.com/india-news/in-a-first-scheme-to-empower-mothers-in-sikkim-who-are-homemakers-3836422]

Norberg, K. & Pantano, J. (2016). "Cesarean Sections and Subsequent Fertility." *Journal of Population Economics, 29*(1): 5-37.

Phan, L. (2013). "Women's Empowerment and Fertility Changes." *International Journal of Sociology of the Family, 39*(1/2): 49-75.

Rai, K. (2023). "Expert Group Deliberates on Declining Fertility Rate in Sikkim." *Sikkim Express,* July 11, 2023 [Accessed on May 4, 2024 https://www.sikkimexpress.com/news-details/expert-group-deliberates-on-declining-fertility-rate-in-sikkim]

Rai, N. (2019). "Women 'Pursuit' for Rights and Empowerment Among Sikkimese Society." *International Journal of Legal Science and Innovation, 1*(2): 1-11.

Roser, M. (2014). *Fertility Rate. Our World in Data* [Accessed on June 22, 2023 https://ourworldindata.org/fertility-rate]

Shah, V. (2019). "The Inspiring Story of How Sikkim Became India's Cleanest State." *Hindu Scriptures,* January 9, 2019 [Accessed on February 18, 2025 https://hinduscriptures.com/the-inspiring-story-of-how-sikkim-became-indias-cleanest-state/]

Sikkim Today (2018). Looking Rural, *Sikkim Today, 12*(4): 1 [Accessed on June 26, 2024 https://ipr.sikkim.gov.in/wp-content/uploads/2018/08/March-April-Sikkim-today-2018.pdf]

Singha, K. & Singh, M.A. (2022). "Political Stability and Its Effect on Economy: Some Lessons from Sikkim Himalaya." *Journal of Social and Economic Development, 24*(2): 340-354.

Statistics Times (2025). "List of Indian States by Population." *Statistics Times,* February 5, 2025 [Accessed on February 18, 2025 https://statisticstimes.com/demographics/india/indian-states-population.php]

Subba, G. (2024). "Women Empowerment in Sikkim Post-2019: A Political Perspective." *Sikkim Express,* October 28, 2024 [Accessed February 18, 2025 https://sikkimexpress.com/news-details/women-empowerment-in-sikkim-post-2019-a-political-perspective]

Subba, B. (2014). "Women 'Quest' for Empowerment in Sikkim's Society." *International Journal of Scientific and Research Publications, 4*(9), (1-5).

UNFPA (1994). Issue 7: Women Empowerment. *ICPD POA,* Cairo, 1994 [Accessed on June 22, 2024 https://www.unfpa.org/resources/issue-7-women-empowerment]

Upadhyay, U.D., Gipson, J.D., Withers, M., Lewis, S., Ciaraldi, E.J., Fraser, A., Huchko, M.J. & Prata, N. (2014). "Women's Empowerment and Fertility: A Review of the Literature." *Social Science & Medicine, 1982*(115): 111-120.

Vandenhelsken, M. (2021). "Ancestrality, Migration, Rights and Exclusion: Citizenship in the Indian State of Sikkim", *Asian Ethnicity, 22*(2): 213-234.

Woldemicael, G. (2009). "Women's Autonomy and Reproductive Preferences in Eritrea." *Journal of Biosocial Science, 41*(2): 161-181.

World Population Dashboard (2024). Total Fertility Rate, Per Woman, 2024. *United Nations Population Fund* [Accessed on May 4, 2024 https://www.unfpa.org/data/world-population-dashboard]

14

The Women's Reservation Act, 2023

A Leap towards Women Empowerment

Chungkham Chingkheinganbi

Introduction

The Women's Reservation Act, also known as the Constitution (106th Amendment) Act, 2023, is a landmark legislation in India which aimed at enhancing the representation of women in legislative bodies. The representation of women in decision-making bodies remained relatively low, despite progress, increasing from 5 per cent in the first Lok Sabha to 15 per cent in the 17th Lok Sabha. By ensuring a significant presence of women in legislative bodies, the Act not only addresses historical inequalities but also promotes a more inclusive, empowering and equitable political environment. The implementation of the Women's Reservation Act in India faces several challenges, both in terms of practical execution and broader political, societal implications. This legislation guaranteed that women hold at least one-third of the seats in legislative bodies. This reservation directly increases the number of women in political positions, addressing the underrepresentation that has been existed in the legislative bodies and will enhance women's representation in political institutions.

Objective and Methodology of the Study

The objective of the study emphasized at whether Women's Reservation Act is a transformative step towards bridging the gender gap in political representation which aimed at increasing women's representation in India's political landscape, thereby fostering gender equality and empowering women in leadership roles so as to a Leap towards Women Empowerment. The study is conducted by systematic analysis of Women Reservation, Constitutional Provisions & Amendments and other relevant challenges in implementation. The materials are collected from Research Articles, Public Documents, Publish Reports including Newspapers and Websites.

Background

As India has also ratified various international conventions and human rights instruments committing to secure equal rights of women for example CEDAW in 1993. But gender inequality persists everywhere, stagnate social progress (Ministry of Law and Justice, 2024). In 2015, the Report on the Status of Women in India noted that the representation of women in state assemblies and Parliament continues to be dismal. 15 per cent of the total members of the 17th Lok Sabha are women while in state legislative assemblies; women on average constitute 9 per cent of the total members. It noted that decision-making positions in political parties have negligible presence of women. It recommended reserving at least 50 per cent seats for women in local bodies, state legislative assemblies, Parliament, ministerial levels, and all decision-making bodies of the government (Joshi,

2023). The National Policy for the Empowerment of Women (2001) had stated that reservation will be considered in higher legislative bodies (United Nations, 2023).

A Brief History of the Bill

The Bills of amending the Constitution have been introduced in 1996, 1998, 1999, and 2008 to reserve seats for women in Parliament and state legislative assemblies (Ministry of Law and Justice). The first three Bills lapsed with dissolution of their respective Lok Sabhas. The 1996 Bill had been examined by a Joint Committee of Parliament, while the 2008 Bill was examined by the Standing Committee on Personnel, Public Grievances, Law and Justice. Both Committees agreed with the proposal to reserve seats for women. Some of the recommendations given by the Committees include: (i) considering reservation for women belonging to other backward classes at an appropriate time, (ii) providing reservation for a period of 15 years and reviewing it thereafter, and (iii) working out the modalities to reserve seats for women in Rajya Sabha and state legislative councils (Ministry of Human Resource Development, 2001). The 2008 Bill was introduced and passed by Rajya Sabha but it also lapsed with the dissolution of the 15th Lok Sabha.

Women's Reservation Act, 2023

This legislation on women's reservation in national and state legislatures is historic as it paves the way for much-needed and much-awaited greater political participation of women in Indian politics (Parliament of India, 2009). Increased presence of women in national and state legislatures not only ensures greater voice of women in legislative deliberations but also increases the overall opportunity for women leaders to access the various institutions of power within the framework of India's parliamentary democracy (Ministry of Law and Justice, 2023). The Act says that despite a number of steps to bring Nari Shakti to the forefront, true empowerment of women will require greater participation of women in the decision-making process as they bring different perspectives and enrich the quality of legislative debates and decision-making (*Times of India*, 2024) (Ghosh, 2023).

The Constitution (One Hundred and Twenty-Eighth Amendment) Bill, 2023 was introduced in Lok Sabha on September 19, 2023 and received parliamentary approval, was finally passed by Parliament on 21st September. It became an Act when it received the President's assent on 28th September, 2023. The Act reserved one-third of the total number of seats in Lok Sabha and state legislative assemblies for women. At the time of the Bill's passage, about 14 per cent of Lok Sabha legislators were women. While that represents India's highest proportion since its Independence, it was far below the global average of 26.5 per cent, or the Central and Southern Asia average of 19 per cent (Wankhade, 2023). Women constituted nearly half of the 95 crore population of the country's registered voters but comprised only 15 per cent of lawmakers in Parliament and 10 per cent in the state assemblies (Joy, 2023).

According to this Act, under Article 330 of the Constitution the reservations for women include the sub-quota of 33 per cent reservations for the Scheduled Castes (SC) and Scheduled Tribes (ST), which have been granted. The Act provides for women's reservation by inserting Article 330A, which places these reservations under the ambit of the previous law (UN Women, 2023). As the allocation of SC/ST seats is under the purview of the Delimitation Commission, this also necessitates a review of women's reservation by the same body. Likewise, women's reservation in State Legislative Assemblies has been introduced under Article 332A, while Article 332 is the provision for the reservation of SC/ST general seats. In both cases, the implementation of women's reservation will be subject to the same delimitation process as SC/ST reservations as it is a pre-requisite for the earlier reservations. The 2023 Act mentions that women's reservation will commence after the first delimitation exercise post the Act's passing (Mehrotra, 2023). However, the reservation will be implemented after the new census and delimitation (Ghosh, 2023).

Highlight of the Provisions of the Act

The Women's Reservation Act provides one-third reservation of all seats for women in the Lok Sabha and the state legislative assemblies. The allocation of reserved seats shall be determined by such authority as prescribed by Parliament. Reservation for women: The Bill reserves, as nearly as may be, one-third of all seats for women in Lok Sabha (Art. 330A), state legislative assemblies (Art. 332A), and the Legislative Assembly of the National Capital Territory of Delhi (Art. 239AA).

Commencement of Reservation: Under Article 334A, the reservation will be effective after the census is conducted and the delimitation is undertaken. Based on the census, delimitation will be undertaken to reserve seats for women. The reservation will be provided for a period of 15 years. However, it shall continue till such date as determined by a law made by Parliament.

Rotation of Seats: Seats reserved for women will be rotated, after each delimitation, as determined by a law made by Parliament. Reservation of seats for women shall cease to exist 15 years after the commencement of this Amendment Act (Singh, 2023).

Implementation Timeline: The reservations will be implemented after the completion of the 2024 national census and the subsequent delimitation exercise, which involves redrawing electoral boundaries to reflect updated population data (Ghosh, 2023).

However, the delay in implementation due to the conditionality's that have been imposed, such as the conduct of a delimitation exercise can cause significant delay, as the lack of a specific timeline remains a cause for concern amongst the Indian community (Ministry of Law and Justice).

Reservation for Women and Women Empowerment

Women's reservation and gender quotas in political representation are supported by several international agreements and conventions aimed at promoting gender equality and women's empowerment. Article 253 of the Constitution provides for Legislative powers of the government that gives the Parliament the special power to legislate and pass laws in order to implement international agreements. India is a signatory to various international treaties and conventions, such as Convention on the Elimination of All Forms of Discrimination against Women (CEDAW) which obligate the country to take measures to promote gender equality in all spheres, including politics (Mallick, 2023). Adopted by the United Nations General Assembly in 1979, CEDAW is often described as an international Bill of rights for women. CEDAW also encourages the use of temporary special measures, such as quotas, to accelerate the achievement of substantive equality between men and women. Beijing Declaration and Platform for Action (1995) is a comprehensive policy agenda for women's empowerment (Singh, 2024). It calls on governments to ensure women's equal access to full participation in power structures and decision-making, includes setting specific targets and implementing measures such as quotas to increase the number of women in political bodies. Goal 5 of the Sustainable Development Goals (SDGs)

(UN Human Rights Instruments, 1979), adopted by all United Nations Member States in 2015, aims to achieve gender equality and empower all women and girls. Target 5.5 specifically calls for ensuring women's full and effective participation and equal opportunities for leadership at all levels of decision-making in political, economic, and public life (Inter-Parliamentary Union (IPU) (UN Women Office Publishing, 2015). Initiatives, actively promotes gender equality in Parliaments worldwide. It provides guidelines and supports measures like gender quotas to increase the representation of women in parliaments. The IPU's Plan of Action for Gender-sensitive Parliaments encourages the adoption of gender quotas as an effective strategy to enhance women's political participation.

Some Asian countries are doing much better on this count. Example, The Philippines, among the first countries in the world to introduce reservations for women, has crossed the global average with 28 per cent. Bangladesh, Pakistan, Nepal and South Korea all have reservations for women in the latter two countries, as many as 50 per cent of seats are reserved (United Nations, 2015). Women's equality in power sharing and active participation in decision-making, including decision-making in political process at all levels will be ensured for the achievement of the goals of empowerment. All measures will be taken to guarantee women's equal access to full participation in decision-making bodies at every level, including the legislative, executive, judicial, corporate, statutory bodies, as also the advisory Commissions, Committees, Boards, Trusts etc. Affirmative action, such as reservations or quotas, including in higher legislative bodies, will be considered whenever necessary on a time bound basis. Women friendly personnel policies will also be drawn up to encourage women to participate effectively in the developmental process (Inter-Parliamentary Union).

India is ranked 127 out of 146 countries in the Global Gender Gap Report, 2023 having Wide Gender Gap and faces the perennial issue of "missing women" from the workforce which is a wicked problem. Women-led development promotes inclusive decision-making structures that involve women in community planning, resource allocation, and policy formulation. Women in Panchayati Raj Institutions have initiated and implemented various community development projects. This includes initiatives related to water management, sanitation, rural infrastructure, and poverty alleviation (Ministry of Human Resource Development, 2001). It is also observed that women's representation in the urban and rural structures of local government has improved considerably in the last three decades after the implementation of the 73rd and 74th Amendment Acts. The provision of reserved seats at the local level ensured remarkable political empowerment of women at the grassroots. As the latest report reveals, around 44 per cent of seats in the local bodies are held by women in India.[2] (United Nations India, 2024). It is a significant record that makes India one of the top performing nations in the world in facilitating women's political empowerment at the local level, leaving behind other major countries like France, the United Kingdom, Germany, and Japan. This record is also higher than the global average of 34.3 per cent. Investing in women's leadership is crucial. "In response to the aspirations of women in our country, today, out of over 3.1 million elected representatives, more than 1.4 million are women", said Ambassador Ruchira Kamboj at the 57th session of the United Nations Economic and Social Commission for Population Development (CPD57) in her opening remarks (United Nations, 2023). The political sphere has also seen significant progress, with over 14 lakh elected women representatives in local bodies, making up a substantial portion of total representatives. Legislation like the Women's

Reservation Act, 2023 aims to further empower women leaders at all levels of governance (Ghosh, 2023).

Discussions and Findings

In the discussion, it is deliberated about challenges in implementation of the reservation for women by analysing the provisions of Women's Reservation Act and its challenges and how it would be effective and enhance women empowerment. As women currently hold only about 15 per cent of seats in the Lok Sabha and even fewer in many state assemblies, the Women's Reservation Act is a significant step towards women empowerment, gender equality and politics in India. The reservation policy focus to increase women's political participation in the legislative process, thereby addressing issues specific to women more effectively. Ensuring the effective implementation of the Women's Reservation Act, will require overcoming deep-seated cultural biases, logistical hurdles, and political resistance to create a more inclusive and equitable political environment in India. By reserving 33 per cent of seats in legislative bodies for women, the Act ensures that women have a stronger voice in political decision-making. This increased representation can lead to policies that better addressed women's issues and promote gender equality (*Hindustan Times*). One of the major criticisms of the reservation policy is its failure to include specific quotas for women from Other Backward Classes (OBC), Scheduled Castes (SC), Scheduled Tribes (ST), and minority communities. This has led to concern that the benefits of reservation may not reach the most marginalized groups of women (*Supreme Court Observer*) (*India Today*, 2023). Critics also argued that the rotation of reserved seats could discourage long-term constituency development, as the rotation of reserved seats might reduce incentives for MPs to develop their constituencies if they are unsure of re-election prospects due to changing reservation statuses (PRS Legislative Research). Nonetheless, the Bill represents a historic move towards enhancing women's representation in India's political landscape. To address these challenges, there needs to be a concerted effort from all stakeholders, including political parties, government bodies, civil society, and the judiciary.

Increasing women's representation in politics can gradually change societal attitudes towards women's capabilities and leadership potential as Women legislators are more likely to advocate for issues directly affecting women, such as healthcare, education, and gender-based violence. This ensures that the needs and perspectives of women are considered in policy-making processes, leading to more inclusive and equitable policies. Political empowerment often translates into economic empowerment. Women in leadership positions can influence policies that promote women's access to education, employment, and entrepreneurial opportunities, thereby improving their economic status and independence (The United Nations in India). Political systems often have informal barriers that make it difficult for women to enter politics, such as patriarchal norms, gender biases, and lack of resources. Reservation policies help to overcome these barriers by creating spaces specifically for women, thereby normalizing their presence in political arenas (*ibid.*).

The Women's Reservation Act aligns India with international norms and best practices regarding gender equality. Many countries have implemented similar measures to improve women's political representation, demonstrating the effectiveness of such policies in achieving political equality (The United Nations in India). Ensuring that women candidates are not just token representatives but are empowered and capable leaders requires significant investment in capacity building, training, and support systems (*Supreme Court Observer*). With more women in visible political roles, the Act can inspire greater political participation among women at all levels of society. This increased participation can lead to a more inclusive political culture and ensure women's voices and concerns are heard more broadly. Studies have shown that diverse legislative bodies tend to be more effective and equitable. By including more women, the Act contributes to more balanced decision-making processes, reflecting a wider range of perspectives and experiences (The United Nations in India).

Some critics argue that reservation might lead to tokenism, where women are elected but do not hold real power or influence within their parties or legislative bodies. Resistance from within political parties and male-dominated structures could hinder effective participation of women even after being elected. Simply increasing the number of women in legislative bodies is not enough. It is crucial to ensure that these women have the necessary support, training, and resources to participate effectively and influence policy decisions. Ensuring that women candidates are not just token representatives but are empowered and capable leaders requires significant investment in capacity building, training, and support systems (*Supreme Court Observer, 2023*).

Various aspects of the reservation law, including its implementation framework, have been subject to legal scrutiny and challenges in the courts, which can create uncertainties and delays (*Hindustan Times*) (*India Today*). Legal experts and critics have raised concerns about the delays introduced by tying the implementation to the census and delimitation. Some argue that these requirements are unnecessary and could be used to delay the actual implementation of women's reservations (*India Today*) (*Hindustan Times*). To implement this reservation, a delimitation exercise is necessary. Article 82 of the Constitution mandates this readjustment for both Lok

Sabha and state legislative assemblies after each census. Similarly, Article 170(3) deals with the composition and adjustment of state legislative assemblies. Thus, changes to these articles are essential for the effective execution of the women's reservation. Moreover, the implementation of the Women's Reservation Act is tied to the next census and subsequent delimitation process, which will redraw constituency boundaries based on the latest population data. This process, though potentially delaying the Act's impact until 2029, ensures that the reservations are fairly distributed across constituencies. However, media coverage has also pointed out certain controversies and challenges associated with the Bill. Critics have noted the Bill's dependency on the completion of the next census and subsequent delimitation (redrawing of constituency boundaries), which some argue could delay its implementation by several years. This delay has led to skepticism about the immediate impact of the Bill, with some viewing these provisions as tactics to postpone the Bill's effects (*Hindustan Times*).

The Supreme Court of India has been involved in several key cases related to women's reservation, primarily focusing on legislative and policy issues surrounding the reservation of seats for women in various political bodies. The Court has periodically nudged the Central Government to take definitive stands on women's reservation issues. For instance, in a Public Interest Litigation (PIL) regarding the Women's Reservation Bill, the Supreme Court pressed the government to clarify its position, indicating judicial impatience with legislative delays (*Hindustan Times*). These cases reflect the ongoing judicial involvement in ensuring that legislative measures for women's reservation are implemented effectively. The Court's interventions highlight the balancing act between respective legislative processes and addressing delays and resistance to gender equality in political representation. The Supreme Court has also dealt with issues at the local governance level, such as in Nagaland, where the implementation of 33 per cent reservation for women in urban local bodies has faced significant resistance. The Court has urged the state government to enforce these reservations, emphasizing the need for compliance with constitutional mandates (*Hindustan Times*).

While quotas are effective in increasing the number of women in political positions, their implementation must be carefully monitored to ensure that they lead to substantive changes rather than merely token representation. Ensuring that women in political roles are empowered to influence policy and governance is crucial for the success of these measures. Many countries have adopted gender quotas for political representation, leading to significant increases in women's participation in politics. Examples include Rwanda, where women hold over 60 per cent of the seats in the lower house of Parliament, and Nordic countries, which have high levels of women's representation due to proactive gender equality policies and quotas. Critics argue that reserving seats for women might undermine the principle of meritocracy, as women in reserved constituencies might be perceived as less competent compared to their male counterparts. This could potentially perpetuate unequal status rather than eliminating it (PRS Legislative Research). Some believe that reservation alone will not lead to true political empowerment of women. Comprehensive electoral reforms are needed, including measures to combat the criminalization of politics, increase internal democracy within political parties, and regulate the influence of money in elections (PRS Legislative Research). Rotating reserved seats can discourage elected representatives from nurturing their constituencies, as they may not be able to seek re-election from the same area. This could affect long-term development and accountability (PRS Legislative Research). The Bill's implementation is contingent upon the completion of the next census and subsequent delimitation, which could delay its practical effect (UN Women). These arguments collectively underscore the critical need for women's reservation to foster a more just, democratic, and prosperous society.

Conclusion

The Women's Reservation Act represents a major shift towards gender parity in Indian politics. While it promises significant benefits in terms of representation and empowerment, its success will depend on effective implementation and overcoming structural and societal challenges. The Act's potential delay in implementation, due to the prerequisite census and delimitation, underscores the need for sustained advocacy and vigilance to ensure that its objectives are fully realized. The broader implications of this legislation could set a precedent for more inclusive governance, ultimately benefiting Indian society as a whole. In the primary findings the issues and challenges in implementation with the provisions of the law is still a long journey as the commencement will depend on the delimitation based on the census to be conducted. Its success will depend on addressing the aforementioned challenges and ensuring that the implementation process is smooth and effective. The reservation policy aims to enhance women's participation in governance and create a more inclusive political environment in India. The long-term benefits of increased gender equality and diversified policy focus can enhance the overall effectiveness and responsiveness of governance in India. To address these challenges, there needs to be a concerted effort from all stakeholders, including political parties, government bodies, civil society, and the judiciary. Ensuring the effective implementation of the Women's Reservation Act will require overcoming deep-seated cultural biases, logistical hurdles, and political resistance to create a more inclusive and equitable political environment in India.

Women's reservation is not just a matter of social justice but also a pragmatic approach to improve governance and democratic functioning. It ensures that the perspectives and needs of half the population are represented, leading to more balanced and effective policy-making. Women's reservation in political bodies has the potential to significantly enhance gender equality and women's empowerment. The implementation of the reservation of women in the urban and rural structures of Local Government considerably empowered women. Women's Reservation Act is also speculated to improve the status of woman. It will impact on enhancing women's participation in governance and decision-making processes at various levels as it will ensure at least 33 per cent representation from the current 15 per cent of the participation in the Lok Sabha which is a major step if implemented effectively within stipulated time. By ensuring a substantial presence of women in legislative and governance roles, reservations can promote inclusive and diverse decision-making. However, to maximize the benefits and mitigate the drawbacks, it is essential to implement these policies effectively, address underlying socio-economic barriers, and create an enabling environment for women's political participation. The legal provisions for women's reservation in India are rooted in the Constitution and reinforced by various legislative measures. These provisions aim to ensure adequate representation of women in political and public life, thereby promoting gender equality and empowering women. In fact, Women's Reservation Act is a leap towards women empowerment as this will directly increase the number of women in political position, what we need is a political will and sincere effort from all stakeholders.

REFERENCES

Ghosh, Ambar Kumar (2023, October 16). *Women's Reservation Act: An Imperative for Women's Greater Political Participation*, Observer Research Foundation. Retrieved from https://www.orfonline.org/expert-speak/womens-reservation-act

Ghosh, Poulomi (2023, September 29). "Women's Reservation Bill Signed into law by President Droupadi Murmu", *Hindustan Times*. Retrieved from https://www.hindustantimes.com/india-news/womens-bill-signed-into-law-by-president-droupadi-murmu-101695987639732.html

Ghosh, Poulomi (2023, September 29). "Women's Reservation Bill Signed into Law by President Droupadi Murmu", *Hindustan Times*. Retrieved from https://www.hindustantimes.com/india-news/womens-bill-signed-into-law-by-president-droupadi-murmu-101695987639732.html

Goals 5 Achieve Gender Equality and Empower all Women and Girls (2015). *Gender Equality and Women's Empowerment,* UN. Retrieved from https://sdgs.un.org/goals/goal5

Ghosh, Ambar Kumar (2023, October 16). *Women's Reservation Act: An Imperative for Women's Greater Political Participation*, Observer Research Foundation. Retrieved from https://www.orfonline.org/expert-speak/womens-reservation-act

India Today. (2023, September 21). "Women's Reservation Bill: NDA's Gender Quota *versus* INDIA Bloc's Caste Politics." *India Today.* Retrieved from https://www.indiatoday.in/opinion/story/womens-reservation-bill-ndas-gender-quota-versus-india-blocs-caste-politics-2438657-2023-09-21

Inter-Parliamentary Union (n.d). *Gender Equality.* Retrieved on May 5 2024, from https://www.ipu.org/impact/gender-equality

Joshi, Kritika (2023, October 11). "Charting the Path to Gender Equality in Indian Politics: The Women's Reservation Bill and Beyond', Student Commentary", *Jurist.* Retrieved from https://www.jurist.org/commentary/2023/10/kritika-joshi-womens-reservation-bill-india/

Joy, Shemin (2023, September 19). "Nari Shakti Vandan Adhiniyam: top takeaways from the Women's Reservation Bill." *Decan Herald.* Retrieved from https://www.deccanherald.com/india/nari-shakti-vandan-adhiniyam-top-takeaways-from-the-womens-reservation-bill-2692636

Krithiha and Patnaik, Sushovan (2023 September 25). "The Women's Reservation Bill has a Long History of Arguments and Stakes". *Analysis, Supreme Court Observer*. Retrieved from https://www.scobserver.in/journal/the-womens-reservation-bill-has-a-long-history-of-arguments-and-stakes/

Mallick, Ashesh (2023, December 16). "Women's Reservation Bill to Come Into force after 2024 Census: Nirmala Sitharaman." *India TV*. Retrieved from https://www.indiatvnews.com/news/india/women-reservation-bill-to-come-into-force-after-2024-census-nirmala-sitharaman-centre-pm-narendra-modi-latest-updates-2023-12-16-907553

Mehrotra,Vani. India Today (2023, November 3). "Very Difficult to Strike Down Part of Women's Reservation Law: Supreme Court", *Press Trust of India*. Retrieved from https://www.indiatoday.in/law/story/supreme-court-says-very-difficult-to-strike-down-part-of-women-reservation-law-2457589-2023-11-03

Ministry of Human Resource Development, Department of Women & Child Development (2001), *National Policy for the Empowerment of Women*, Government of India. Retrieved from https://prsindia.org/files/bills_acts/bills_parliament/2008/bill184_20080923184_National_policy_for_empowerment_of_women.pdf

Ministry of Law and Justice, Legislative Department, Official Language Wing (2024, May 1) p. 37 & p. 38, *Constitution of India,* Government of India. Retrieved from https://legislative.gov.in/constitution-of-india/

Ministry of Law and Justice, Government of India, *Women's Reservation Bill 2023 [The Constitution (one Hundred Twenty-Eighth Amendment) Bill, 2023]*. Retrieved on May 10 2024, from https://prsindia.org/billtrack/the-constitution-one-hundred-twenty-eighth-amendment-bill-2023

Ministry of Law and Justice, Legislative Department, Government of India, (2023 September 28), *Gazette of India, Extraordinary, Constitution (one Hundred and Sixth Amendment) Act, 2023*, Retrieved from https://egazette.gov.in/WriteReadData/2023/249053.pdf

Parliament of India (2009, December). *The Constitution (One Hundred and Eight Amendment) Bill, 2008*, Rajya Sabha Secretariat. Retrieved from https://prsindia.org/files/bills_acts/bills_parliament/2008/scr_Women_Reservation_Bill_2009.pdf

Singh, Rashmi (2023, December 5). "Women's Reservation Act and its Unsettled Details." *The India Forum*. Retrieved from https://www.theindiaforum.in/gender/womens-reservation-act-and-its-unsettled-details

Singh, Tiya (2024, March 20). "Women's Reservation Act of 2023: A Symbolic Gesture or a Significant Stride towards Empowerment?" *Engage EPW*. Retrieved from https://www.epw.in/engage/article/womens-reservation-act-2023-symbolic-gesture-or-0

The Sustainable Development Goals Report (2023). *Goal 5: Achieve Gender Equality and Empower All Women and Girls*, UN. Retrieved from https://www.un.org/sustainabledevelopment/gender-equality/

Times of India (2024). "India Moving towards Viksit Bharat by 2047 has Laser Focus on Women-led Development: Ruchira Kamboj Story", *News Desk*. Retrieved from https://www.msn.com/en-in/news/India/india-moving-towards-viksit-bharat-by-2047-has-laser-focus-on-women-led-development-ruchira-kamboj/ar-BB1kcoFp

TOI News Desk (2024, March 20). "India Moving towards Viksit Bharat by 2047 has Laser Focus on Women-led Development: Ruchira Kamboj." *Times of India*. Retrieved from https://timesofindia.indiatimes.com/india/india-moving-towards-viksit-bharat-by-2047-has-laser-focus-on-women-led-development-ruchira-kamboj/articleshow/108636824.cms

United Nations Organisation (2003). *Goal 5: Achieve Gender Equality and Empower all Women and Girls*, Retrived May 10, 2024. Retrieved from https://www.un.org/sustainabledevelopment/gender-equality/

UN Human Rights Instruments (1979, December 18). *Convention on the Elimination of All forms of Discrimination against Women New York*, United Nations General Assembly. Retrieved from https://www.ohchr.org/en/instruments-mechanisms/instruments/convention-elimination-all-forms-discrimination-against-women

UN Women (2023, October 4). "India Passes Law to Reserve Seats for Women Legislators". *Feature*. Retrieved from https://www.unwomen.org/en/news-stories/feature-story/2023/10/india-passes-law-to-reserve-seats-for-women-legislators

UN Women Office Publishing (2015). *Beijing Declaration and Platform for Action, Beijing +5 Political Declaration and Outcome*. UN Women. Retrieved from https://www.unwomen.org/en/digital-library/

publications/2015/01/beijing-declaration

UN India (2024, May 23). "Indian Women Leaders in the Spotlight at CPD57." *Story*, https://india.un.org/en/269474-indian-women-leaders-spotlight-cpd57V

Wankhade, Satyendra (2023, September 20). "Lok Sabha Passes Women's Reservation Bill with 454: 2 Majority." *News, Bar and Bench*. Retrieved from https://www.barandbench.com/news/lok-sabha-passes-womens-reservation-bill-with-4542-majority

15

Women Reservation Act, 2023

Fair Equality of Opportunity through a Rawlsian Lens

Konsam Romabati

Introduction

Globally, women's political participation is of concern, especially in the Indian context. An overwhelming presence of male politicians dominates Indian politics. The country, right after its Independence, has been advocating for a more active participation of women in politics. To make the desired political participation a reality, the Government of India came up with the 73rd and 74th Constitutional Amendment Acts, 1992, which reserved one-third of seats for women in local governance of panchayats and municipal bodies in order to have inclusive participation and promotion of women's decision-making power. Initially, it was criticized as a piecemeal approach, but over the years, research shows that it has achieved remarkable feats and resulted in greater participation and representation of women in local governance. There are cases of agendas like sanitation, cooking fuel, drinking water, dowry, and sale of liquor, which were never a part of governance discourse, highlighted by women representatives (First Post, 2024, March 31). This Act gave the marginalized and disadvantaged women greater voice and bargaining power. Now, the encouraging figure of women in local representation stands at 1.4 million women, where 44 per cent of all local seats are held by women, making India among the best country in the world.

Indian women, since Independence, have made their mark in education and workforces, became more politically aware, and asserted their electoral rights. However, enthusiasm needs to be created when it comes to women's political representation and participation. To address this issue, the government has resorted to reserving seats with the recently passed Women Reservation Act, 2023 (hereafter WRA) by the Indian Parliament. The idea of reservation being used as a means of delivering social justice and achieving equality is undoubtedly a familiar one, as is evident from the 73rd and 74th Constitutional Amendments Acts. Women have been underrepresented and kept at a distance from decision-making positions globally, and this is particularly true in the Indian context. This reality has become a part of the mainstream discourse in the Indian Parliament after the passing of the Act to fill up the lacunae in women's politics. The discourse on the values of equality, non-discrimination, and inclusivity of women has gained momentum since the passing of this Act. This Act takes cognizance of historical discrimination, subjugation, and the disadvantaged position that women have been put into. The government has ended this debate by putting forth the reservation as the most viable solution to reinforce women's political participation.

Women Reservation Act, 2023

Politics has a gender problem, which is all the more peculiar to India. According to reports, only 15 per cent of Indian

Parliamentarians are women's representatives, and the share is even more abysmal in the state houses, where it is only around 9 per cent (PRS Legislative Research). This seat occupation is far below the global average of 22-23 per cent. According to the report in the *Indian Express*: "India currently ranks 142 among 193 countries when it comes to women representation in Parliament" (Roychowdury, 2024). Despite the constitutional provisions provided by the 73rd and 74th Constitutional Amendment Acts, the representation and participation of women still need to be improved and remain confined at the local level, failing to facilitate a bottom-up approach. The abysmal reality is that as we go up the hierarchy in politics, women's representation becomes all the more less.

The Indian Parliament passed the Women Reservation Act of 2023, which reserves one-third of all electoral seats for women in the Lok Sabha, State Legislative Assemblies, and Union Territories. The reservation will be provided for fifteen years and extended further. The Act is expected to ensure women's empowerment in all social, economic, and political spheres. The WRA, with all its provisions, has the potential to fundamentally revamp the country's political landscape and challenge the existing *status quo* in unprecedented ways.

Historically, women have always maintained a safe distance from politics. This is even though ancient Indian texts like *Arthashastra* emphasized the role of women in politics, and there are strong female characters like Draupadi in the Mahabharata who played a crucial role in deciding whether the *Pandava* was to go to war. Even though women played an unofficial role in policy-making and diplomacy in the subcontinent, they were rarely given officially recognized political positions. Leaders like Sarojini Naidu, Herabai Tata, and Mithan Lam are prominent women figures in Indian politics pre- and post-Independence. Further, in 1964, Sucheta Kripalni was the first woman Chief

Minister of independent India from Uttar Pradesh. Fast forward to the present scenario, there are 28 states and 8 UTs, but only one woman Chief Minister in West Bengal. This raises a big troubling question about women's positions in political leadership. The solution for this trouble lies in successfully implementing WRA, 2023. The task is to locate the WRA in the larger political philosophy that appeals to equality, justice, and democracy through the Rawlsian perspective of fair equality of opportunity.

Fair Equality of Opportunity

The agenda of delivering political justice to Indian women with the WRA can traced to its resonance with the idea of justice of the American moral and political philosopher John Rawls' theory of justice. His theorizing was fundamentally animated by a desire to address the political injustice in modern constitutional democracies. He attributes justice to be the most essential virtue in a society. He emphasized that "justice is the first virtue of social institutions, as truth is of systems of thought. A theory, however, elegant and economical, must be rejected or revised if it is untrue; likewise, laws and institutions, no matter how efficient and well-arranged, must be reformed if they are unjust" (Rawls, 1999a: 3). It speaks volumes of the primacy given to the virtue of justice in a democratic society.

Accordingly, Rawls states that "a society is a cooperative venture for mutual advantage; it is typically marked by a conflict as well as an identity of interests" (1999a: 4). He defines the necessities of principles of social justice as "they provide a way of assigning rights and duties in the basic institutions of the society, and they define the appropriate distribution of the benefits and burdens of social cooperation" (Rawls,1999a: 4). The WRA of the Indian subcontinent appeals to this basic sense of justice.

His idea of social justice is particularly applicable to major institutions like the political constitution and the principle of economic and social arrangements. He acknowledges that despite the desire for a just society, in reality, a society is laden with "deep inequalities" given the varied social and economic backgrounds that one belongs to. His notion of social justice specifically targets these inequalities (Rawls, 1999a: 7). Thus, it can be understood that Rawls' idea of social justice includes political justice and is not merely confined to distributive aspects of economic benefits, which is popularly misconceived.

Furthermore, Rawls' idea of the "veil of ignorance" requires that the person in the initial situation choose two positions: the first requires equality in the delivery of fundamental rights and duties. This, he argues, is the "original position", which is the best hypothetical position to decide on the question of justice in a society. In this original position, "none are known to be advantaged or disadvantaged by social or natural contingencies" (Rawls, 1999a: 17). The second holds that social and economic inequalities only occur if they result in compensating benefits for everyone, particularly for the least advantaged member. Rawls' theory of justice justifies and defends this kind of positive discrimination on the ground that "there is no injustice in the greater benefits earned by a few provided that the situations of persons not so fortunate are thereby improved" (1999a: 13). His theory of justice offers a political theory that gives all the members of society an agreed-upon minimal set of rights and liberties, which ensure that they are able to participate as fully functioning members of society.

In summary, Rawls's theory of justice has three basic principles: equal basic liberties, fair equality of opportunity, and the difference principle. The first principle of equal basic liberties, according to Rawls's own description, is:

> The basic liberties of citizens are, roughly speaking, political liberty (the right to vote and to be eligible for public office) together with freedom of speech and assembly, liberty of conscience, and freedom of thought; freedom of the person along with the right to hold (personal) property; and freedom from arbitrary arrest and seizure as defined by the concept of the rule of law (1999a: 61).

In conformity with the values of the first principle of basic liberties, Rawls expressed his other two principles of justice: the principle of "fair equality of opportunity" and the "difference principle". The two principles are, namely:

> *First Principle:* Each person has the same indefeasible claim to a fully adequate scheme of equal basic liberties, which scheme is compatible with the same scheme of liberties for all; *Second Principle:* Social and economic inequalities are to satisfy two conditions: They are to be attached to offices and positions open to all under conditions of fair equality of opportunity. They are to be the greatest benefit to the least-advantaged members of society (the difference principle) (1999a: 60).

According to Rawls, between the two principles, the implementation of the first principle takes priority over the fulfilment of the second, and within the second, the fair equality of opportunity takes priority over the difference principle. Further, he emphasized that "those with similar abilities and skills should have similar life chances... the expectations of those with same abilities and aspirations should not be affected by their social class" (Rawls, 1999a: 73). Moreover, Rawls states that "the intuitive idea is that the social order is not established and secure the more attractive prospects of those better off unless doing so is to the advantage of those less fortunate" (1999a: 75). Then, it is a clear indication that marginalized and discriminated groups should be given priority. According to Rawls, equality of opportunity is the basic principle that no discrimination or limitation exists on who can fill an open position. Suppose there are past cases of discrimination and limitation exhibited by any group. In that case, affirmative or positive discrimination might be incorporated to make up for the failure to provide equality of opportunity by intentionally choosing candidates who have been denied that opportunity. These ideas are perfectly in sync with the reservation for women in politics provided by WRA.

In effect, Freeman observes that the two principles of justice for Rawls can be interpreted as "the less advantaged should be in a position to participate in politics and influence public life on a par with the more advantaged" (2018: 16). Here, the "greatest benefit to the least advantaged," Rawls means that "inevitable inequalities"—in income, wealth, and powers and positions—are to be arranged to make the least advantaged class better off than they would be under any alternative social and economic system (Rawls, 2001: 59-63). Then, coming to the inequality experienced by women, Rawls added that " regarding inequality of opportunity of women due to childbearing and their assuming the predominant burden of childbearing: Rawls says that childbearing within the family is 'socially necessary labour', and that women's or men's share of childbearing either should be equalized, or they should be compensated for it (1999b: 600). This would be personal compensation in addition to family allowances intended to benefit children by fair equality of opportunity and the difference principle (Rawls, 1999a: 243).

In recognition of the idea of women having the predominant burden of childbearing responsibilities taken cognizance by Rawls, Gheaus observes that:

> In most societies, women appear to have a lesser share of benefits than men, a greater share of burdens than men, or both: even in countries where women enjoy the same legal rights as men, there are large disparities among men and women with respect to wealth, income, and the holding of desirable social positions such as well-paid or high-status jobs and political functions. Worldwide, more women than men live in poverty (2018: 389).

The above observations are more pertinent in the Indian context as Gheaus continues to emphasize that "the gender pay gap—that is, the fact that women on aggregate earn less than men—and women's under-representation in positions of responsibility and power appear especially problematic in those societies where women have started to outperform men educationally" (2018: 389). Here, Rawls idea of distributive justice is interpreted by Gheaus as "the inequalities of outcome between men and women with respect to all these goods could be indicative of gender injustice, especially if gender turns out to negatively influence the women's opportunities to secure desirable social positions" (2018: 390).

While the WRA is being proposed as a positive discrimination or affirmative action to mitigate the gender gap in political participation in the country, there are still other dimensions to be looked after simultaneously for a more inclusive representation of women in politics as Gheaus suggested the requirements such as "abolishing sexist upbringing and the gender division of labour" (2018: 391). The main issue of gender norms is that they associate the subordination of a class of individuals to another. "Gender norms are the rules, formal or informal, explicit or implicit, concerning the way in which women and men ought to be and behave; they shape not only social interactions but also individual's expectations and preferences (and hence, indirectly, our bodies too) (2018: 392). The societal expectations of perceiving men as the primary breadwinners and women as the caregivers only aggravate the problems of gender norms.

Moreover, one strong reason for dissuading women from entering politics as a profession is explained by Gheaus as "it is likely that expected interactions with potential co-workers dissuade some women from seeking jobs they would otherwise want; in an important sense they have less opportunity than men to enter and remain in such professions"(2018: 393). The artificial construct between gender segregation of 'feminine' and 'masculine' jobs and the assumption that politics is dirty and a man's job is another fact on the gender-biased institutional arrangements. So, ultimately, it boils down to patriarchal mindsets, which also need to be challenged. With the prejudiced mindset of politics being conceived as dirty, women have this fear psyche of facing far more sexual comments than their male counterparts. Thus, it is equally pertinent to battle these biases, which breed misogyny, sexual slurs, and character assassination in Indian politics. There are cases of women being remarked as temperamental and reduced to their *bindis*, *sarees*, handbags, and looks. In general, women rising to power are constantly questioned, which is also a stereotypical approach that must be addressed. *The Hindu* report, which highlights some of the current biases against women in politics, is reported as follows: "Female candidates of both the parties (BJP and Congress) had a relatively low strike rate if they had to face male candidates of the other party. This also proves the existence of a vote bloc which wants to see a man as their representative. This is why there is lack of winnability of women candidates" (Anekant, 2024).

Furthermore, Iris Young, in her *Justice and the Politics of Difference*, emphasized the need to expand the idea of justice to accommodate oppression and lack of recognition, which come in different expressions and are forms of injustice towards women at least as significant as an unfair distribution of natural resources (Iris, 1990). She expressed that "justice is the primary aim subject of political philosophy" (*ibid.*: 3). The above statement can imply that this WRA appeals to the more inclusive idea of justice, which challenges or modifies the traditional conception of justice. It is crucial to expand the understanding of justice to accommodate the often neglected decision-making paradigm and gender-based division of labour. In coherence with the provisions of WRA, Young also argues that "social justice requires explicitly acknowledging and attending to those group differences in order to undermine oppression (*ibid.*, 1990: 3). Also, there is a need to explore the seat reservation in politics from the angle of justice as Young states that "the concept of justice is coextensive with the political" (*ibid.*, 1990: 9). It is pertinent to look at the larger role played by politics in society and how it affects the well-being of individuals. Additionally, this idea of politics is echoed in Unger's thoughts, which is reflected in the definition of politics as a "struggle over the resources and arrangements that set the basic terms of our practical and passionate relations. Preeminent among these arrangements is the formative institutional and imaginative context of social life" (1981: 145). A better representation of women in Indian politics will have ripple effects in institutional organizations and decision-making. The significance of this reservation also resonated in Pitkin's definition of politics as "the activity through which relatively large and permanent groups of people determine what they will collectively do, settle how they will live together, and decide their future, to whatever extent that is within human power" (1981: 343). Further, Pitkin's stresses that "politics is also about defining relative status and power and privilege, which also defines the nature of our community and the norms and principles by which we shall live" and it reinstates the need of better representation of women in politics (1981: 346). Thus, the benefits of the WRA will not be limited only to governmental acts but will uplift the overall social status of women in India.

In congruent with Rawls' Theory of Justice, many scholars have defended affirmative action from the perspective of fair equality of opportunity. Harris and Narayan endorse this perspective as:

> Our position in that affirmative action is best understood as an attempt to promote equality of opportunity in a social context marked by pervasive inequalities, one in which many institutional criteria and practices work to impede a fair assessment of the capabilities of those who are working-class, women, or people of colour. Thus, affirmative action is an attempt to equalize opportunity for people who continue to face institutional obstacles to equal consideration and equal treatment (2014: 452).

Thus, it can be understood that according to Rawls' concept of seat reservation for women in politics, not only as a means of compensating for past discrimination but also as a measure of reducing the current competitive handicap caused by past discrimination and making a way of regenerating equal access to the benefits of the societal progress and in claiming social justice. In Young's words, this affirmative act of seat reservation of women is essential "not on grounds of compensation for past discrimination, but as important means for undermining oppression, especially oppression that results from unconscious aversions and stereotypes from the assumption that the point of view of the privileged is neutral" (1990: 12).

Conclusion

In a society that has perfectly implemented Rawls' theory of justice, there would be no need for reservation or affirmative action. However, the society is far from perfect and ideal. So, Rawls' fair equality of opportunity can be used to identify those who have been denied this opportunity and lift them from this disadvantaged position. It also provided avenues for affirmative measures to overcome this denial of opportunity in society. To an extent, affirmative action is usually confined and discussed in university admissions and employment, and this expansion to the political domain is significant in combating the inequality women face across generations. The Indian Parliament has taken a giant leap in the right direction of promoting women's empowerment through the Women Reservation Act of 2023. If successfully implemented, this Act might open new opportunities for women and bridge the gender gap in politics. Also, this Act is a precondition for other aspects of development to follow suit, thus instigating the much-needed call for a change in political practice in the country. Unlike the unpopular opinion, conclusively, it can be comprehended that this Act is not only a tokenistic gesture but one laden to question many misogynistic and patriarchal values of the country. Apart from mitigating the gender gap in politics, it will have the far-reaching benefits of achieving gender equality and women empowerment and instilling confidence across generations. In favour of the Reservation Act of women, Rawls' Theory of Justice states that less advantaged and marginalized women have political and career opportunities to develop their capacities.

REFERENCES

Adams, M. (2021). "Nonideal Justice, Fairness, and Affirmative Action." *Journal of Ethics and Social Philosophy, 20*(3). Retrieved from https://doi.ord/10.26556/jesp.v2oi3.1630

Anekant, V., Sanjay, K. (2024, February 12). "How Women can be Represented in Politics." *The Hindu.* Retrieved from https://www.thehindu.com/opinion/op-ed/how-women-can-be-represented-in-politics/article67835144.ece

Freeman, S. (2018). "Rawls on Distributive Justice and the Difference Principle." in Serena Olsaretti (Ed.), *The Oxford Handbook of Distributive Justice* (pp.13-40). Oxford University Press.

First Post (2024, March 31). *Why are there so Few Women in Indian Politics?* [Video]. Youtube. Retrieved from https://youtu.be/6LeaJswZrfy?si=IKAsE2xOWbp7Yerk.

Gheaus, A. (2018). "Gender." in Serena Olsaretti (Ed.), *The Oxford Handbook of Distributive Justice* (pp. 389-414). Oxford University Press.

Harris, L.C. & Narayan U. (2014). "Affirmative Action as Equalizing Opportunity: Challenging the Myth of Preferential Treatment." in LaFollette, H. (Ed.), *Ethics in Practise: An Anthology* (pp. 422-433). Wiley-Blackwell.

Lippert- Rasmussen, K. (2023). "Equality of Opportunity and Affirmative Action." in Sardoc, M. (Ed.), *Handbook of Equality of Opportunity*. Springer. Retrieved from https://doi.ord/10.1007/978-3-319-52269-2_87-1.

Olsaretti, S. (2018). *The Oxford Handbook of Distributive Justice.* Oxford University Press.

Pitkin, H. (1981). "Justice: on Relating Public and Private." *Political Theory*, *9*(3): 327-352. Retrieved from http://links.jstor.org/sici?sici=0090-5917%28198108%299%3A3%3C327%3AJORPAP%3E2.0.CO%3B2-6

PRS Legislative Research (2023). *Vital Stats: Women in Parliament and State Assemblies*. Retrieved from https://prsindia.org/parliamenttrack/vital-stats/women-in-parliament-and-state-assemblies

Rawls, J. (1999a). *A Theory of Justice* (Rev. ed.), Harvard University Press.

Rawls, J. (1999b). *Collected Papers* (Samuel, Freeman, Ed.). Harvard University Press.

Rawls, J. (2001). *Justice as Fairness: A Restatement* (Erin, Kelly, Ed.). Harvard University Press.

Roychowdhury, A. (2024, May 18). "With just 14% Women in Lok Sabha Members, India still behind its Neighbours." *The Indian Express*. Retrieved from https://indianexpress.com/article/research/with-14-women-lok-sabha-members-india -still-behind-its-neighbours-9336769/

Unger, R. (1987). *Social Theory: Its Situation and Its Task.* Cambridge University Press.

Young, Marion I. (1990). *Justice and the Politics of Difference.* Princeton University Press.

16

Performance of Power in Politics and Administration in Royal Court

Women in B.M. Maisnamba's Ningthemnubee

Elangbam Priyokumar Singh and *Ph. Jayalaxmi*

Introduction

"One is not born, but rather becomes, a woman" (Beauvoir, 1973: 361). Simone de Beauvoir distinguishes sex and gender, suggesting that gender is an aspect of identity gradually acquired. The existence of differences between males and females and explaining the reason for these differences documented the area of focusing on sex and gender issues. Society has demarcated men and women based on their social roles, capabilities, and associated traits. Sex is understood to be the biological aspect, while gender is the cultural implications. With this view, it can be concluded that 'being' female and 'being' a woman are two very different concepts. The instance of subjugation on the basis of gender is extensively found in many societies where women are excluded from different fields. Gerda Lerner argued that women were portrayed as victims in the historical situation and were never cited for their contributions. She said, "Women are essential and central to creating society; they are and always have been actors and agents in history" (1986: 5). Women's advancement is always hindered due to the ideological construct of "patriarchy", which privileges men and places the power and authority of everything on men.

Manipur, one of the north-eastern states of India, has a rich history and tradition. It has a legacy of women's movements and contributions in constructing a peaceful society. Women are forerunners in society but are deceptively silenced in the historical records. Concerning women's position in ancient times, history books and chronicles have inadequately recorded women's roles. Jamini Devi also raised the ineffective records on Meitei women and put forth that "*Cheitharol Kumbaba* or the *Manipuri Royal Chronicle* records more about the male progenies of kings and much less about the princesses..." (2010: ix). Even while examining Manipuri literature, it is found that men used to write for female experiences and women writers were absent from the literary scenario. Manipuri Literature as a proper establishment began in the early twentieth century with the works of eminent male writers like Hijam Anganghal, Khwairakpam Chaoba, Lamabam Kamal and many more. These writers drew the actual facet of Manipur society of the time, embodying women's issues and social instabilities, mostly the emergence of nationalism. Following the tradition, eminent modern writers like Elangbam Nilakanta, Pacha Meitei, Hijam Guno, Arambam Samarendra, B.M. Maisnamba, Thanjam Ibopishak, Saratchand Thiyam and others started shaping the modern Manipuri Literature representing the post-war period. The aspects of female consciousness struck the literary tradition of Manipur in the late 1960s and 1970s with writing of first-generation women writers like Thoibi Devi, M.K. Bonodini, Arambam Ongbi Memchoubi, Khaidem Pramodini, and others.

They represented the pioneering women literary figures who wrote about women's issues in the Manipuri literary tradition. Women's writing in Manipur came very late in the literary convention and literature was mostly engaged by the male writers. The reason for the late entrance of women writers in Manipuri literature was predominantly because of the education system, which was not accessible to women. It was only after the introduction of education that women writers emerged in the literary scene. Women's writing in Manipur has its phases, starting from the oral literature to this modern period, and the thematic contents also vary with each phase.

While tracing the growth of Manipuri literature, Nahakpam Aruna said that the early Manipuri literary works existed "in the form of royal chronicles, ritual songs, tales of heroism and allegories written in archaic *Meitei Mayek script* by anonymous, unmade male authors" (2019: 19). The role of rituals and customs in literary texts was palpable in the writings. However, the question of how such influences have an impact on female writers remains a contestable issue. Regardless of whether the oral narratives influenced the female writers or not, Arambam Ongbi Memchoubi, in her book *Manipuri Sahityada Nupeegee Khonjen* (2003), opines that the fact is without any argument from the early time it was evidently visible that it was through the *maibis* (local women shaman) that gods and goddesses communicated with the people for the well-being of the Meitei community (my trans. 2003: 7). Women's position in society is highly regarded and they have played fundamental roles in the upliftment of society since time immemorial.

This present chapter proposes to highlight the role of women in politics and administrations in ancient times by analyzing the women in B.M. Maisnama's *Ningthemnubee (Ladies in the Palace)* (2006, 2023). B.M. Maisnamba, is a modern Manipuri writer, whose writings reflected a challenging attitude to the traditional values associated with women in society. He is also among the acclaimed historical writers in Manipuri literature, and he is known for representing historical elements in fiction, focusing on historical recreation, political intrigues, and, notably, women's issues. The idea of 'powerful women' or 'women in power politics' are essential in most of his novels. His expertise lies in giving voices to the subdued females. The male writer writing about female characters is always confrontational in nature, which is the reason why Hélène Cixous always advocates, "Woman must write herself; must write about women and bring women to writing" (1976: 875), and men should write for men; and "it's up to him to say where his masculinity and femininity are at" (1976: 877). However, Maisnamba is one such male author who writes about feminine sensibilities. His construction of femininity is overpoweringly explained in every female characterization that he created.

For the analysis, his novel, *Ningthemnubee,* has been taken to illustrate the aspects of women in politics in the historiography of Manipur. The novel is the first and foremost trilogy ever produced in Manipuri literature. It consists of three parts—Ningthemnubee: A Woman in the Bondage, Ningthemnubee: A Woman in the Political Trap, and Ningthemnubee: A Woman in the Historical Court. The combined volume of the three related titles is popularly known as *Ningthemnubee* or *Ningthemnubee Trilogy*, which was presented with four literary awards in Manipuri Literature because of its historical re-creation with literary touch in charming language and its superb narrative style, characterisation and plot. It is based on the reign of Ningthempishak, Chandrakiriti Maharaj (1833-1844 AD and 1850-1886 AD), especially in his second rule. For a short period, the king lived at the palace of Langthabal and then shifted to Kangla. Behind the king, there were many women who played reflective roles in ruling the kingdom but were subjected to the peripheral position. Therefore, this chapter will investigate the role of those women in power politics during that time and their representation in the historiography of Manipur. As the title indicates, it narrates the stories of different ladies in the palace, consisting of Mamashija (Queen Ponglenkhombi), other Queens, royal attendants, concubines and their respective roles, duties, political conspiracy and sacrifice for safeguarding the kingdom of Manipur. It depicts a forgotten chapter of history with a deep sense of historical elements, the background of the ancient royal palace of Langthabal, the old Capital of Manipur.

Power Politics and Subjugation of Women

Gerda Lerner says, "Women's history is indispensable and essential to the emancipation of women" (1986: 3). For a long time, the voices of women were imprisoned and were never the subject of history. Historically women were rendered invisible in historical narratives. The question remains: who will write for women? Therefore, questioning what history is, Lerner distinguishes between "the unrecorded past—all the events of the past as recollected by human beings—and History—the recorded and interpreted past." She says, "Like men, women are and always have been actors and agents in history" (1986: 4). Women are relegated to the peripheral position despite sharing equal responsibilities and duties in the maintenance of the state.

B.M. Maisnamba's *Ningthemnubee* is a historical account delineating the women characters who played central roles but were shoved into the margins to give men the centre stage in the historical narratives. The novel accurately represents women in power and palace politics in ancient Manipur, showcasing many untold stories of unrecognized *Ningthemnubees* like the character of Puyanu and others. Usually, the term *Ningthemnubee* was a title given to the wives of the king, and in more extensive interpretation, the term also extended to the royal maidservants and concubines in earlier times. It was used to denote the Ladies of Ningthem (the king) or the 'Ladies in the Palace', individually or collectively. However, the position of women in the royal palace is demarcated by the power hierarchy among the Ladies in the Palace. For instance—the Chief Queen was also known as *Leimarenbi* or *Meeren Ningthemnubee*, and other queens were given the titles like *Yoibu Ningthemnubeee, Yohen Ningthemnubee, Apambi, Apambi Naha, Leima Khubi, Leima Khubi Naha* etc., according to their status and duties assigned to them. In those days, the King kept many wives or *Ningthemnubees* openly or secretly, under some customary laws, for personal needs or as part of political strategy.

Historical narratives always perceive the anguish of the victims subjectively. Frequently, we find that the narrator of history is male and male-centric. History is permeated with the narratives of many people, like women, servants, children, workers, armies, and others. But few stories become the subjects of the historians. In the history-making process, only those incidents have been recorded which have caught the fancies of the historians. Gerda Lerner also argues the fact that "these historians have been men, and what they have recorded is what men have done and experienced and found significant. They have called this History and claimed universality for it. what women have done and experienced has been left unrecorded, neglected, and ignored in interpretation" (1986: 4). The story of *Ningthemnubee* recounts one particular Ningthemnubee, Puyanu, and her journey inside the royal palace. Although Puyanu is presented as a fictional character in the novel, she is the representative of many unheard voices of women whose experiences were never recorded in the royal chronicles. In the introduction to *Ningthemnubee*, Maisnamba penetrates the skeletons of history to re-narrate the incidents and happenings of the past by infusing lives into the apparitions of history. The narrative of Ningthemnubee is constructed from the lost clue that the writer got from *Puya*, an ancient manuscript. Puyanu is presented as the subjugated being who raised against her perpetrators who attempted to subdue her as part of the political intrigues. Thus, the author writes:

> "Oh Ladies!
> Ladies living in the Palace!
> I am the bird of the cage, my life,
> My leg is in chain…!" (Maisnamba, 2023:10)

Though Puyanu is an imaginary character, her sufferings are the actuality of most of the "Ningthemnubees" who become the victims of palace politics. She adorned many faces in the novel to counter the subjugation and resist the male hegemony. Sometimes, she was disguised as Nuyam Saphabee, the royal maidservant, and sometimes Nuyam Saphabee Puyanu, a woman in the political trap. She was used as a political *Laibar* (agent) by the mother of the king to prevent internal wars among the royal family.

The novel deals with her journey and struggle to become the Chief Queen of Ningthempishak, Chandrakriti Maharaj. She has been portrayed as a strong, beautiful, and kind-hearted woman. She was born from an incestuous relationship between Pamheibi (Pychola) and Panthoi, who belonged to the same family clan, the Puyam. From ancient times, marriage between the same clan was substantial and punishable. The story of Panthoi and Pamheibi has been recorded in the *Ningthourel Puya* as "Panthoi and Pamheibi-Kiyamgei taba (settlers of Kiyamgei) are the grandsons of Puyam Chukon". (p. 29). Fearing social exclusion from their clan, Puyanu and her mother had been left by Panthoi in Chasat Hill. So, Puyanu was brought up under the care of the Chasat King, Lanthouyang (a tribal king), where she learnt enormous martial arts skills. This story of Puyanu's bravery and deftness has reached Ponglenkhombi's ear. Therefore, during the *Mera Hou Chongba Festival,* which marks the loving brotherhood relationship between hill tribes and valley people, she planned to see Puyanu with her own eyes. So, she invited Lanthouyang along with his daughter for the celebration. After witnessing Puyanu, she concluded that Puyanu possessed every quality of a queen and wanted her to be the wife of her son, Ningthem Pishak. Puyanu was brought to the palace, and decided to make marriage arrangements for Puyanu as her daughter-in-law. However, when Ponglenkhombi asked about the identity of Puyanu and her parents during the marriage ceremony. Puyanu refused to disclose the truth as she would like to save her parents. Meanwhile, one older man disclosed Puyanu's true identity, and upon hearing that, Queen Ponglenkhombi lost her temper and cancelled her son's marriage to Puyanu. Then, she ordered her female soldiers to shave Puyanu's hair and to keep her in *Leinungshang* (prison) because of her stubbornness and her illicit origin. She was not allowed to be the Chief queen under Manipuri customary law. Puyanu accepted the verdict with unexpressed inner dialogues.

Through the narratives, Maisnamba has brought up the issue of incestuous relationships, which was disdained in Meitei society and how it created impediments for Puyanu. Even though royal lineage was polluted with impure blood, the royal archives attempted to hide such contentious matter and Puyanu was shown as a victim of such conspiracy. Thus, she represents women's voices restrained and subjugated in the political conflict. Consequently, she wanted to reform the royal palace, particularly the polygamy tradition of the Manipuri Kings. She protested against the system for keeping women in chains and bondage against their own will for sexual and political purposes. Many other women like Puyanu were exploited in the political game in the Meitei palace. In order to fulfil her mission, Puyanu had to face *Pacha Loishang*, the Royal Court of Women, bravely and wisely. In the end, she completed her mission and took revenge against the injustices meted out to women by sacrificing her own life.

In history, there were also women who resisted the authoritarian regime of the monarchy. However, their stories were never told as fascinatingly as the stories of men were narrated. B.M. Maisnamba also stated that many records of *Ningthemnubees* were not found. The *Sanggei Phamang* (ancient book) was rewritten during the reign of Meidinggu Ninthem Pishak Chandrakriti in which the stories of numerous *Ningthemnubees* were left out, and the names of nine *Ningthemnubees* of Ningthem Nungleinkhombi were not found (2023: 12). Arousing the feminist consciousness in his fictional works, Maisnamba challenges the royal records which fail to address or even mention some powerful women rendering them voiceless and invisible. Through his recreation of indiscernible women, Maisnamba stimulates feminist awareness by delineating strong and powerful women who defy the royal convention. As Gerda Lerner (1993) argues that:

> It was under patriarchal hegemony in thought, values, institutions and resources that women had to struggle to form their own feminist consciousness. I define feminist consciousness as the awareness of women that they belong to a subordinate group; that they have suffered wrongs as a group; that their condition of subordination is not natural, but is societally determined; that they must join with other women to remedy these wrongs; and finally, that they must and can provide an alternate vision of societal organization in which women as well as men will enjoy autonomy and self-determination. (p. 14)

Maisnamba makes an effort to give an alternative space where women could retaliate against the royal hierarchal power structure, which put women on trial who failed to follow and serve the royal indictment. Puyanu's victory in avenging her enemies has emphasized the autonomy and self-determination of a woman who survives the royal domination.

Women in Power and Palace Politics: The Ku(s)

History captures only the bravery of men but not that of women. History is all about male rulers, male doings and male activities but seldom projects the reality of women's lives. Even if women played significant roles, they were excluded from the annals, which muffled women's voices. While considering the position of Manipuri women, Manipuri women played a pivotal role in a vast spectrum of society by contributing prominently to political, economic and cultural aspects. While highlighting the active participation of women in various movements, N. Lokendra (1998) states that:

> In fact, in many of the movements, the participation of the women was much more than their male counterparts and in certain instances, they often took the leadership.... The active role of the women in the political movements of Manipur valley may be understood in the framework of the crucial role that they play in the society and economy of the state... (pp. 247-48).

In comparison to other women's counterparts, Meitei women are more independent, courageous, skilled, and hardworking. Hence, the Manipuri women contributed significantly to every part of social activities. T.C. Hodson, the then Political Agent in Manipur, exclaims in his book *The Meitheis* about the association of Manipuri women in social and political affairs. He reflected on women holding "a high and free position in Manipur". Women managed the internal trade and exchange. Women had set up bazaars at convenient spots by the roadside and congregated at an early hour without spending leisure time (1908: 23). Women weaved all their clothes and exhibited their ability to have a better economic position. The active participation of women in social, economic and political sphere is quite evident while analysing the history of Manipur. However, due to the lack of records, the bravery and heroism of Manipuri Queens have not been recorded. While considering the political position of women, Ksh. Bimola Devi (2001) accentuates the necessity of understanding social norms, customs and societal structures. In order to understand women in politics, she felt the need to examine women in two categories—an individual and a group. She mentioned the role of Chief Queen Laisana in ancient Manipur 33AD and how "she headed the women's court called *Patcha* where all women-related cases were taken up and settled." Numerous women took an active part in the administration and political affairs of the state. She also mentioned the role of Maharani Linthoingambi who played a crucial part in the absence of her husband in 1443. Maharani Gomti Devi is another instance of women taking part in the political strategy in controlling the political administration. Maharani Kumudini, wife of Gambhir Singh, who, after the death of her husband, went to the extent of protecting her minor son, Chandrakirti, from the royal conspiracies for the throne. Furthermore, in a monarchical system, the direct participation of women was not encouraged. However, during the *Lallup* system (when all males went out of the palace for service), women had come out to shoulder the social responsibilities apart from managing the household activities. In groups, they would fight against injustice and influence the king (pp. 113-14). Thus, as individuals or in groups women have exhibited their astuteness in decision-making and had shouldered the social obligations.

In the history of Manipur, Maharani Kumudini plays a significant role in protecting and safeguarding her son, Ningthem Pisak. Even in the fictional world of B.M. Maisnamba, she is shown as one of the authoritative women known as (Ku's) under whose supremacy the royal court performed. Maisnamba's powerful ladies (Ku's) include Loukram Chanu Kumudini, Khuraijam Chanu Kumudini and Maisnam Kumudini, and the author attempted to show the authority of the royal women in this novel. They represented women in power politics in the palace and controlled the palace. They were also the jury of the ladies' court (which is known as *Pacha Loishang* in the ancient Manipur Capital). Maisnam Kumudini, also known as Ponglenkhombi, represents the most commanding woman in the novel. Whenever an emergency occurred inside the Palace, the information should be given to her first, even though there was the King or many brave soldiers; under her plans and strategies, steps would be taken to rule the reign peacefully. During that time, there were also sibling rivalries among the royal blood for the throne and power, and women played a significant role in the political intrigues. They took firm steps and measures to protect the throne from the enemies, conspiracies, and unwanted forces which threatened the royal power to protect the throne of Ningthem Pishak, King Chandrakriti, from many internal or external invaders. They sometimes took the role of a mediator and sometimes assumed the role of forceful and violent rulers. Ponglenkhombi taught her son, King Chandrakriti, about political intrigue and governance so that nobody could take his place. Ponglenkhombi, as a female ruler, exercised her power in the political and internal matters of the state. As quoted in 'Maharani Kumudini' Wikipedia (n.d.),

> After the death of her husband at an early age, she took full responsibility to protect her minor son, Prince Chandrakirti, from the evil plots of palace intrigues. After her son ascended the throne of the Manipur kingdom, she is best known for being the most extraordinary royal lady holding the utmost powers in history.

Therefore, after the death of her husband, King Gambhir Singh, she entrusted Narasingh and Debendra, whom her husband trusted the most, to rule the Palace. With their support, she made her only two-year-old son Ningthem Pishak, the King of Manipur. Nevertheless, she was an astute woman who was cautious in protecting the royal Palace from power politics. She exclaimed, "Whatever it may be, I have to save the throne of my son! I am Aboklembee! We have to send one Nonthangleima" (p. 193). To maintain peace in the imperial court, these women (Ningthemnubees) used women (Ningthemnubees) in their political games as a weapon to negotiate with the opposite troops during many wars. As represented in the past chronicles of Manipur, women can be used in treaties with other dynasties or communities. The Ku(s) believed that women could cause wars; at the same time, they could also prevent them. They were instrumental in the political system of the monarchy, using women for sexual purposes to entice or gratify men. The subjugation of women of lower rank was quite apparent in Manipuri history, and they were utilised to make deals among the warring enemies or even gifted to the kings. In history, another Ningthemnubee called Nongthonbee intercepted the war between Narasingha and Chourajeet. Induprava, the daughter of Maharaj Budhachandra, was betrothed to the son of Cachar King to extend the ties between the two kingdoms. Women are instrumental in this power politics. As Ponglenkhombi exclaims, "All these are administrative policies, Aboklembee! If there is administrative acumen, we can play politics on the woman:

it is the highest politics, it is the only means for controlling enemy" (p. 194). Moreover, it is a fact that politics changes from time to time, and this is in the hands of these women in power. Khuraijam Kumudini is also one of the women in power who takes a more significant role in administration inside the Palace. She saved Puyanu from the terrible punishment of Ponglenkhombi. In the novel, she sided with Puyanu, who became the victim of royal politics. These powerful ladies had the power to punish or forgive a convict easily. Puyanu has been given another life to serve their purposes as they are in power. She was trained to avenge the system for the humiliation she suffered at the hands of the women in authority.

Conclusion

Maisnamba's narrative may be understood as a fiction coming out from the imagination of an artist. However, he aptly raised the issue of women's subjugation in the royal intrigues and also pointed out the powerful women who were never mentioned in the royal records. Women in Manipur have suffered a lot throughout the historical phases. Women have been marginalised in all possible ways in the male-dominated society. The idea that women are concerned with only keeping the household to look after children is being challenged by many, and many young women are now stepping out to take part in academics, social activism, entrepreneurship and politics. So, this novel, *Ningthemnubee,* redefines women's power and promotes the necessity of recreating the historical aspects of Manipuri history to give voices to women.

REFERENCES

Aruna, Nahakpam (2019). "The Journey of Women's Writing in Manipuri Literature", in Thingnam Anjulika Samom (Ed.). *Crafting the Word: Writings from Manipur*. Zubaan.

Beauvoir, Simone de (1973). *The Second Sex*. Vintage Book.

Cixous, Hélène (1976). "The Laugh of the Medusa" (Keith Cohen and Paula Cohen, trans.) in Signs, *1*(4). (Summer, 1976), pp. 875-893. http://links.jstor.org/sici?sici=00979740%281976 22%291%3A4%3C875%3ATLOTM%3E2.0.CO%3B2-V

Devi, Jamini (2010). *Cultural History of Manipur: Sija Laioibi and the Maharas* (Sheela Devi Chaudary, Trans.). Mittal Publications.

Devi, Prof. Ksh. Bimola (2001). "The Role of Women in Manipur Politics", in C. Joshua Thomas, R. Gopalakrishnan and R.K. Ranjan Singh (Eds). *Constraints in Development of Manipur.* Regency Publications.

Hodson, T.C (1908). *The Meitheis.* London: Wiliam Clowes and Son.

Lerner, Gerda (1986). *The Creation of Patriarchy.* New York: OUP.

Lerner, Gerda (1993). *The Creation of Feminist Consciousness: from the Middle Ages to Eighteen-seventy.* New York: OUP.

Maisnamba, B.M (2023). *Ningthemnubee* (E. Priyokumar Singh. Trans.) Uma Publication. (Original Work published 2006).

Memchoubi (Thounaojam Chanu Ibemhal) (2003). *Manipuri Sahityada Nupeegee Khonjel.* New Delhi: Sahitya Akademi.

'Maharani Kumudini' Wikipedia. (n.d.). Accessed on 27th May, 2024, retrieved from https://simple.wikipedia.org /wiki/Maharani_Kumudini

Singh, N. Lokendra (1998). *The Unquiet Valley: Society, Economy and Politics in Manipur (1891-1950).* Mittal Publications.

Section-IV
Gender-based Policies, Challenges and Ways Forward

17

Women in Decision-making

Current Scenario & Issues Ahead

Rajesh Gill

Introduction

Even after decades of consistent action-oriented programmes towards gender parity undertaken by countries all over the globe, the current situation is far from satisfactory. Theoretically speaking, there has been enormous development, in terms of the loud rhetoric around gender equality and even the legal structures supporting gender parity in most of the countries. However, in many cases, even the legal and institutional structures have failed to be implemented on ground, leaving much to be desired. For illustration, the recently released Report on Women, Business and Law 2024 by the World Bank, based on an analysis of 190 economies, underscores the huge gap between the legal rights granted to women on paper and the reality they face on the ground (World Bank, 2024). The Report states that women have just two-thirds of the rights of men in the workplace. Further, just 98 of the 190 economies have put in place legislation mandating equal pay for women. Only 35, i.e. fewer than one in five have adopted enforcement mechanisms to address the gender pay gap. As a consequence, women on an average earn just 77 cents for every dollar earned by men. The Report, shockingly, finds that a large number of countries are yet to enact laws prohibiting sexual harassment at workplace, domestic violence, child marriage, feticide etc. Introducing two new indicators of gender equality, i.e. child care and safety, the Report underlines the differences in the experiences of men and women while travelling in mass transit, travelling across countries, child care, career graph and so on, making it most difficult for women to have prosperous career. Women spend nearly two and a half more hours a day on unpaid work than men, much of it in childcare. This results in only half of women participating in the global workforce, in comparison to three quarters of men.

Gender Inequality in Decision-making Positions: The Current Status

Till date, India has had just one-woman Prime Minister, two Presidents and fifteen Chief Ministers since Independence, i.e. 1947. Interestingly, however, despite a large proportion of female students in Law colleges in the country, India's Supreme Court has not had a single woman Chief Justice so far, while till 2023, there were three women judges out of the sanctioned strength of 34 in the Apex Court and 106 women Judges in the High Courts out of 788. If all goes well, Justice B.V. Nagarathna is due to become the first woman Chief Justice of India in the year 2027. Women remain a minority in all the male dominated professions, particularly Defence and Police services. Women constitute just 11.7 per cent of the 2.1 million strong police force. On the positive side, India has the highest proportion of women pilots in the world at 15 per cent against the 5 per cent at the global level.

The situation is not very different in the corporate sector, too. Women are reported to be occupying 18.2 per cent of Board seats at NIFTY 500 companies in 2023. Women are occupying top managerial posts in only 8.9 per cent firms in the tech industry (Boben, B. & Jain, R., 2023).

Situation in the political arena is actually a bit more confusing, in so far as the women's participation at decision-making positions is concerned. The Lok Sabha, whose term ended in 2024, had just 15 per cent women Parliamentarians, while their proportion in State Legislative Assemblies is only 9 per cent. Although Women's Reservation Act, 2023, is expected to increase the proportion of women in both these political bodies, its implementation will take a few years due to the delimitation exercise. Moreover, no provision for reservation for women in the Upper House, i.e. Rajya Sabha, has been made. Despite these limitations, the new Law is bound to send a large number of women to the Central and State decision-making bodies.

Numbers are not Sufficient for Effective Participation

A more pertinent question that follows the increased number of women coming into decision-making positions relates to their effective participation in these decision-making bodies. The empirical evidence so far, not only from India, but even from other countries, indicates that mere numbers hardly matter and many of the women who came up as Village Panchayat members or *Pradhans*, or even as members of Parliament etc., have remained silent spectators, while men in their families have been the decision makers. The phenomenon has been termed as *'Rubber Stamp Politics'* in the name of political empowerment. Elected women's experiences of discrimination have been recorded in countries like Uganda and Rwanda, the latter leading the world with the highest proportion of women in parliament. Quota-elected women in Uganda have been reported to be less recognized, suggesting lack of respect and negotiating power (Porfido and Horgan, 2020). In Rwanda, too, female participation in parliament is being questioned as *"rubber stamp politics"*. Observing similar trends in Indian politics, a fundamental question that remains is whether placing a larger number of women in key positions in political, educational and other structures essentially signifies gender equality. Does the democratic secular Indian system—political and social, have sufficient tolerance for women who are independent and critical of patriarchy that celebrates masculinity at the cost of all other genders? So long as clear answers evade us, gender equality shall remain a mirage. In recent cases of women's violation in India, we have hardly heard voices of our women representatives in local bodies, more than a million in numbers. Even the women representatives in Parliament, Legislative Assemblies and other Women based Statutory Bodies prefer to remain mum and tow party lines. Under the circumstances, can we really call participation of women in politics as political empowerment? Even the voting patterns among women, a majority of whom come from villages and poor backgrounds with a *ghunghat* intact, hardly show an agency, thus making it difficult to call it political empowerment. Actually, in recent times, even women who matter, have shied away from directly speaking out against real cases of gender violence, which is not a very encouraging trend. Therefore, India's position on the latest Global Gender Gap Report (2023) on political empowerment appears to be misleading. The quantification of political empowerment in terms of number of women who have entered by virtue of the reservation in Rural and Urban Local Bodies, fails to reflect the ground reality, with a clear divergence between positions of power and exercise of power.

Women in Decision-Making Positions in HEIs

All the regions of the world have seen a considerable increase in female enrolment in tertiary education, which tripled globally between 1995 and 2018, growing at a higher rate than male enrolment over the period (UNESCO, 2020). This phenomenon has been termed as the "female advantage" in higher education (Buchmann & DiPrete, 2006). While it is generally presumed on the basis of an impressive enrolment of girls in education at all levels, even in erstwhile masculine disciplines, across the world, that gender gaps in education have vanished, I would like to argue here that irrespective of disciplines, education has hardly enabled women to assume a role in economic workforce, especially in technologically the most sophisticated areas, equal to men and statistics support this reality. According to the data released by Ministry of Education in the All India Survey on Higher Education (AISHE, 2022), the percentage of female enrolment to total enrolment has increased, so as the Gender Parity Index. Interestingly, the female enrolment in North Eastern States is higher than that of the males, i.e. 104 female students for 100 males in NER. Further, at the national level, female students outnumber male students in Science Stream. Although female students outnumber males in Under-graduate, Post-graduate and M.Phil. courses, what is indeed more important is that female students are fewer in B.Com. (48.5%), still fewer in B.Tech. (28.7%) and Bachelor of Engineering (28.5%). Female students outnumber males in Arts Stream both at undergraduate and post-graduate levels. Interestingly, girl students enrolled in Education comprise 64.4 per cent.

Generally, it is presumed that the expansion of science and technology brings greater gender equality and therefore, nations have been found to invest more and more into it in order to forge gender parity. It is imperative in this context to cite some statistics from STEM (Science, Technology, Engineering, and

Mathematics) in terms of gender representation. Maldives has less than 1 per cent women in STEM, while they comprise 43 per cent in India, the highest in the world. Globally in over two-thirds of countries, one can find that less than a quarter of the students of Engineering, Manufacturing and Construction or ICT are female. By contrast, education, health, arts, humanities and social sciences tend to see an overrepresentation of women (UNESCO, 2020). More interestingly, within STEM, there are significant gender variations. For example, in Engineering & Technology, girls are only 29.3 per cent at all levels put together. Female participation in professional courses is lower in comparison to academic courses both at undergraduate and postgraduate levels. According to UNESCO Report 2020, only 22 women have won the Nobel Prize in any branch of science historically. In Latin America and the Caribbean, women represent less than 30 per cent of all researchers in science. Empirical evidence has refuted the explanation that women are underrepresented in STEMM (Science, Technology, Mathematics, and Medicine) because of innate incompetence in these areas (NASEM, 2007; Pawley, 2011). Instead, studies have demonstrated that implicit and explicit biases discourage women from entering STEMM careers (Cheryan *et al.*, 2015). In addition to undermining the advancement of women in STEMM to positions of leadership, masculine values can signal to women that they do not belong in these fields in the first place (Bian *et al.*, 2017).

The structural biases against women professionals and leaders appears to be ill-founded in view of the empirical evidence showing women physicians to be more competent than their male counterparts, Tsugawa (2017), in such a study, has observed that when treated by female physicians, more than one million elderly hospitalized patients were less likely to die within 30 days of admission or to be readmitted within 30 days of discharge than those cared for by male physicians. The author further noted that if male physicians could achieve the same outcomes as their female colleagues, there would be 32,000 fewer deaths each year among Medicare patients. Despite such data, the fact remains that women in medicine have failed to occupy the leadership positions, indicating a 'leaking pipeline' phenomenon. According to a study, in a typically female dominated field, obstetrician gynaecologists women face barriers in getting to leadership positions and earn $36,000 per year less than men in the same field (Hughes and Bernstein, 2018). Women physicians reported spending 8.5 more hours a week on domestic chores in comparison to male colleagues and were more likely than male colleagues to have spouses or domestic partners who were employed full-time (Jolly *et al.*, 2014).

Studies have also confirmed higher incidences of sexual harassment of women at multiple career levels. More than sexual harassment, gender harassment has been found to be the most common and harmful form of sexual harassment (NASEM, 2018). The same author has observed that sexual harassment undermines women's professional and educational attainment and mental and physical health, leading to negative career outcomes. Women's entry into leadership and their positions is also inhibited due to 'Microaggressions', which implies as under:

> "The everyday verbal, non-verbal and environmental slights, snubs, or insults, whether intentional or unintentional, which communicate hostile, derogatory, or negative messages to target persons based solely upon their marginalized group membership. In many cases, these hidden messages may invalidate the group identity or experiential reality of target persons, demean them on a personal or group level, communicate they are lesser human being, suggest they do not belong with the majority group, threaten and intimidate, or relegate them to inferior status and treatment" (Sue, 2017).

The most prominent example of the above stated phenomenon is the prevalence of 'bro-culture' in the corporate sector, often reflecting patriarchal practices in networking, communications, work assignments, partying etc., all at the cost of women employees. All the expectations from the corporate sector, of encouraging a gender—just work culture, have actually been belied, as indicated by the enormous empirical evidence from all over the globe. The gendered language and jargons in vogue, despite the rhetoric of gender equality, at the workplaces as well as in public spheres, contribute in keeping alive the significance of gender over and above merit and competence.

Glass Ceiling in Higher Education

Studies have revealed that there are factors other than individual agency which actually contribute to educational and career outcomes. Educational choices are not gender free and are often shaped by students' rational cost-benefit calculations combined with social influences that set expectations early during gender socialization. Male students continue to choose higher-paying degrees and receive higher earnings after graduation than women (Conger & Dickson, 2017). What is most important is that the 'female advantage' may be an illusion, noting that women's educational successes have not translated into socio-economic achievement (Niemi, 2017). Instead of vertical gender segregation, horizontal gender segregation has been stable over time.

Just 30 per cent of the world's researchers at universities are women (UNESCO, 2019). Examining the trend from a gender lens, one finds that in most cases, men publish on average more articles than women, in every country, leading to gender publication gap, being most pronounced in top journals. Elsevier's 'Gender Report' analyzed the research publications, career progression and perceptions across the European Union and 15 countries globally in 26 subject areas. On an average, women researchers author fewer publications than men in every country, regardless of authorship. One of the most industrially advanced country, Japan, had the lowest ratio of women to men among authors in all subject areas, i.e. 18 women per 100 men, whereas Argentina was the closest to gender parity among authors overall (Elsevier, 2020). These data certainly do not reflect the lower competencies of women scientists or academicians, instead, these points at the disrupters, which target women much more than men, putting the former into severe disadvantage.

Data across the countries shows that there are fewer women at the senior most positions in the universities, though their proportion is higher at the lower levels. In countries like Canada and US, too, there are fewer women at the level of professor in the universities. Female Professors are underrepresented in STEM careers. The H.E. sector is among those industries that are still struggling to bridge the gender gap. Globally women occupy only 25 per cent of seats in Parliament and 36 per cent of senior private sector management positions (World Economic Forum, 2020).

Barriers Obstructing Women from Decision-making Positions

The World Bank Report, 2024 on Women, Business and Law, confirms that safety, child-care responsibilities, gender-based violence and lack of mobility are the most prominent barriers, which come in the way of women in career. Further, Women face greater obstacles in accessing credit, training, networks, and information and in starting businesses (Jones and Clifton, 2017; Piacentini, 2013). Out of 190 economies assessed in the Report, only in 62 economies, quality child care services are provided by law, leaving 128 economies without established quality assurance standards for centre-based childcare services. Moreover, only 24 economies require a legally binding gender quota for corporate boards. Despite a growing body of knowledge on the performance benefits of gender-balanced decision-making (Garcia and Herrero 2021; Kang *et al.,* 2022), women hold only about 20 per cent of corporate board positions (EIGE, 2020). In 2003, Norway set a significant precedent, becoming the first economy globally to establish a binding gender quota for corporate boards.

Unless the *'leaky pipeline'* is plugged by putting in place the support structures for women professionals, so that they do not have to leave their career midway, women shall not be able to reach to the top positions, either in the professional or the political fields. The invisible institutional biases in the corporate sector, which is expanding in the current scenario, has always worked against women, resulting into the segregation of women in non-executive positions, with no participation in decision-making process.

It is due to these barriers that even the reservation for women in rural and urban local bodies in India, has failed to push the women as decision makers. Instead, due to the persistent patriarchal structures, most of these women have been used mainly by men in their families, to usurp political power and prestige. Criminalization of politics has been an important factor pushing women out of political decision-making. Scrupulous use of muscle power and loads of money further makes it difficult to women to venture into the electoral politics. The new Act of 2023 granting Reservation to women in Lok Sabha and State Legislative Assemblies, would also meet the same fate, if no efforts are made to ensure that women are inducted not just as showpieces, but they are absorbed in the political system as active decision-making members.

It is, in fact, the responsibility of the State to facilitate the institutional and structural support for an active participation of women in decision-making system. In an interesting study, Sadia Hussain (2022) studied about 4 lakh responses taken from both male and female Members of Parliament. She contested the simplistic assumption that women only take up 'softer issues' such as women and child development, food processing, health and sanitation. Contrary to that, she found that women are likely to speak on issues of prime importance to all, including the hardcore issues of home, foreign affairs, railways and intra-structure. Women in decision-making positions have been found to promote policy of transformative finances, e.g., 'Alcohol-free villages in Maharashtra' and stopping the diversion of wheat for the production of beer in Punjab for its distribution through PDS among the poor, utilizing the Panchayat funds for the installation of *gobar* gas plant, piped water at homes, toilet blocks for women, creation of schools, shelter homes, hostels and health centres etc. It is common for the political parties to ignore women workers while shielding candidates for elections, even though these women have spent their whole lives in campaigning, public meetings, demonstrations, community work etc. The most often cited plea against these women is the problem of their 'win-ability'. In reality, it is the patriarchy, which obstructs women, who comprise almost 50 per cent of the total population, from coming to the centre-stage, well deserved by them. Towing party lines continues to be another major hurdle in the emergence of women leaders in politics, where women members from specific political parties are often seen taking sides according to their political affiliations rather than the issues in hand.

Judicial activism has helped in ways more than one, in getting women their due in the areas such as Defence forces, marriage and family laws, gender violence etc., but the institutionalization of gender-just practices in the fields of employment, education and politics, is still lacking. The gap between theory and practice is yet to be plugged; and till that is done, decision-making positions would keep eluding women in India as elsewhere.

REFERENCES

All India Survey on Higher Education (AISHE) (2022). Ministry of Education, Government of India.

Bian, L., S.-J. Leslie, M.C. Murphy, and A. Cimpian (2017a). "Messages About Brilliance Undermine Women's Interest in Educational and Professional Opportunities." *Journal of Experimental Social Psychology, 76*: 404-420.

Boben, Blassy & Jain, Rupam (2023). "Female Footprint in India's Workforce." *Reuters*, September 20, 2023, Indian Press Information Bureau.

Buchmann, C., DiPrete, T.A. & McDaniel, A. (2008). "Gender Inequalities in Education." *Annual Review of Sociology, 34*: 319-337.

Buchmann, C. and DiPrete, T. (2006). "The Growing Female Advantage in College Completion: The Role of Family Background and Academic Achievement." *American Sociological Review, 7*(4): 515-541.

Cheryan, S., A. Master, and A.N. Meltzoff (2015). Cultural stereotypes as gatekeepers: Increasing girls' interest in computer science and engineering by diversifying stereotypes. *Frontiers in Psychology, 6*: 49-49.

Conger, Dylan & Dickson, Lisa (2017). "Gender Imbalance in Higher Education: Insights for College Administrators and Researchers." *Research in Higher Education, 58*(2).

EIGE (European Institute for Gender Equality). (2020). "Statistical Brief: Gender Balance in Corporate Boards." *EIGE*, Vilnius, Lithuania.

Elsevier (2020). *The Researcher Journey through a Gender Lens: An Examination of Research Participation, Career Progression and Perceptions Across the Globe*. Elsevier: Amsterdam.

Garcia, C. Jos., and Bego.a Herrero. (2021). "Female Directors, Capital Structure, and Financial Distress." *Journal of Business Research, 136* (C): 592-601.

Global Gender Gap Report (2023). World Economic Forum.

Niemi, Nancy S. (2017). *Degrees of Difference—Women, Men and the Value of Higher Education*. Routledge, Taylor & Francis Group.

Hughes, F., and P.S. Bernstein (2018). "Sexism in Obstetrics and Gynaecology: Not just a 'Women's Issue'." *American Journal of Obstetrics & Gynaecology, 219*(4): 364.

Hussain, Sadia (2022). "Performance of Women in Parliament: A Quantitative Study of the Questions asked by Women Members in Lok Sabha (1999-2019)", *Special Article*, in *Economic & Political Weekly, 57*(31).

Jolly, S., K.A. Griffith, R. DeCastro, A. Stewart, P. Ubel, and R. Jagsi. (2014). "Gender Differences in Time Spent on Parenting and Domestic Responsibilities By High-Achieving Young Physician-researchers." *Annals of Internal Medicine, 160*(5): 344-353.

Jones, Karen, and Jonathan Clifton (2017). "Rendering Sexism Invisible in Workplace Narratives. A Narrative Analysis of Female Entrepreneurs' Stories of Not Being Talked to by Men." *Gender, Work, and Organization, 25*(5): 557-74.

Kang Wei, John K. Ashton, Ayan Orujov, and Yang Wang (2022). "Realizing Gender Diversity on Corporate Boards." *International Journal of the Economics of Business, 30*(1): 1-29.

National Academies of Sciences, Engineering, and Medicine (2020). *Promising Practices for Addressing the Underrepresentation of Women in Science, Engineering, and Medicine: Opening Doors*. Washington, DC: The National Academies Press. https://doi.org/10.17226/25585.

NASEM. (2018). *Sexual Harassment of Women: Climate, Culture, and Consequences in Academic Sciences, Engineering, and Medicine*. (Ed.) P.A. Johnson, S.E. Widnall and F.F. Benya. Washington, DC: The National Academies Press.

NASEM. (National Academies of Sciences, Engineering, and Medicine). (2007). *Beyond Bias and Barriers: Fulfilling he Potential of Women in Academic Science and Engineering*. Washington, DC: The National Academies Press.

Niemi, N.S. (2017). *Degrees of Difference: Women, Men, and the Value of Higher Education*. New York: Routledge.

Pawley, A.L., and J. Hoegh, J. (2011). Exploding Pipelines: Mythological Metaphors Structuring Diversity-Oriented Engineering Education

Research Agendas. Paper read at 2011 ASEE Annual Conference and Exposition, Vancouver, BC [quoted in NASEM 2020]

Piacentini, Mario (2013). "Women Entrepreneurs in the OECD: Key Evidence and Policy Challenges." *OECD Social, Employment and Migration Working Paper* 147, Organisation for Economic Co-operation and Development, Paris.

Porfido, Danielle and Abby Horgan (2020). "More Than a Numbers Game: Gender Quotas in Africa's Parliaments." *Gender Policy Journal*, July 9.

Rodrigues, M. & Kathryn Clancy (2020). "Factors that Drive the Underrepresentation of Women in Science, Engineering and Medical Disciplines." in *Promising Practices for Addressing the Underrepresentation of Women in Science, Engineering and Medicine: Opening Doors,* Washington, DC, The National Academies Press.

Sue, D.W. (2017). "Microaggressions: More than just Race." *Psychology today*. Available at: https://www.psychologytoday.com/us/blog/microaggressions-in-everyday-life/201011/microaggressionsmore-just-race

Tsugawa, Y. (2017). "Comparison of Hospital Mortality and Readmission Rates for Medicare Patients Treated by Male *Vs.* Female Physicians." *JAMA Internal Medicine, 177*(2): 206-213.

UNESCO. (2021). *Women in Higher Education: Has the Female Advantage Put an End to Gender Inequalities?* UNESCO.

UNESCO. (2020). *Global Education Monitoring Report 2020: Gender Report, A New Generation: 25 Years of Efforts for Gender Equality in Education*. UNESCO.

World Bank. (2024). *Women, Business and the Law 2024.* Washington, DC, The World Bank Publications.

18

Gender Responsive Budgeting

A Small Reflection

Chinglen Maisnam (Bobo) and *Takhellambam Menaobi Chanu*

Introduction

Women's enjoyment of human rights is severely affected by the cultural construct of gender. Gender-based assumptions and expectations generally place women at a disadvantage with respect to substantive enjoyment of rights such as freedom to act and to be recognized as autonomous, fully capable adults, to participate fully in economic, political, and social development, and to make decisions concerning their circumstances and conditions. Gender-based assumptions about economic, social, and cultural roles preclude the sharing of responsibility in all spheres that are necessary for equality. Economic, social, and cultural rights are critical to survival and the development of full human potential. These rights include adequate food, shelter, health care, education, fair employment, social security, and the right to participate in and benefit from one's culture. They are enshrined in the Universal Declaration of Human Rights, the globally accepted statement of universal rights and freedoms adopted by the United Nations in 1948. Why is progress towards gender equality and the realization of women's social, economic, and cultural rights so slow? In part, this is a failure to attach money to policy commitments. Whilst government budgets have allocated resources in a way that has perpetuated gender biases, budgets also offer the potential to transform gender inequalities. In recent years, gender budget initiatives (GBI) have risen to this challenge. GBIs can significantly contribute to overall objectives like equity, equality, efficiency, transparency, the realization of social, economic, and cultural rights, and good governance. They can offer a practical way of evaluating governmental action—based on the weight of money attached—and of scrutinizing the budget, demanding clearer accountability processes. The increasing marginalization of women, young people, and poor men made clear the need for more gender-sensitive and pro-poor approaches to tackling macroeconomic processes, including through the budget. A study on Gender-responsive budgets will help us determine whether States have taken appropriate steps to achieve economic, social, and cultural rights for women as well as men. Keeping in view the magnitude of gender inequalities, the Government of India supports a series of international commitments that aim at achieving women's empowerment and gender equality, including the "World Plan of Action" adopted at the World Conference of the International Women's Year (1975), the "Convention on the Elimination of All Forms of Discrimination against Women" (1979), the "Beijing Declaration and Platform of Action" (1995) and the United Nations "Millennium Declaration" (2000). However, gender equality is still a distant dream. The rationale for GB arises from recognizing that national budgets impact men and women differently through the pattern of resource allocation. It is also one of the critical tools to tackle the Socio-Economic and Cultural disparity of women. The chapter critically examines the passage of GB in India with special reference to the East. The analysis is based on various sources ranging from official records and reports to related works of literature.

II

The study on gender budgeting has attracted much attention in recent years. It recognizes that the government's budgetary policy has a major role in achieving objectives of gender equality and growth through the content and direction of Fiscal and Monetary Policies. Thus, the system of Gender Budgeting, as a tool for achieving gender mainstreaming, has been put in place by the Government of India. In budget 2005-06, the Union Government, for the first time, included a statement on gender budgeting. Since 2005-06, the Expenditure Division of the Ministry of Finance, Government of India, has been issuing a note on Gender Budgeting as a part of the Budget Circular every year. Many State governments in India have also prepared a Gender Budget Statement and have started reflecting allocations for women in the GB Statement of the State Budgets. Many State governments have stated commitments to mainstreaming gender in their state programmes and have targeted the education, health care, justice, and police sectors as priorities. However, the introduction of the system of Gender Budgeting has still been a distant dream for the North Eastern States. There is still a fair way to go in developing legislation and regulations that enable the implementation of gender equality goals and objectives.

Though India follows high growth trajectories, India's growth has remained dividend and inequitable, and wealth has remained confined to only a small segment of society. It is an urban-centric, consumption-driven, and gender prejudice. Many laws have been enacted, and many inclusionary policies are implemented to empower women economically, politically, and socially.[1] It is a well-known fact that gender equality is guaranteed under the Constitution, and the Government is a signatory to the Convention on the Elimination of All Forms of Discrimination against Women (CEDAW) and has adopted the Millennium Development Goals targets and indicators in national planning. Keeping in view the magnitude of gender inequalities, the government supports a series of international commitments that aim at achieving women's empowerment and gender equality, including the "World Plan of Action" adopted at the World Conference of the International Women's Year (1975), the "Convention on the Elimination of All Forms of Discrimination against Women" (1979), the "Beijing Declaration and Platform of Action" (1995) and the United Nations "Millennium Declaration" (2000). However, gender equality is still a distant dream.

In India, gender sensitivity in the government budget has been gaining ground since the publication of the Committee on the Status of Women report. As the Status of Women in India Report of 1975 demonstrated, in almost all walks of life, education, health, and employment, discrimination against women was rampant. From top-sided sex ratios at all stages of life (produced by the 'customs' of dowry, polygamy, and child marriage) to discriminatory legal frameworks and general neglect of the economic and social contribution of women, the Report underlined how a fundamental inequality was rooted in social structures. It was being exacerbated by the path of development being pursued.[2]

The system of Gender Budgeting, as a tool for achieving gender mainstreaming, has been put in place by the Government of India to ensure a definite flow of funds from the general developmental sectors to women. Gender sensitivity in the government budget was initially featured through the allocation of resources during the Seventh Plan (1987-1992), which started monitoring 27 programmes whose direct beneficiaries were women. The Eighth Plan (1992-1997) focused on ensuring the flow of funds for women-centred programmes. The Ninth Plan (1997-2002) adopted the Women Component Plan as one of the significant strategies. The Eleventh Plan (2007- 2012) envisaged the incorporation of Gender Budgeting.

III

The government mandated setting up gender budget cells in ministries during 2004-05. The government presented the first gender budget statement. From 2004 till 2014, almost all ministries have set up gender budget cells. The number of ministries: 9 in 2005-06, 56 in 2013-14, 43 in 2024-25, and 49 in 2025-26. Evaluating the union budgets since 2008-09, Jhamb, Mishra, and Sinha (2013: 35) reveal that "...barring 2011-12 BE when it registered a marginal jump (6.2%), the magnitude of the GBS has hovered around 5.5 per cent all these years." Reacting to the GB 2013-14, Vibhuti Patel (2013) remarks, "... a look at the Interim Budget through the gender lens reflects its gross inadequacies on most fronts. The government has done nothing to change its shameful track record on gender budgeting." A gender audit of the current Budget 2017-18 to assess whether gender commitments have been converted into budgetary commitments by the Government of India reveals more shortcomings than successes. No steps have been taken to review the format of the Gender Budget Statement. There has been a substantial compression of development expenditure from the Union Budget in several crucial sectors, particularly Rural Development and Health.

The budget starts with an assumption of 11.75 per cent growth in the GDP for 2017-18, calculated over the revised figures of 2016-17. Based on the inflated GDP estimates, the size of the budget as a proportion of GDP has declined from 13.4 per cent in 2015-16 to 12.7 per cent in 2017-18 budget estimates. This will severely affect the lives and livelihoods of most people, especially women. The tall government claims that the aim is to double the farmers' incomes, which is not reflected in its allocations. The FM stated that the allied sector of dairy development and fisheries (which provides livelihood to many women) would receive a significant boost through an increased allocation of Rs. 8,000 crore. However, there is no specific allocation for women in either dairy or fisheries. Further, the only agricultural scheme that has allocations for women in the agricultural sector is the National Food Security Mission, where a nominal increase of Rs. 60 crore has been made in the gender budget, which accounts for less than 30 per cent of the entire allocation. This does not even qualify to be in Part B of the gender budget, and yet it has been listed there. Given the fact that the majority of women are dependent on agriculture for their livelihood, the dismal allocations and absolute cut of 50 per cent in the Mudra and other credit guarantee schemes show the absolute callousness towards women and agriculture, which is a continuing feature of this government's policies. MGNREGA has been allocated a massive sum of Rs. 48,000 crore, which is yet another example of dressing down of facts. In 2015-16, MGNREGA allocated Rs. 47,499 crore in the revised estimates. Thus, the allocation of Rs. 48,000 crore does not entail any substantial increase. This freezing of allocation to MNREGA in this period of adverse impact on employment due to demonetization is not desired. Food (including the allocations under the National Food Security Act), kerosene, and LPG subsidies directly impact women. The share of these in the total budget has decreased from 9.5 per cent in 2015-16 to 7.9 per cent in 2017-18. Moreover, there is no gender budget component in any of these except the LPG subsidy, which is a miniscule of Rs. 3,200 crore. The budget has failed to respond to the issue of rising violence against women. The revised estimate for the Nirbhaya fund in 2016-17 was Rs. 585 crore, which has now been cut to Rs. 400 crore. The freezing of inadequate allocations in real terms to education and health will hit women even further. The gender budget accounted for 5.2 per cent of total government spending, an increase of only 0.4 per cent from 4.8 per cent in 2016-17 (revised estimates). It accounted for 4.5 per cent of budget expenditure in 2016-17; an allocation of Rs. 4.49 lakh crore has been reported for the welfare of women and girls in the gender budget statement of FY 2025-26. This is 37.25 per cent increase over the GBS allocation of Rs. 3.27 lakh crore in FY 2024-25.

This year, 49 ministries/departments and 5 UTs have reported allocations, as compared to 38 ministries/departments and 5 UTs in FY 2024-25. This is the highest number of reports by the Ministries/Departments in the GBS since its inception. Twelve new Ministries/Departments have reported allocations in the GBS 2025-26—the Department of Animal Husbandry & Dairying, Department of Biotechnology, Department of Food & Public Distribution, Department of Financial Services, Department of Fisheries, Department of Land Resources, Department of Pharmaceuticals, Department of Water Resources, RD & GR, Ministry of Food Processing Industries, Ministry of Panchayati Raj, Ministry of Ports, Shipping & Waterways, and Ministry of Railways. These 49 Ministries/Departments and 5 UTs have reported allocations in Parts A, B, and C of the Gender Budget Statement. Rs. 1,05,535.40 crore (23.50% of total GBS allocation) have been reported by 17 Ministries/Departments and 5 UTs in Part A (100% women-specific schemes); Rs. 3,26,672.00 crore (72.75%) have been reported by 37 Ministries/Departments and 4 UTs in Part B

(30-99 per cent allocation for women) and Rs. 16,821.28 crore (3.75%) have been reported by 22 Ministries/Departments in Part C (below 30% allocation for women).

Top 10 Ministries/Departments that have reported more than 30 per cent of their allocations in the Gender Budget for FY 2025-26 are Ministry of Women & Child Development (81.79%), Department of Rural Development (65.76%), Department of Food & Public Distribution (50.92%), Department of Health & Family Welfare (41.10%), Ministry of New & Renewable Energy (40.89%), Department of Social Justice & Empowerment (39.01%), Department of Higher Education (33.94%), Department of School Education & Literacy (33.67%), Ministry of Home Affairs (33.47%) and Department of Drinking Water & Sanitation (31.50%).

Table 18.1: Gender Budget: Trends in Allocation

Year	Gender Budget (India) (Rs. in Crore)	As % of the Total
2025-26	4,49,028.68	8.8
2024-25(RE)	3,762,528.9	7.98
2024-25	3,27,158.44	6.72
2023-24(AE)	3,84,499.61	8.65
2023-24	2,38,219.75	5.29
2022-23(AE)	2,31,333.29	5.2
2022-23	1,71,006.5	4.33
2021-22(AE)	2,09,527.77	5.52
2021-22	1,53,326.3	4.4
2020-21	30,42,230	4.72
2019-20	27,86,349	4.91
2018-19	23,15,113	4.98
2017-18	1,13,326	5.20
2016-17 (RE)	96,331	4.8

(*Contd.*)

Year	Gender Budget (India) (Rs. in Crore)	As % of the Total
2016-17	90,625	4.5
2015-16	79,258	4.46
2014-15	98,029.84	5.40
2013-14	97,134	5.83
2012-13	88,143	5.91
2011-12	78,251	6.22
2010-11	67,750	6.11
2009-10	56,858	5.57
2008-09	27,662	3.68
2007-08	31,178	4.5
2006-07	28,737	5.09
2005-06	14,379	2.79

Source: Ministry of Finance, Government of India.

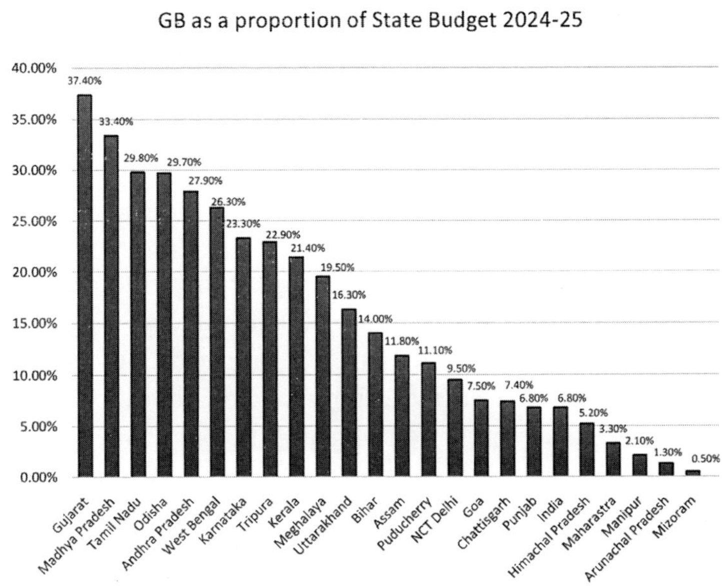

Fig. 18.1: Gender Budget as a Proportion of State Budget 2024-25.

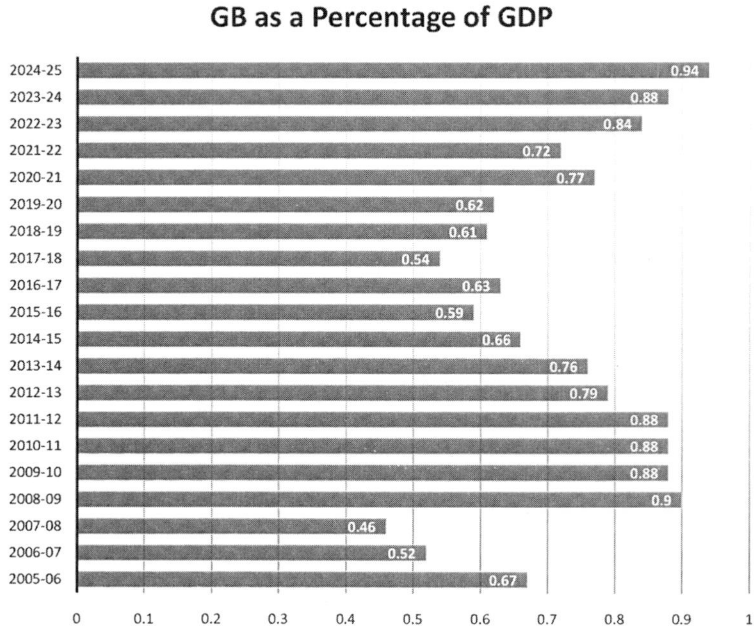

Fig. 18.2: Gender Budget as a Percentage of GDP.

IV

North East Scenario

The system of Gender Budgeting has been put in place by many state governments, including the North East States of Assam, Nagaland, and Tripura. They have also prepared Gender Budget Statements and started reflecting women's allocations in the GB Statement of the State Budgets. The State Governments like Rajasthan, Gujarat, Madhya Pradesh, Karnataka, Odisha, Kerala, Bihar, Chhattisgarh, Uttar Pradesh and Uttarakhand have also adopted Gender Budgeting.[3] Regarding the sustainable use of the Women Component Plan as a strategy at the Centre or the State level, the Planning Commission, Government of India, has clarified that "Women Component Plan should no longer be used as a strategy either at the Centre or at the State level. In its place as already initiated by the Ministry of Finance and Ministry of Women and Child Development, we should adopt Gender Responsive Budgeting or Gender Budgeting only". The Secretary, Planning Commission, Government of India,[4] has written to Chief Secretaries of all States/UTs that, "To accelerate the process (of GB), State Finance Departments could set up Gender Budget Cells on the lines of the Charter for Gender Budget cells issued by the Ministry of Finance. The State Planning Departments may also be instructed to include the need for gender budgeting as a part of their annual plan circular". However, the introduction of the system of Gender Budgeting has still been a distant dream for many of the North Eastern States. As pointed out, GB Statements are prepared only in Tripura, Nagaland and Assam. Recently, Mizoram, along with Assam and Tripura, adopted the Results Framework Document (RFD) policy and is at various stages of implementation.[5] In March 2009, the Committee on Welfare of Women and Children, Manipur Legislative Assembly, recommended the state government introduction of gender budgeting with special allotment of funds for women and children in all departments and framing of a state policy on Women, among others.[6] But, so far, no step has been taken in this regard.

The present chapter urges all the remaining states of the region to introduce gender budget statements as part of their state budgets and also to make a sufficient allocation for women with appropriate gender budgeting by all departments besides guaranteeing accountability and transparency in executing the schemes.

Table 18.2: Initiatives on Gender Budgeting: NE & Selected States

State	Year of Approving Gender Budget	Year of Introducing Gender Budget Statement
Assam	2008-09	2008-09
Tripura	2005-06	2005-06
Nagaland	2009	—
Chhattisgarh	2007-08	2007-08
Karnataka	2006-07	2007-08
Kerala	2008	2008-09
Maharashtra	2011-12	---
Rajasthan	2005-06	2012-13
Uttarakhand	2007-08	2007-08
Manipur	2020	2020-21

Source: Media Reports.

Initiatives on Gender Budgeting: North-East

Tripura

- Officially adopted Gender Budgeting in 2005-06.
- The Social Welfare and Social Education Department is the nodal Department.
- Gender Budget Cells have been formed in the State in 17 Departments.
- Introduced Gender Budget Statement as part of State Budget 2005-06.
- The budget allocation in Gender Budget Statement has increased from Rs. 149.82 crore in 2005-06 to Rs. 337.45 crore in 2012-13.

Nagaland

- Officially adopted Gender Budgeting in 2009.
- Set up a Task Force for "Engendering State and District Plans" headed by the Additional Chief Secretary in 2009 with members from the Departments of Health and Family Welfare, Finance, Rural Development, Development Commissioner, SIRD, ATI, Nagaland University, and Additional Director, Women Development is member secretary.
- Constituted a Gender Budgeting Cell under the Planning and Coordination Department.
- Gender Budgeting is a subject of the training calendar of ATI (Administrative Training Institute) and SIRD (State Institute of Rural Development). The task force also developed a Gender Budgeting manual customized to local requirements in collaboration with UNDP.

Assam

- Assam government reported allocated under Gender Budget Statements (GBS) on 2017-18.
- 2028-29: 18 departments reported allocations.
- 2019-20: 20 departments reported allocation under GBS, objectives of the reported schemes were introduced as a part of GBS.
- 2020-21; 20 departments reported allocated under GBS.
- 2021-22; 25 departments reported allocation under GBS. Department reported targeted age group for the schemes under GBS. The actual expenditure reported for the first time.
- 2022-23: Reported allocation under GBS and bilingual statement.

Manipur

- In October 2020, the Manipur government initiated gender budgeting.
- 5th February, 2021, the First GRB statement was introduced in the legislative assembly.
- GB is mandated under the gender budget cell.
- Gender budgeting cells are formulated in all 48-line departments as of April 2022.
- The convergence of finance with social welfare seamlessly successfully implements GRB in the state.
- Since budget call circular 2022-23, the government added another mandatory proforma on gender-disaggregated data with two parts: A (For beneficiary-oriented) and B (for beneficiary-oriented).
- The state has mandated all government departments to report gender-specific achievements and challenges in the annual report.

Table 18.3: Percentage of GB Out of total Expenditure in Manipur

Year	BE/RE	% of GB out of total expenditure
2020-2021	BE	2.95
2020-2021	RE	3.01
2021-2022	BE	2.56
2022-2023	BE	6.50
2022-2023	RE	2.95
2023-2024	BE	2.45
2024-2025	BE	2.08

Meghalaya

- Meghalaya government's first-ever gender budget in 2022-23.
- 14 per cent of total expenditure in 2022-23 shared by GB and 15 per cent in 2023-24.

- A total of 18 departments contribute to the gender budget 2023-24 with 250 schemes.
- Total of 10 departments for Part A and 13 departments for Part B for the year 2023-24.

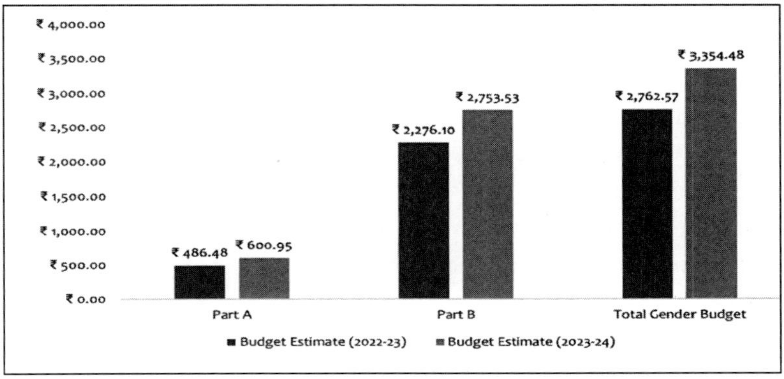

Source: State Budget Document, Meghalaya.

Fig. 18.3: GB for the Financial Year, 2023-24 in Meghalaya.

Mizoram

- Mizoram introduced the gender budget 2024-25, a total of Rs. 74 crore, 1 per cent of the total expenditure of the Financial Year 2024-25.
- 78 per cent of the gender budget is spent on the Social Welfare Department. Rs. 42 crore spent on Anganwadi services.
- Rs. 13 crore on education and Rs. 4 crore on police department.

V

Conclusion

Although the Gender Budgeting exercise is meant to empower women by ensuring each ministry has allocations made for women, a few fundamental concerns have been raised. Many ministries do not have women-specific programs, and anything remotely benefiting women is clubbed under gender budgeting. Furthermore, the utilization of funds meant to benefit women remains blurred. The percentage of allocations for the gender budget remained static, and it is less than 6 per cent of the total budget. From 2004 to 2014, 56 ministries have set up Gender Budget cells. However, making their fiscal policy gender responsive has been an uphill task. Galloping inflation has adversely affected the toiling poor women of India, whose real wages have declined sharply. Due to the withdrawal of the state from the social sector, women's work burden in the unpaid care economy (cooking, cleaning, nursing, collecting fuel, fodder, water etc.) has increased many-fold. The subordinate status of women manifests in declining child sex ratio, i.e. the 'missing girls phenomenon,' deteriorating reproductive and child health, feminization of poverty, increased violence against women, enhanced mortality and morbidity among girls and women, and deplorable condition of elderly women.

A look at India's Union Budgets since the introduction of GB through the gender lens reflects its gross inadequacies on most fronts. These budgets need to be understood in the historical context of the country's social parameters. India's record for achieving the Millennium Development Goals has been abysmal compared to several African, Latin American, and Asian Countries. In the international arena, despite the attempt to portray a 'Shining India', the country has been named and shamed continuously for not being able to reduce its maternal and child mortality rates, widespread anaemia and malnutrition among women and children, starvation deaths in certain pockets, skyrocketing prices of essential goods, namely food, water, and cooking fuel.

It is in this context one must examine the Union Budgets and GBs. The factors that affect gender inequality are a complex combination of economic structure, politics, culture, society, history, and geography specific to the country and region. Therefore, sex-disaggregated information on beneficiary groups, needs, and project impact should be assessed during the project planning process to attain outcomes that are equitably beneficial for both women and men. From this perspective, the integration of gender perspective into ex-ante evaluation will be strengthened, and studies for analyzing women's social and economic roles and situations will be implemented as needed. At the same time, considerations will be given to promote women's and men's participation in decision-making at the planning and implementation stages of policies and projects that may affect their lives. In addition, efforts must be made at project implementation and post-completion stages to conduct monitoring, evaluation, and effective feedback based on gender perspective. We reiterate that efforts to close the gender gap and make growth more equitable depend on making resources available to women. This is essential to achieving social advancement and deepening democracy. Given this, the chapter urges all the North Eastern Region state governments to also enhance gender-specific resource allocation for women and ensure that funds under these heads are not diverted. It concludes by calling for an urgent need for institutionalizing gender budgeting in the north-eastern region and for making adequate provisions for women with proper gender budgeting by all departments, besides ensuring accountability and transparency in implementing the schemes. GBIs can significantly contribute to overall objectives like equity, equality, efficiency, transparency, the realization of social, economic, and cultural rights, and good governance. They can offer a practical way of evaluating governmental action based on the weight of money attached and scrutinizing the budget, demanding more evident accountability processes. The increasing marginalization of women, young people, and poor men made clear the need for more gender-sensitive and pro-poor approaches to tackling macroeconomic processes, including through the budget. The Gender-responsive budget should be one of the steps to achieve economic, social, and cultural rights for women as well as men.

NOTES

1. The country's concern in safeguarding the rights and privileges of women found its best expression in the Constitution of India, covering fundamental rights and the directive principles of state policy. Articles 14, 15, 15(3), 16, 39, 42, 51 (A)(e) contain various types of provisions for equal rights and opportunities for women and eliminate discrimination against women in different spheres of life. Apart from the constitutional provisions, a large number of laws have been enacted to protect the Human Rights for Women. The women-specific Legislations are the Immoral Traffic (Prevention) Act, 1956, The Dowry Prohibition Act, 1961, The Indecent Representation of Women (Prohibition) Act, 1986. The Commission of Sati (Prevention) Act, 1987, Domestic Violence Act, 2005. Besides, there are as many as forty one Women related legislations.
2. For a fuller crtical account, see Sundararaman, S. (2006).
3. For further details visit http://www.wcd.nic.in/gb/material/index.htm
4. Planning Commission (GOI, 2012), *vide* D.O. No. PC/SW/1-3(13)/09-WCD, dated 18th October, 2012.
5. for a comprehensive report, IIPA (2013).
6. *Hueiyen Lanpa,* March 19, 2009.

REFERENCES

CBGA (2012). *Recognising Gender Biases, Rethinking Budgets: Review of gender-responsive budgeting in Union Government and Select States,* Centre for Budget and Governance Accountability, New Delhi.

CBGA (2014). *Brief Response to Interim Budget 2014-15,* Centre for Budget and Governance Accountability (CBGA), February 17, 2014, Available at www.cbgaindia.org (Accessed on 22-02-2014).

CBGA (2018). *Of Hits and Misses; An Analysis of Union Budget 2018-19*, Centre for Budget and Governance Accountability (CBGA), February, 2018, New Delhi. Available at: www.cbgaindia.org (Accessed on 22-02-2014).

GoI (2004). "Classification of Government Transactions: Report of the Expert Group Constituted to Review the Classification System for Government Transactions", Ministry of Finance, Government of India.

GoI (2010). Planning Commission, Government of India, letter, *vide* D.O. no. PC/SW/1-3(13)/09-WCD, dated, 5th January, 2010,

GoI (2012). Planning Commission, Government of India, letter, *vide* D.O. no. PC/SW/1-3(13)/09-WCD, dated, 18th October, 2012.

GoI (2016). *Annual Report 2015-16,* Government of India, Ministry of Women and Child Development, Available at www.wcd.nic.in/gb/material/index.htm

GoI. *Union Budget Documents (various years).* Ministry of Finance: Government of India.

Huiyen Lanpao (March 19, 2009). "Gender Budgeting Recommended", *Hueiyen Lanpao,* Local Vernacular (English Version).

IIPA (2013). *Report of the Workshop on Gender Budgeting for Officials of State Departments of Finance, Planning and WCD/Social Welfare* (June 2013). Indian Institute of Public Administration, New Delhi.

IMF (November 2016). "The Influence of Gender Budgeting in Indian States on Gender Inequality and Fiscal Spending", International Monetary Fund, *Working Paper* WP/16/227.

Janet, G. Stotsky (2006). "Gender Budgeting", *IMF Working Paper* No. 06/232, Washington, DC.

Singh, Bobo & Thoudam, Prabha (2010). "Socioeconomic Exclusion and development deficits: Some Reflections on Manipuri Women." *RMS Journal of Management & IT, 4*(5): 3-13.

Sundararaman, Sudha (2006). *Achieving Gender Equality-An Unfinished Agenda.* All India Democratic Women's Association, New Delhi, available at aidwaonline.org.htm (Accessed on 22-02-14).

United Nations (2018). *Turning Promises into Action: Gender Equality in the 2030 Agenda for Sustainable Development,* available at http://www.unwomen.org/en/news/in-focus/women-and-the-sdgs.

World Bank (2018). *The Cost of Gender Inequality Unrealized Potential: The High Cost of Gender Inequality in Earnings,* Washington, DC: The World Bank, May 2018.

Gender Responsive Planning and Budgeting: State Journeys Across India. UN Women—Asia-Pacific. Retrieved from https://asiapacific.unwomen.org/en/digital-libraryhttps://finance.mizoram.gov.in/uploads/attachments/2024/02/5e558629ebdb90a73a50d6775537bcfd/posts-107-gender-budget-statement-2024-2025.pdf/publications/2024/02/gender-responsive-planning-and-budgeting-state-journeys-across-india.

https://megfinance.gov.in/budget_documents/2024-2025/others/gender_budget.pdf

https://finance.assam.gov.in/documents-detail/gender-budget-fy-2024-25

https://finance.tripura.gov.in/sites/default/files/Gender%20Budget%20 2022-23.pdf

https://ebudgetmanipur.mn.gov.in/

https://finance.mizoram.gov.in/uploads/attachments/2024/02/5e558629ebdb90a73a50d6775537bcfd/posts-107-gender-budget-statement-2024-2025.pdf

https://pib.gov.in/PressReleaseIframePage.aspx?PRID=2098912

19

Dissenting Voices

Critiques and Challenges of Women's Reservation Policies in India's Political Arena

Sandeep Gupta

Introduction

Pursuing inclusive government and gender equality has been a major motivator and a divisive topic in Indian politics. Women's reservation policies, which are legal measures intended to rectify the historically low representation of women in political decision-making processes, are at the centre of this discussion. These laws, which seek to increase the representation of women in public offices, have the potential to change the balance of power and promote more just societies. However, they can provoke contentious discussions, bringing criticism from various sources and provoking opposing viewpoints that cast doubt on their effectiveness, equity, and unforeseen consequences. This chapter takes readers on a tour of the complex issues and criticisms surrounding women's reservation legislation in Indian politics. It traverses the historical currents, legislative turning points, and socio-political environments that have influenced these policies' development. It explores the nuances of female representation, affirmative action, and democratic government, delving into the complicated arguments and differing points of view that drive the debate. This study employs a systematic literature review to examine the historical context, critiques, challenges, and ways forward for the issue of women's reservation in India. It entails thoroughly searching scholarly databases that address women's political engagement in India. Key themes and findings are retrieved using a standardised form, and thematic analysis is used to uncover common difficulties. The outcomes are then combined to create a logical story. The study examines the intersections of gender, caste, class, and identity to shed light on the complex aspects of women's reservation legislation. It examines the criticisms that call into question these programmes' fundamental beliefs and goals, analysing their effects on social justice, democracy, and meritocracy. It addresses the difficulties of putting women's reservation policies into practice, ranging from institutional resistance to cultural norms. It also wrestles with the intricacies of determining how they will affect political dynamics and societal transformation.

As we traverse this terrain of dissent and dialogue, we confront fundamental questions about power, privilege, and representation in democratic societies. We confront the tensions between equality of opportunity and equality of outcome, between diversity and merit, inclusion and tokenism. Ultimately, we confront the imperative of forging a more just and inclusive political order—one that honours the voices of all citizens, regardless of gender, and empowers them to shape their collective destinies.

Historical Context and Evolution of Women's Reservation Policies in India

In the tapestry of India's socio-political history, the struggle for women's rights and political representation has been a persistent thread woven into the fabric of movements for social justice and democratic reform. The quest for gender equality in governance found its roots in the early twentieth century, as Indian women mobilised alongside their male counterparts in the struggle against colonial rule. The participation of women in the nationalist movement, exemplified by figures like Sarojini Naidu and Kamala Nehru, laid the groundwork for broader demands for political empowerment and social emancipation. The post-Independence era witnessed significant milestones in the advancement of women's rights as the newly established Indian state grappled with the task of nation-building and democratic consolidation. The Constitution of India, adopted in 1950, enshrined the principles of equality and non-discrimination, laying the groundwork for progressive legislation and policy interventions to address gender disparities. Article 14 of the Constitution guaranteed equality before the law, while Article 15 prohibited discrimination based on religion, race, caste, sex, or place of birth.

Despite these constitutional guarantees, women faced systemic political participation and representation barriers. Patriarchal norms and social hierarchies entrenched within Indian society limited women's access to education, employment, and public life, perpetuating their marginalisation in decision-making processes. Recognising the need for affirmative action to redress historical injustices and promote gender equity, policymakers explored mechanisms to enhance women's representation in elected bodies (Thomasn & Kaunain, 2023). The journey towards women's reservation policies in India can be traced back to the early decades of independence, marked by incremental steps towards greater gender inclusion in politics. In 1955, the first-ever committee on the status of women, chaired by Hansa Mehta, was established to examine issues related to women's rights and recommend policy measures for their advancement. Subsequent years saw the formulation of legislative initiatives such as the Dowry Prohibition Act (1961) and the Equal Remuneration Act (1976), which aimed to address specific forms of gender-based discrimination (Kumar,1993).

However, not until the 1990s did the demand for women's reservation in legislative bodies gain significant momentum, propelled by grassroots activism and advocacy campaigns led by women's organisations and civil society groups. The landmark Beijing Declaration and Platform for Action (1995), adopted at the Fourth World Conference on Women, provided a global impetus for gender mainstreaming and affirmative action, inspiring renewed calls for legislative reforms in India. In response to mounting pressure from women's groups and political allies, the Indian government introduced the Women's Reservation Bill in Parliament in 1996, seeking to reserve one-third of the seats in the Lok Sabha (Lower House) and state legislative assemblies for women. The bill, however, faced vehement opposition from various quarters, including within the political establishment, where concerns about the impact on existing power structures and electoral dynamics loomed large.

Despite several attempts to pass the Bill over the years, it languished in parliamentary limbo, caught in the crossfire of partisan politics and ideological wrangling. The contentious nature of the debate surrounding women's reservation reflected deeper fissures within Indian society, encompassing issues of caste, class, and regional identity. Opponents of the Bill raised questions about its implications for democracy, meritocracy, and the autonomy of political parties in candidate selection. Nevertheless, the persistence of women's movements and the growing recognition of the need for gender-sensitive governance propelled the issue back into the spotlight in the early twenty-first century. In 2008, the Women's Reservation Bill was once again introduced in Parliament, with a historic amendment proposing to reserve one-third of the seats for women within the existing reservation for Scheduled Castes and Scheduled Tribes. While the Bill passed in the Rajya Sabha (Upper House) amidst scenes of jubilation and celebration, it has yet to be ratified by the Lok Sabha and enacted into law. The protracted saga of the Women's Reservation Bill underscores the complexities and challenges inherent in pursuing gender equality and political representation in India. It reflects the tensions between democratic ideals of equality and justice and the realities of entrenched power structures and vested interests. Moreover, it highlights the interplay of social movements, institutional dynamics, and political calculations in shaping the trajectory of policy reform (Misra, 2012).

The historical context and evolution of women's reservation policies in India reflect a tumultuous journey marked by progress, setbacks, and ongoing struggles. From the early pioneers of the women's movement to contemporary activists and policymakers advocating for change, the quest for gender equity in governance continues to animate Indian democracy, challenging entrenched norms and reshaping the contours of political power. As the nation marches on the path of progress and development, the imperative of realising the full potential of half its population remains a pressing priority, demanding concerted action and collective resolve (Deshpande, 2004; Pai, 2009).

Critiques of Women's Reservation Policies in India: Unpacking the Controversies

Women's reservation policies in India have been subject to many critiques, reflecting the complex interplay of gender dynamics, political exigencies, and socio-cultural norms within the country's diverse and dynamic democracy. While proponents argue that such policies are essential for promoting gender equality and enhancing women's political representation, opponents raise many concerns regarding their efficacy, fairness, and unintended consequences. The critiques of women's reservation policies in India are an attempt to engage in debates surrounding their implementation, impact, and implications for democratic governance.

Erosion of Meritocracy

The critique of the erosion of meritocracy stems from the concern that women's reservation policies may prioritise gender over qualifications, leading to the selection of candidates based on their gender rather than their competency or track record. Critics argue that in a democracy, political leaders should be chosen based on their ability to represent the interests of their constituents and govern competently and effectively. By introducing quotas for women, there is a risk that less qualified candidates may be elected simply because of their gender, undermining the merit-based principles fundamental to democratic governance. This critique raises important questions about the criteria for selecting political leaders and the balance between diversity and merit in representative bodies. Advocates for women's reservation policies counter this critique by emphasising the systemic barriers and discrimination faced by women in accessing political opportunities, which may result in talented women being overlooked in favour of less qualified male candidates. They argue that quotas are necessary to address historical inequalities and ensure a more inclusive and representative political system (Kishwar, 1996).

Tokenism and Elite Capture

Tokenism and elite capture are concerns associated with women's reservation policies, particularly in contexts where quotas are implemented without accompanying measures to promote genuine empowerment and representation. Critics argue that while quotas may increase women's numerical representation in politics, they may not necessarily lead to substantive empowerment or meaningful participation. Instead, there is a risk that reserved seats may be captured by elite women from privileged backgrounds, who may not truly represent the interests and concerns of marginalised communities. This critique highlights the importance of ensuring that women's reservation policies are accompanied by measures to promote diversity, inclusivity, and accountability within political institutions. Advocates stress the need for mechanisms to support women from diverse backgrounds and ensure their meaningful participation in decision-making processes. This may include provisions for capacity-building, mentorship, support networks, and efforts to address systemic barriers to women's political participation (Rai, 1999; Rao, 2005; Phillips, 1998).

Undermining Democratic Principles

Critics of women's reservation policies raise broader concerns about their compatibility with democratic principles of equality, fairness, and individual rights. They argue that quotas based on gender violate the principle of equal treatment under the law and discriminate against male candidates who may be equally deserving of political office. Moreover, they contend that quotas undermine the notion of political representation as a voluntary mandate entrusted by voters, instead imposing artificial constraints on the electoral process that may distort democratic outcomes. This critique challenges the notion of quotas to promote social justice and inclusive governance, suggesting that they may instead perpetuate inequalities and undermine the legitimacy of democratic institutions. Advocates for women's reservation policies counter this critique by emphasising the systemic nature of gender discrimination and the need for targeted interventions to address historical injustices and promote gender equality. They argue that quotas are necessary to break down entrenched barriers to women's political participation and ensure that all citizens have equal opportunities to engage in the democratic process (Deshpande & Gupta, 2021).

Reinforcing Stereotypes and Stigmatization

Critics argue that women's reservation policies may inadvertently reinforce gender stereotypes and perpetuate the stigmatisation of women in politics. By designating certain seats exclusively for women, quotas may suggest that women require special treatment or protection, reinforcing the perception of them as a homogenous group with distinct interests and abilities. This can contribute to the marginalisation of women candidates, who may be perceived as beneficiaries of preferential treatment rather than as competent leaders in their own right. This critique underscores the importance of addressing cultural attitudes and societal norms that perpetuate gender stereotypes and inhibit women's political participation. Advocates for women's reservation policies stress the need for comprehensive strategies to challenge discriminatory beliefs and promote positive representations of women in leadership roles. This may involve media campaigns, educational initiatives, and community outreach efforts to challenge stereotypes and foster a more inclusive and equitable political culture (Kapur, 2001).

Divisive Politics and Backlash

The introduction of women's reservation policies has often sparked divisive political debates and resistance from entrenched interests, particularly within male-dominated political parties and institutions. Critics argue that quotas may exacerbate existing fault lines within society, pitting different groups against each other and fuelling identity-based politics. Moreover, they warn of potential backlash from male politicians and voters who may perceive quotas as threatening their interests and privileges, leading to resistance and obstructionism in implementing such policies.This critique highlights the political challenges and resistance that women's reservation policies may face in practice, particularly in contexts where they are perceived as threatening existing power dynamics and entrenched interests. Advocates for women's reservation policies emphasise the importance of building coalitions and mobilising support for gender equality and inclusive governance. This may involve engaging with political parties, civil society organisations, and other stakeholders to address concerns and build consensus around the need for affirmative action to promote women's political participation (Franceschet *et al.*, 2012).

Insufficient Focus on Structural Reform

Another critique of women's reservation policies is that they may offer a superficial solution to deeper structural problems related to gender inequality and political exclusion. Critics argue that while quotas may increase women's numerical representation in elected bodies, they do not address the underlying barriers to women's political participation, such as limited access to education, economic resources, and social networks. As such, quotas alone may not be sufficient to bring about meaningful change in the *status quo*, requiring complementary measures to address structural inequalities and empower women at all levels of society. This critique underscores the importance of taking a holistic approach to promoting gender equality and political empowerment, addressing both the symptoms and root causes of women's underrepresentation in politics. Advocates for women's reservation policies acknowledge the need for complementary measures to address systemic barriers and promote women's leadership development. This may include initiatives to improve access to education and training, strengthen women's economic empowerment, and reform electoral systems to ensure greater transparency and accountability (Yadav, 2000).

Lack of Intersectional Perspective

Critics also point to the limitations of a one-size-fits-all approach to women's reservation policies, highlighting the need for a more nuanced and intersectional understanding of gender inequality. They argue that quotas based solely on gender fail to account for the intersecting forms of discrimination and marginalisation experienced by women from different socio-economic, regional, and cultural backgrounds. As a result, women from marginalised communities, such as Dalits, Adivasis, and religious minorities, may continue to face multiple barriers to political participation despite the existence of quotas. This critique underscores the importance of taking an intersectional approach to gender equality and political representation, recognising the diverse experiences and identities within the category of "women". Advocates for women's reservation policies stress the need for targeted interventions to address marginalised women's challenges and ensure their meaningful participation in political processes. This may involve initiatives to promote leadership development, provide support services, and address systemic inequalities that intersect with gender to perpetuate exclusion and marginalisation (Rao, 2005).

Challenges in Implementation and Impact Assessment of Women's Reservation in India

Women's reservation policies in India have been hailed as a crucial step towards promoting gender equality and enhancing women's representation in political decision-making. However, implementing these policies and their impact on governance and social dynamics has been challenging. This chapter explores the complexities involved in the implementation and impact assessment of women's reservations in India, examining the hurdles faced in translating policy intentions into meaningful outcomes.

Logistical Hurdles and Institutional Resistance

The effective implementation of women's reservation policies requires overcoming various logistical challenges, from candidate selection to electoral logistics. Identifying suitable candidates to fill reserved seats involves navigating a pool of potential representatives and ensuring they are qualified, capable, and willing to serve. This process can be complex, particularly in regions with limited political participation among women or where societal barriers hinder women from entering politics. Moreover, electoral logistics such as voter education, ballot design, and polling station accessibility must accommodate the inclusion of women candidates, which may require additional resources and planning. Furthermore, institutional resistance within political parties and government bodies can hinder implementation. Political parties may face internal opposition or reluctance to comply with reservation quotas due to concerns about disrupting existing power dynamics or losing control over candidate selection processes. Bureaucratic inertia and administrative challenges can also impede the effective execution of reservation policies, as government agencies may lack the capacity or resources to enforce compliance and monitor adherence to quotas (Roy, 2018; Kalam, 2014; Htun & Weldon, 2010).

Cultural and Societal Norms

Cultural and Societal norms play a significant role in shaping attitudes towards women's political participation and can pose significant challenges to implementing reservation policies. Patriarchal values and gender stereotypes often limit women's access to political opportunities, reinforcing the perception of politics as a male-dominated sphere. Women who challenge traditional gender roles by entering politics may face social stigma, discrimination, or even violence, particularly in conservative or patriarchal communities. Moreover, intersectional factors such as caste, class, and religion intersect with gender dynamics to further marginalise certain groups of women. Women from marginalised communities, such as Dalits, Adivasis, or religious minorities, may face compounded barriers to political participation due to systemic discrimination and social exclusion. As a result, reservation policies aimed at enhancing women's representation may not fully address the intersecting forms of inequality experienced by these groups, necessitating broader social reforms and targeted interventions to address structural inequalities (Hasan, 2010; Kishwar, 1996; Rao, 1998).

Political Backlash and Opposition

The introduction of women's reservation policies often triggers political backlash and opposition from various quarters, including within the political establishment. Male politicians and dominant interest groups may perceive reservation quotas as threatening their power and privilege, leading to resistance and obstructionism in the implementation process. Political parties, particularly those dominated by men, may resist adopting quota systems due to concerns about losing control over candidate selection or facing internal dissent from party members. Additionally, ideological differences and partisan politics can exacerbate tensions surrounding reservation policies, making consensus-building and cooperation difficult to achieve. Opposition parties may use reservation policies as a political tool to mobilise their base or discredit the ruling party, further complicating the implementation process. As a result, reservation policies may become entangled in political manoeuvring and gridlock, delaying or impeding their effective implementation (Gupta & Desai, 2020; Kumar, 2012; Sharma, 2018).

Tokenism and Symbolic Representation

Critics of women's reservation policies often raise concerns about tokenism and symbolic representation, whereby the mere presence of women in elected bodies fails to translate into substantive empowerment or meaningful participation. In contexts where quotas are implemented without accompanying measures to address structural barriers and promote women's leadership development, there is a risk that reserved seats may be filled by elite women from privileged backgrounds who do not genuinely represent the interests and concerns of marginalised communities. This phenomenon, known as elite capture, perpetuates existing power imbalances and undermines the goal of inclusive governance. Moreover, token representation of women may reinforce stereotypes and stigmatisation, as women in politics are perceived as figureheads or tokens rather than competent leaders. To mitigate these risks, reservation policies must be accompanied by measures to support women's political empowerment, such as capacity-building programmes, mentorship initiatives, and efforts to address systemic barriers to women's participation in politics (Kishwar, 1996; Mohanty *et al.*, 1991).

Intersectional Challenges

Women's reservation policies face intersectional challenges arising from the diverse experiences and identities within the category of "women". While quotas may increase the numerical representation of women in politics, they may not adequately address the intersecting forms of discrimination and marginalisation experienced by women from different socio-economic, regional, and cultural backgrounds. Women from historically marginalised communities, such as Dalits, Adivasis, and religious minorities, face multiple barriers to political participation, including caste-based discrimination, economic marginalisation, and social exclusion. As a result, reservation policies alone may not be sufficient to ensure their meaningful representation in elected bodies, necessitating targeted interventions and intersectional approaches to address their specific needs and challenges (Pal & Ray, 2019; Chattopadhyay & Duflo, 2004).

Lack of Comprehensive Impact Assessment

Despite implementing women's reservation policies, there is often a lack of comprehensive impact assessment to evaluate their effectiveness and outcomes. While reservation quotas may increase women's numerical representation in elected bodies, their impact on governance, policy outcomes, and social dynamics requires systematic evaluation. Impact assessment efforts must go beyond quantitative representation measures to examine the quality of women's participation, their influence on decision-making processes, and how reservation policies have contributed to broader goals of gender equality and inclusive governance. This requires robust data collection, monitoring, evaluation mechanisms, and stakeholder engagement to understand their perspectives and experiences. Furthermore, impact assessment efforts must adopt an intersectional lens to capture women's diverse experiences and identities affected by reservation policies. This includes examining the differential impact of quotas on women from different socio-economic, regional, and cultural backgrounds and assessing their implications for broader goals of social justice and inclusive development.

Addressing these challenges requires a multi-faceted approach that combines legal reforms, institutional capacity-building, public awareness campaigns, and targeted interventions to address structural barriers to women's political participation. By addressing these challenges, India can harness the full potential of women's leadership to promote inclusive governance and advance the principles of democracy and social justice (Rai & Spary, 2018; Deshpande, 2004).

Intersectionality and Inclusivity

Intersectionality, a term coined by legal scholar Kimberlé Crenshaw, refers to the interconnected nature of social categorisations such as race, class, gender, and sexuality, which create overlapping and interdependent systems of discrimination or disadvantage. In the context of women's reservation policies in India, intersectionality highlights women's diverse experiences and identities affected by reservation quotas. It underscores the need for inclusive approaches that address intersecting forms of discrimination and marginalisation (Crenshaw, 1991). In India, women's reservation policies are often framed in terms of gender representation, aiming to address the historical underrepresentation of women in political decision-making processes. However, gender intersects with other social identities, such as caste, class, religion, ethnicity, and disability, to shape individuals' experiences and opportunities. Women from marginalised communities, such as Dalits, Adivasis, religious minorities, or economically disadvantaged backgrounds, face compounded forms of discrimination and marginalisation that affect their access to political participation and representation (Pal & Ray, 2019; Chattopadhyay & Duflo, 2004, Rao, 2005).

Recognising Diversity within Women

Intersectionality highlights the diversity within the category of "women" and the need to recognise the intersecting identities and experiences of women from different socio-economic, regional, and cultural backgrounds. Multiple factors like caste, class, religion, ethnicity, language, geography etc. shaped women's experiences of discrimination and exclusion. Therefore, women's reservation policies must adopt an inclusive approach that accounts for the diverse needs, perspectives, and interests of women from various social groups.

Addressing Multiple Forms of Discrimination

Women from marginalised communities face multiple forms of discrimination and exclusion based on intersecting social identities. For example, Dalit women may face discrimination based on both gender and caste, while Muslim women may face discrimination based on both gender and religion. These intersecting forms of discrimination create unique barriers to political participation and representation, which must be addressed through targeted interventions and inclusive policies.

Ensuring Representation and Empowerment for all

Inclusive approaches to women's reservation policies aim to ensure representation and empowerment for all women, regardless of their social background or identity. This requires measures to address marginalised women's needs and challenges, including access to education, economic opportunities, healthcare, and social support services. It also involves promoting leadership development and capacity-building programmes that empower women from diverse backgrounds to participate meaningfully in political processes.

Overcoming Structural Barriers

Intersectionality highlights the importance of addressing structural barriers to women's political participation and representation, including socio-economic inequalities, cultural norms, institutional biases, and systemic discrimination. Inclusive approaches to women's reservation policies seek to overcome these barriers by promoting social justice, equity, and inclusion across multiple dimensions. This may involve legal reforms, policy interventions, awareness campaigns, and advocacy efforts to challenge discriminatory practices and promote equal opportunities for all.

Engaging with Marginalized Communities

Inclusive approaches to women's reservation policies require engaging with marginalised communities and ensuring their meaningful participation in decision-making processes. This involves consulting with community leaders, civil society organisations, and grassroots activists to understand marginalised women's specific needs and concerns and develop tailored strategies to address them. It also involves building partnerships and alliances with marginalised communities to advocate for their rights and promote inclusive governance.

Intersectional Impact Assessment

Intersectional impact assessment is essential for evaluating the effectiveness and outcomes of women's reservation policies in addressing the needs and concerns of marginalised women. This involves collecting disaggregated data, monitoring implementation processes, and conducting qualitative research to understand the differential impact of reservation quotas on women from different social groups. It also involves engaging stakeholders to gather their perspectives and experiences and using this information to inform policy development and decision-making.

Hence, intersectionality and inclusivity are central principles in designing and implementing women's reservation policies in India. By adopting an intersectional approach that recognises the diversity within the category of "women" and addresses intersecting forms of discrimination and marginalisation, India can ensure that reservation policies promote meaningful representation and empowerment for all women, regardless of their social background or identity.

Public Discourse and Political Narrative

Addressing the issue of women's reservation in India requires a multifaceted approach encompassing public discourse and political narratives to raise awareness, build consensus, and mobilise support for policy reform. This chapter explores the key elements of public discourse and the required political narrative for advancing the cause of women's reservation in India. Public discourse plays a crucial role in framing the issue of women's reservation in a way that resonates with diverse audiences and fosters understanding of its importance. Framing the issue as a matter of social justice, gender equality, and democratic representation can help garner public support and mobilise grassroots activism. Highlighting the historical injustices and systemic barriers women face in politics can underscore the urgency of addressing the issue and galvanise public opinion for policy reform (Rao, 2005).

Building Awareness

Public discourse and political narratives are instrumental in building awareness about the need for women's reservation and its potential benefits for society as a whole. Educational campaigns, media outreach, and community engagement efforts can help disseminate information about the underrepresentation of women in politics, the barriers they face, and the importance of diverse representation in decision-making bodies. Public discourse can mobilize public support and create momentum for policy change by raising awareness about the issue.

Engaging Stakeholders

Effective public discourse and political narratives require engaging a wide range of stakeholders, including policymakers, political leaders, civil society organisations, and the general public. By fostering dialogue and collaboration among diverse stakeholders, public discourse can generate innovative ideas, build consensus, and identify common ground for policy reform. Political narratives that emphasise the importance of bipartisan cooperation, inclusive governance, and collective action can facilitate constructive engagement and build momentum for change (Kishwar, 1996).

Amplifying Marginalized Voices

Public discourse and political narratives must amplify the voices of marginalised women and communities most affected by the lack of political representation. By centring the experiences and perspectives of marginalised groups, public discourse can highlight the intersectional nature of gender inequality and underscore the importance of inclusive policies that address the needs of all women. Political narratives prioritising marginalised communities' voices can build solidarity, foster empathy, and mobilise support for policy reform efforts (Pal, 1999; Kishwar, 1996).

Mobilising Support

Political narratives are crucial in mobilising support for women's reservation policies among various stakeholders, including policymakers, political leaders, civil society organisations, and the general public. Through strategic messaging and advocacy efforts, political actors can highlight the benefits of women's political representation, such as improved governance, enhanced legitimacy, and greater responsiveness to diverse perspectives. By framing women's reservation policies as a means to achieve these goals, political narratives can mobilise support and build momentum for policy reform.

Challenging Stereotypes

Public discourse and political narratives are essential for challenging stereotypes and changing societal attitudes towards women in politics. Historically, women have been stereotyped as unfit for leadership roles or lacking in the qualities required for effective governance. Public discourse can challenge these stereotypes and debunk myths about women's suitability for political leadership positions by highlighting women leaders' capabilities, achievements, and leadership qualities. Political narratives that celebrate the accomplishments of women leaders and highlight their contributions to society can inspire other women to enter politics and pursue leadership positions, fostering a culture of inclusivity and empowerment within the political arena.

Fostering Dialogue and Collaboration

Public discourse and political narratives foster dialogue and collaboration among diverse stakeholders, creating opportunities for engagement and consensus-building. By fostering dialogue and collaboration among diverse stakeholders, public discourse can generate innovative ideas, build consensus, and identify common ground for policy reform. Political narratives that emphasise the importance of bipartisan cooperation, inclusive governance, and collective action can facilitate constructive engagement and build momentum for change.

Addressing Misconceptions and Opposition

Public discourse and political narratives also address misconceptions and opposition to women's reservation policies. Critics may raise concerns about the erosion of meritocracy, fears of tokenism, or resistance to change within the political establishment. By addressing these concerns head-on and providing evidence-based arguments in support of women's reservation policies, public discourse can challenge misconceptions and build support for policy reform. Therefore, public discourse and political narratives are essential tools for shaping attitudes towards women's reservation policies in India. By framing the debate, mobilising support, challenging stereotypes, amplifying marginalised voices, fostering dialogue, and addressing opposition, stakeholders can effectively navigate the complexities surrounding women's reservation policies and drive meaningful change towards a more inclusive and representative democracy. It can also drive policy reforms and advance the cause of gender equality and inclusive governance (Kudva, 2003; Pal,1999; Kishwar, 1996; Jayal, 2006).

Conclusion

In the dynamic landscape of Indian politics, women's reservation policies are a beacon of hope for achieving gender equality and inclusive governance. Despite their noble intentions, however, these policies have been met with many critiques and challenges, reflecting the complex realities of India's socio-political landscape. As this chapter has explored, understanding the nuances of these critiques and challenges is essential for advancing the cause of gender equality and women's empowerment in India's political arena. One of the central critiques of women's reservation policies revolves around the erosion of meritocracy and concerns about tokenism. Critics argue that by prioritising gender over qualifications, reservation policies may undermine the principles of fairness and competence in political representation. Moreover, some fear reserved seats may be captured by elite women from privileged backgrounds, perpetuating existing power imbalances and failing to address the needs of marginalised communities. Addressing these critiques requires a nuanced approach that balances the imperative of diversity with the principles of meritocracy and accountability.

Implementation challenges further complicate the realisation of women's reservation policies in India. Logistical hurdles, institutional resistance, and cultural barriers pose significant obstacles to effectively implementing these policies. Moreover, the complexities of assessing the impact of reservation quotas on gender representation, governance effectiveness, and socio-economic outcomes add another layer of complexity to the implementation process. Overcoming these challenges requires concerted efforts to strengthen institutional capacity, build political will, and foster a culture of inclusivity and accountability within the political system. Intersectionality and inclusivity are essential considerations in advancing women's reservation policies in India. Recognising the diverse experiences and identities within the category of "women" is crucial for ensuring that reservation policies address intersecting forms of discrimination and marginalisation. Women from marginalised communities, such as Dalits, Adivasis, and religious minorities, face compounded barriers to political participation and representation, necessitating targeted interventions and inclusive approaches to address their specific needs and challenges. Public discourse and political narratives shape attitudes towards women's reservation policies. By framing the debate in terms of social justice, gender equality, and democratic representation, public discourse can mobilise support and galvanise grassroots activism. Moreover, political narratives that celebrate the accomplishments of women leaders and highlight their contributions to society can inspire other women to enter politics and pursue leadership positions, fostering a culture of inclusivity and empowerment within the political arena.

In conclusion, the journey towards gender equality and inclusive governance in India's political arena is fraught with challenges but worth undertaking. By addressing the critiques and challenges surrounding women's reservation policies and embracing intersectionality and inclusivity, India can pave the way for a more equitable and representative democracy. It is imperative that policymakers, civil society organisations, and citizens alike work together to build a future where every voice is heard, and every woman has the opportunity to participate fully in shaping the nation's destiny.

REFERENCES

Chattopadhyay, R. & Duflo, E. (2004). "Women as Policy Makers: Evidence from a Randomised Policy Experiment in India." *Econometrica*, *72*(5): 1409-1443.

Crenshaw, K. (1991). "Mapping the Margins: Intersectionality, Identity Politics, and Violence against Women of Colour." *Stanford Law Review*, *43*(6).

Deshpande, A. & Gupta, A.S. (2021). "Economic Empowerment of Women in India." *World Development*, *142*: 105377.

Deshpande, A. (2004). "Affirmative Action in India and the United States." *The Journal of Asian Studies*, *63*(3): 843-847.

Deshpande, R. (2004). "Women's Reservation Bill: Politics and Stalemate." *Economic and Political Weekly*, *39*(42): 4491-4493.

Franceschet, S., Krook, M.L. & Piscopo, J.M. (2012). *The Impact of Gender Quotas*. Oxford University Press.

Gupta, S. & Desai, S. (2020). "Political Backlash and the Impact of Women's Reservation in India." *Journal of South Asian Studies, 34*(2): 123-145.

Hasan, Z. (2010). *Gender, Religion, and Democratic Politics in India.* Oxford University Press.

Htun, M. & Weldon, S.L. (2010). "Challenges to Women's Political Participation in India." *Women's Studies International Forum, 33*(1): 1-12.

Jayal, N.G. (2006). "Representing India: Ethnic Diversity and the Governance of Public Institutions." *Ethnic and Racial Studies, 29*(5): 884-905.

Kalam, M.A. (2014). "Women's Reservation and Electoral Politics in India." *Journal of Political Studies, 21*(2): 123-135.

Kapur, R. (2001). "Law and the 'Woman Question' in India: Examining the Constituent Assembly Debates." *Social and Legal Studies, 10*(3): 383-406.

Kishwar, M. (1996). "Women and Politics: Beyond Quotas." *Economic and Political Weekly, 31*(43): 2875-2880.

Kishwar, M. (1996). "Women's Reservation Bill: A Debate in Need of Direction". *Economic and Political Weekly, 31*(42).

Kishwar, M. (1996). "Women's Reservations: Beyond Symbolism." *Economic and Political Weekly, 31*(43): 2871-2874.

Kudva, N. (2003). "Engineering Elections: The Experiences of Women in Panchayati Raj in Karnataka, India." *International Journal of Politics, Culture, and Society, 16*(3): 445-463.

Kumar, R. (1993). *The History of Doing: An Illustrated Account of Movements for Women's Rights and Feminism in India 1800-1990.* Zubaan Books.

Kumar, S. (2012). *Women's Reservation in India: Politics, Policy, and Practice.* Sage Publications.

Misra, M. (2012). "A Historical Overview of Women's Reservation in India." *International Journal of Social Science and Interdisciplinary Research, 1*(6): 38-47.

Mohanty, C.T., Russo, A. & Torres, L. (1991). *Third World Women and the Politics of Feminism.* Indiana University Press.

Pai, S. (2009). "Women's Political Representation in India: Dissecting the Puzzle." *The Journal of Legislative Studies, 15*(4): 565-578.

Pal, M. & Ray, P. (2019). *Women in Indian Politics.* Sage Publications.

Pal, M. (1999). "Women's Representation and Political Participation in India: A Study of Local Urban Bodies in Haryana and Delhi." *The Indian Journal of Political Science, 60*(3): 485-502.

Phillips, A. (1998). "Democracy and Difference: Contesting the Boundaries of the Political." *Feminist Politics and Democratic Values*, pp. 123-144.

Rai, S.M. & Spary, C. (2018). *Performing Representation: Women Members in the Indian Parliament.* New Delhi: Oxford University Press.

Rai, S.M. (1999). "Political Representation and Women's Empowerment: The Quota Debate in India." *Democratization*, 6(3): 84-103.

Rao, N. (1998). "Representation and Political Space: Gender and Politics in India." *Economic and Political Weekly, 33*(2): 89-98.

Rao, N. (2005). "Reservation for Women in Legislative Bodies: Perspectives." *Economic and Political Weekly, 40*(40): 4396-4399.

Rao, N. (2005). *Reservation for Women in India: Contemporary Context and Prospects.* Manak Publications.

Roy, A. (2018). *Gender Quotas in Indian Politics: Pathways to Action.* Oxford University Press.

Sharma, R. (2018). *Gender Quotas and the Indian Political Landscape.* Routledge.

Thomas, V. & Kaunain, S. (2023). "The Intersection of Culture and Politics: Understanding Women's Underrepresentation in Indian Democracy." *Journal of Asian and African Studies, 0*(0).

Yadav, Y. (2000). "Understanding the Second Democratic Upsurge: Trends of Bahujan Participation in Electoral Politics in the 1990s." *Transforming India: Social and Political Dynamics of Democracy*, pp. 120-145.

20

Struggle for Voice

Women Leaders in Punjab's Local Governance

Rajni Bala

Introduction

The 73rd Constitutional Amendment of 1992 marked a transformative step in India's democratic framework, aiming to decentralize governance and empower marginalized sections of society. Among its most significant provisions was the mandatory reservation of one-third of all seats in Panchayati Raj Institutions (PRIs) for women, including positions of leadership such as Sarpanches (village heads). This legislative intervention was not just about increasing the numerical presence of women in governance but about enabling their active participation in decision-making processes that directly affect their communities. By doing so, the amendment sought to challenge the patriarchal structures that have historically excluded women from public life and governance. Punjab, a state renowned for its agricultural prosperity and vibrant culture, offers a particularly intriguing case for examining the intersection of gender, governance, and empowerment. While the reservation policy has undoubtedly succeeded in increasing the visibility of women in Punjab's local governance structures, the translation of this representation into substantive leadership remains a significant challenge. Deeply entrenched patriarchal norms, socio-economic dependencies, and institutional biases often limit women's ability to exercise real authority.

One of the most pervasive issues in Punjab's PRIs is the phenomenon of proxy leadership, colloquially termed the "Panchayat Pati" syndrome. Here, male relatives—often husbands—wield the actual power, reducing elected women leaders to figureheads. This practice undermines the very essence of the 73rd Amendment, which was designed to empower women as independent leaders and decision-makers. Coupled with economic dependency, restricted mobility, and limited access to political networks, this phenomenon highlights the systemic barriers that continue to impede women's leadership in the state. Despite these challenges, the potential of women's leadership in governance remains undeniable. Research has consistently demonstrated that women leaders in governance prioritize issues such as health, education, sanitation, and welfare, which are often neglected by male counterparts. These contributions underscore the importance of fostering an enabling environment where women can exercise their authority without interference or constraints.

Punjab's case also reveals the critical role of intersectionality in understanding the barriers to women's empowerment. Women from marginalized castes or economically disadvantaged backgrounds face compounded challenges, as their gender intersects with other axes of social disadvantage. Addressing these intersecting inequalities requires targeted interventions that go beyond generic solutions and are tailored to the specific socio-cultural and economic realities of this region. The involvement of women in governance through the 73rd Amendment has created an important starting point for addressing gender inequality. However, as this study explores, representation alone is insufficient for achieving true empowerment. A comprehensive approach that includes capacity-building programmes, legal reforms, economic support mechanisms, and efforts to dismantle patriarchal norms is essential for enabling women to lead effectively.

This chapter examines the dynamics of women's leadership in Punjab's PRIs, focusing on the complex interplay of empowerment and marginalization. By analysing primary and secondary data, it identifies, the barriers, that women face and the strategies needed to overcome them. The findings aim to contribute to the broader discourse on gender and governance, offering insights into how social and institutional reforms can complement legislative measures like the 73rd Amendment to create a more inclusive and equitable political landscape.

Objectives

- To find out Socio-economic and Institutional Challenges for women leaders in PRIs.
- To assess the opportunities for women leaders in PRIs.
- To examine the Role of intersectionality in women's leadership in PRIs.
- To propose strategies for the empowerment of women leaders in PRIs.

Methodology

The present study has used both qualitative and quantitative techniques. Semi-structured interviews were conducted with 30 women leaders from PRIs across rural and semi-urban areas in Punjab. These interviews explored their experiences, challenges, and perceptions of leadership. Detailed case studies of selected women leaders who have successfully navigated systemic barriers were documented to highlight best practices and success stories, government reports, including data from the Ministry of Panchayati Raj and Punjab State Election Commission. Previous research studies, academic articles on women's participation in governance and the impact of the 73rd Amendment, Census data and reports from NGOs, were also considered. By using Purposive Sampling, women leaders in PRIs were selected based on their leadership roles (Sarpanch, Panchayat member) and geographical diversity across Punjab. Efforts were made to include leaders from different caste groups and socio-economic backgrounds to ensure the representation of marginalized communities. Informed consent was obtained from all participants before conducting interviews or surveys and anonymity and confidentiality were maintained to ensure the privacy of respondents.

Review of Literature

The role of women in governance has been a subject of extensive academic inquiry, particularly in the context of developing nations like India, where structural and cultural barriers significantly hinder women's political participation. The 73rd Constitutional Amendment, introduced in 1992, was a watershed moment in India's democratic evolution. It mandated the reservation of one-third of seats in Panchayati Raj Institutions (PRIs) for women, marking a significant policy shift towards inclusive governance. The amendment aimed not merely to increase women's numerical representation but to provide a platform for their active involvement in decision-making processes, particularly at the grassroots level. However, the impact of this legislation has varied across states, shaped by unique socio-cultural and economic dynamics. Punjab, with its deeply entrenched patriarchal norms, presents a compelling case for examining the challenges and potential of women's leadership in local governance.

The transformative potential of the 73rd Amendment has been highlighted in various studies. Chattopadhyay and Duflo (2004) conducted a seminal randomized policy experiment in India, demonstrating that women leaders in PRIs prioritized investments in public goods such as water, sanitation, and roads. Their research underscored the distinctive governance styles of women, focusing on community welfare and inclusive development. Similarly, Beaman *et al.* (2012) found that women's leadership in PRIs inspired higher aspirations among young girls, fostering educational attainment and challenging traditional gender roles. These studies indicate that when women are empowered to lead, they bring transformative changes to governance, benefiting entire communities. Yet, the practical realization of such potential often remains constrained by systemic barriers, particularly in regions like Punjab.

Punjab's socio-economic and cultural landscape creates unique challenges for women in governance. Despite its agricultural prosperity and relatively high literacy rates, the state is marked by deeply entrenched patriarchal norms that restrict women's agency. Singh and Kaur (2020) examined the challenges faced by women leaders in Punjab's PRIs, identifying factors such as patriarchal resistance, limited mobility, and economic dependency as significant barriers. One of the most striking phenomena observed in Punjab is the prevalence of proxy leadership, commonly referred to as the "Panchayat Pati" syndrome. In this practice, male relatives, often husbands, exercise actual decision-making power, reducing elected women leaders to symbolic figures. This undermines the very intent of the reservation policy, which seeks to foster independent female leadership. The prevalence of proxy leadership is supported by survey data from Punjab University (2023), which found that 50 per cent of women leaders in the state reported that male relatives exerted significant control over their official responsibilities.

The limitations of women's leadership in Punjab's PRIs are not confined to patriarchal resistance. Economic dependency further exacerbates these challenges, as many women lack financial autonomy, making them reliant on male family members for resources and support. This economic dependence translates into restricted decision-making power, as women are unable to assert themselves without financial leverage. Krook (2010) highlighted that the exclusion of women from political networks further limits their ability to navigate governance structures effectively. In Punjab, this exclusion is compounded by socio-cultural barriers that coerce women's participation in public life, particularly in rural areas. Rai (2017) argued that such barriers are not merely individual challenges but systemic issues that require targeted interventions to be dismantled.

The intersection of gender, class and caste further complicates the experiences of women leaders in Punjab. Intersectionality, as explored by Bhavnani (2009), reveals how women from marginalized castes or economically disadvantaged backgrounds face compounded challenges in asserting their leadership. In Punjab, caste dynamics often intersect with gender biases, which further limit the access to opportunities and resources for women leaders from lower castes. This highlights the urgent need to address these intersecting forms of discrimination.

While these challenges are significant, the potential of women's leadership to drive positive change cannot be ignored. Bardhan, Mookherjee, and Parra Torrado (2010) demonstrated that women-led PRIs in West Bengal were more effective in targeting anti-poverty programmes, improving outcomes for marginalized communities. Although Punjab presents a different socio-cultural context, similar studies suggest that empowering women in governance could lead to better prioritization of social welfare issues. Jayal (2006) emphasized the importance of capacity-building programmes to equip women leaders with the skills and confidence needed to navigate the complexities of governance. Such initiatives are particularly critical in Punjab, where many women leaders lack formal training in financial management, public speaking, and governance processes.

Community engagement and awareness campaigns also play a pivotal role in challenging patriarchal norms and fostering acceptance of women leaders. Singh and Kaur (2020) highlighted the success of community-driven initiatives in changing societal attitudes, particularly when local influencers and male allies are involved. These campaigns have the potential to create an environment where women leaders are not only elected but are also respected and supported in their roles.

Data from the Punjab State Election Commission (2023) provide a quantitative backdrop to these discussions, showing that while women occupy 50 per cent of seats in PRIs, only 45 per cent of these women actively participate in decision-making. Moreover, in higher leadership positions such as Sarpanch, the participation rate drops to 35 per cent, indicating a vertical segregation in leadership roles. These figures illustrate that while the reservation policy has increased women's visibility, it has not fully translated into empowerment or leadership effectiveness. Proxy leadership, patriarchal resistance, and socio-economic barriers remain significant obstacles to achieving the goals envisioned by the 73rd Amendment.

The body of literature underscores the need for a comprehensive approach to address these challenges. Simply increasing the numerical representation of women in governance is insufficient. Empowerment requires dismantling systemic barriers through targeted policies and programmes. Capacity-building initiatives, economic support mechanisms, and institutional reforms must be complemented by efforts to change societal attitudes towards women in leadership. As Clots-Figueras (2011) argued, genuine empowerment is achieved not just by placing women in positions of power but, by enabling them to exercise that power effectively.

Hence, the literature on women's leadership in PRIs highlights both the progress made and the persisting challenges. By synthesizing these insights, this study aims to contribute to the ongoing discourse on gender and governance, offering recommendations for bridging the gap between representation and empowerment in Punjab's PRIs.

Women Leaders in Punjab's Panchayati Raj Institutions: Challenges and Opportunities

The implementation of the 73rd Constitutional Amendment in 1992, mandating the reservation of one-third of seats in Panchayati Raj Institutions (PRIs) for women, represented a significant milestone in India's democratic journey. However, the lived realities of women leaders in these governance structures reveal a complex interplay of challenges and opportunities. Punjab, with its deeply entrenched patriarchal norms, presents a compelling case study to understand these dynamics. While the amendment has enabled a greater numerical presence of women in local governance, systemic and cultural barriers continue to limit their substantive empowerment. At the same time, there are emerging opportunities that hold the potential to transform local governance and foster gender equality.

Challenges for Women Leaders in Punjab's PRIs

Patriarchal Resistance: One of the most pervasive challenges faced by women leaders in Punjab is the deeply entrenched patriarchal norms that shape societal attitudes. Governance has historically been a male-dominated domain, and the entry of women into PRIs has been met with resistance. Traditional gender roles, which view women primarily as caregivers confined to the domestic sphere, often lead to skepticism regarding their capabilities as leaders. Studies, such as those by Singh and Kaur (2020), indicate that 78 per cent of women leaders in Punjab reported encountering patriarchal resistance in their communities. This manifests in various forms, including reluctance from male colleagues to collaborate, lack of respect for women's authority, and outright hostility.

Proxy Leadership: The phenomenon of proxy leadership, colloquially referred to as the "Panchayat Pati" syndrome, is a significant impediment to women's empowerment in Punjab. In many cases, the real power is wielded by male relatives—husbands, fathers, or brothers—of elected women leaders, reducing them to figureheads. Ban and Rao (2008) highlighted this issue as a widespread practice that undermines the intent of the reservation policy. Data from the Punjab State Election Commission (2023) revealed that nearly 50 per cent of women leaders in the state function under the influence of male proxies. This practice not only perpetuates patriarchal control but also limits women's ability to gain the experience and confidence needed to emerge as independent leaders.

Economic Dependency: Economic independence is critical for effective leadership, yet many women leaders in Punjab lack financial autonomy. Women often rely on male family members for resources, which constrain their decision-making power and undermine their authority in governance. Krook (2010) emphasized that economic dependency directly impacts women's capacity to participate meaningfully in governance. In Punjab, the intersection of economic dependency with social norms further exacerbates this challenge, leaving many women unable to assert their leadership roles.

Limited Mobility and Public Engagement: Restrictions on women's mobility, particularly in rural areas, pose another significant challenge. Social norms often discourage women from travelling alone or interacting with male colleagues, limiting their ability to attend meetings, participate in training programmes, or engage with their constituencies. This restriction not only hampers their professional development but also isolates them from critical political networks that are essential for effective governance. Surveys conducted by NGOs in Punjab (2023) indicate that 60 per cent of women leaders reported limited mobility as a barrier to their leadership.

Institutional Barriers: Institutional barriers within PRIs also hinder women's participation. These include a lack of gender-sensitive policies, inadequate training programmes, and limited access to resources such as information and funding. Many women leaders are not provided with the necessary tools to understand governance processes, manage finances, or implement development projects. Jayal (2006) argued that without institutional support, women's presence in governance structures risks being reduced to token representation rather than substantive leadership.

Intersectional Discrimination: Women leaders from marginalized castes and economically disadvantaged backgrounds face compounded challenges. Intersectionality, as explored by Bhavnani (2009), highlights how caste, class, and gender intersect to create unique forms of discrimination. In Punjab, lower-caste women leaders often encounter additional barriers, such as exclusion from decision-making spaces and lack of access to resources. These intersecting forms of disadvantage further marginalize already vulnerable groups, limiting their ability to participate effectively in governance.

Harassment and Discrimination: Harassment and discrimination against women leaders are prevalent in Punjab's

PRIs. Instances of verbal abuse, intimidation, and social ostracization discourage women from asserting their authority. Singh and Kaur (2020) documented widespread harassment, with 50 per cent of surveyed women leaders reporting experiences of discrimination. Such hostile environments not only undermine women's confidence but also deter potential leaders from entering governance.

Opportunities for Women Leaders in Punjab's PRIs

Legislative Framework: The 73rd Amendment provides a strong legal foundation for women's participation in governance. The reservation of seats ensures women's numerical presence in PRIs, creating a critical mass that can influence decision-making. By normalizing women's participation in governance, this policy has the potential to challenge traditional gender roles and pave the way for greater acceptance of women as leaders.

Role Models and Community Impact: Women leaders who overcome barriers serve as role models, inspiring others to aspire to leadership positions. Beaman *et al.* (2012) found that the presence of women leaders in PRIs positively impacts the aspirations of young girls, fostering educational attainment and challenging gender stereotypes. In Punjab, case studies of successful women leaders demonstrate how their contributions to health, sanitation, and education have transformed communities.

Capacity-Building Programmes: Various government and non-governmental organizations have initiated capacity-building programmes to enhance the leadership skills of women in PRIs. These programmes focus on areas such as financial management, governance processes, and public speaking, equipping women with the tools needed to navigate the complexities of governance. Singh and Kaur (2020) emphasized that such initiatives have shown promising results in increasing women's confidence and competence.

Economic Empowerment Initiatives: Providing women leaders with economic resources and financial independence can significantly enhance their ability to lead. Microfinance schemes, entrepreneurship training, and access to government subsidies can reduce dependency on male family members and enable women to assert their authority. Bardhan, Mookherjee, and Parra Torrado (2010) demonstrated that women-led PRIs with access to resources were more effective in implementing development projects.

Intersectional Approaches: Addressing the unique challenges faced by marginalized groups through intersectional approaches is critical. Policies that specifically target lower-caste and economically disadvantaged women can help bridge the gap in access to resources and opportunities. Bhavnani (2009) emphasized that intersectional strategies are essential for ensuring equitable representation and participation in governance.

Digital Technology and Networking: The increasing penetration of digital technology presents a unique opportunity for women leaders to connect with broader networks, access information, and participate in online training programmes. Digital platforms can also serve as spaces for advocacy, enabling women leaders to amplify their voices and share best practices.

The challenges and opportunities for women leaders in Punjab's PRIs reflect the broader tensions between structural barriers and the transformative potential of inclusive governance. While patriarchal resistance, proxy leadership, and socio-economic dependency continue to limit women's substantive empowerment, the legislative framework, capacity-building programmes, and community support mechanisms offer pathways for progress. By addressing these challenges through targeted interventions and leveraging emerging opportunities, Punjab can move closer to realizing the vision of gender-equal governance envisioned by the 73rd Amendment. Empowering women leaders in PRIs is not just a matter of fulfilling legal mandates but a critical step towards building inclusive, effective, and transformative local governance.

Data Collection and Analysis: Contextualizing the Case Studies

The challenges and opportunities in Punjab's Panchayati Raj Institutions (PRIs) provide a nuanced understanding of the dynamics between representation and empowerment in the case of women leaders. While systemic barriers such as patriarchal norms, proxy leadership, and economic dependency continue to undermine women's substantive participation, emerging opportunities through capacity-building programmes and community initiatives hint at the transformative potential of inclusive governance. To further illustrate these dynamics, it is critical to examine real-life case studies that demonstrate both the challenges and successes of women leaders in Punjab's PRIs. These qualitative accounts not only validate the broader trends but also shed light on individual and collective strategies adopted by women to navigate and overcome systemic obstacles.

Some Case Studies

As a researcher delving into the dynamics of women's leadership in rural governance, my primary objective was to understand the extent of power and influence wielded by women panchayat leaders in the villages around Batala city, Punjab. The specific focus was on assessing whether these women leaders have a genuine voice in decision-making, whether their opinions are heard and respected, and if they are content with their roles.

To explore these questions, I conducted a series of interviews with women sarpanchs in various villages. This study includes twelve detailed case studies, each providing a unique glimpse into the experiences of these women leaders. The interviews aimed to uncover the realities of their leadership, the challenges they face, and the societal and familial dynamics that affect their ability to govern effectively. Are these women truly empowered, or do they remain figureheads under the shadow of a patriarchal system? How do their male counterparts and family members influence their roles? And importantly, are these women satisfied with their positions, or do they face constant resistance and frustration? To keep the identity of the respondents, their names have been changed.

The findings from these interviews reveal a complex interplay of empowerment and marginalization. While some women exhibit resilience and determination, others are relegated to passive roles, with their leadership curtailed by deeply entrenched gender norms. These case studies provide critical insights into the socio-political landscape of rural Punjab and the ongoing struggle for genuine female empowerment in local governance.

Case 1: The Passive Sarpanch

In a village near Batala city, the position of sarpanch is reserved for women, and the current sarpanch hails from an upper-caste Jat Sikh family. However, during our meeting, it became apparent that she had very little knowledge about the functioning of the panchayat or its finances. When questioned, she explained that women in the village are burdened with daily household chores, leaving little time for governance. Consequently, important village matters are managed by the male members of her family, who approach her solely for her signature. This scenario underscores the superficial empowerment of women in leadership roles, where the title of sarpanch is held by a woman, but the actual power remains firmly in the hands of men.

Case 2: The Invisible Sarpanch

In another village, our attempts to contact the woman sarpanch were repeatedly thwarted by her husband, who always answered the phone. He consistently promised to relay our messages but never facilitated a direct conversation with her. When we finally spoke to her, she deferred all inquiries to her husband, stating that he handles such matters. This case highlights the invisibility of female leaders, where societal norms and family dynamics restrict their direct participation in governance, rendering their roles nominal at best.

Case 3: The Silenced Sarpanch

We met a woman sarpanch who was initially pleased by our visit. However, throughout the conversation, her husband dominated the discussion, answering all questions on her behalf. Whenever she attempted to speak, he would ridicule her, reducing her contributions to mere kitchen duties. Despite her evident dissatisfaction with this treatment, she did not openly oppose him. This case illustrates the pervasive patriarchal attitudes that belittle and undermine the authority of women in leadership positions, preventing them from effectively fulfilling their roles.

Case 4: The Oppressed Sarpanch

A woman sarpanch from a lower caste, elected to a reserved seat, faced severe domestic abuse and societal challenges. Her husband, a visible presence in the panchayat, mistreated and physically abused her. She had three sons; all addicted to drugs, and her husband was involved in drug peddling, leading to numerous incarcerations in the village. The community expressed doubt about her returning for another term. This case starkly portrays the intersection of caste, gender, and substance abuse issues, where the sarpanch's ability to lead is crippled by personal and societal adversities.

Case 5: The Determined Sarpanch

Despite facing continuous criticism and sarcasm from her husband, a bold woman sarpanch in another village stood firm in her resolve to bring positive changes. She recounted her efforts to improve the village, undeterred by her husband's negative remarks. Although it was her first term, she was determined to work hard and serve the community. This case demonstrates the resilience and determination of women leaders who, despite facing patriarchal resistance, strive to make a difference. These case studies collectively reveal the pervasive patriarchal mindset that hampers the effective participation of women in governance. Reserved seats for women in panchayats are often symbolic, with real power remaining in the hands of male family members. Women sarpanchs face varying degrees of marginalization, from passive involvement and complete invisibility to overt ridicule and abuse. However, there are also instances of resilience and determination, where women strive to fulfil their roles despite significant opposition. This analysis underscores the need for deeper societal changes and supportive mechanisms to truly empower women leaders and ensure their meaningful participation in governance.

Conclusion

The 73rd Constitutional Amendment marked a historic step towards gender-inclusive governance by mandating the reservation of seats for women in Panchayati Raj Institutions (PRIs). However, this study reveals that the journey from representation to substantive empowerment remains an ongoing struggle, particularly in Punjab, where deeply entrenched patriarchal norms and socio-cultural dynamics present significant barriers. Through a combination of qualitative and quantitative research, this chapter has examined the nuanced realities of women's leadership in PRIs, offering critical insights into both the challenges and transformative potential of these roles.

The findings underscore the persistent challenges that undermine the empowerment of women leaders in Punjab's PRIs. Proxy leadership, where male relatives assume *de facto* control of governance, is one of the most pervasive obstacles. This practice not only diminishes the agency of women leaders but also perpetuates patriarchal control within the very structures designed to challenge it. Economic dependency further exacerbates this issue, as financial autonomy is often a prerequisite for effective leadership. Women from marginalized castes and economically disadvantaged backgrounds face compounded challenges, highlighting the importance of addressing intersectionality in governance reforms.

The case studies provided in this research illuminate the lived experiences of women leaders and expose the structural and cultural barriers they face. For instance, the stories of passive, invisible, and silenced women Sarpanchs demonstrate how entrenched gender roles and societal norms limit women's decision-making capacities. Yet, these narratives are counterbalanced by examples of resilience and determination, such as the determined Sarpanch who defied patriarchal norms to bring tangible improvements to her community. These cases highlight the dual reality of women's leadership: a landscape fraught with obstacles but also filled with the potential for transformative change.

Despite these challenges, the study identifies significant opportunities for fostering meaningful empowerment. Capacity-building programmes, community awareness campaigns, and the integration of digital technology emerge as pivotal tools for equipping women leaders with the skills and resources needed to assert their authority. Programmes that engage male allies and community influencers hold promise for challenging patriarchal norms and fostering broader acceptance of women in leadership roles. Moreover, leveraging digital platforms for networking and advocacy offers a way to overcome traditional barriers of mobility and access. The analysis also reveals that while systemic barriers persist, the presence of women in governance has the potential to create ripple effects that extend beyond the individual. Women leaders bring unique perspectives and priorities to governance, often focusing on issues such as health, education, and sanitation, which directly impact community well-being. Their success stories inspire future generations of women to aspire to leadership roles, thereby gradually shifting societal perceptions and challenging the *status quo*.

To bridge the gap between representation and empowerment, a multi-faceted approach is essential. Policymakers and practitioners must focus on creating supportive ecosystems that enable women leaders to thrive. This includes providing comprehensive training programmes that cover governance processes, financial management, and public speaking; offering economic incentives and resources to reduce dependency; and enacting institutional reforms that promote gender-sensitive governance. Additionally, addressing intersectional barriers requires targeted interventions that account for the unique challenges faced by women from marginalized communities. The findings also emphasize the importance of monitoring and evaluation mechanisms to ensure the effectiveness of interventions. For example, capacity-building programmes should include metrics for measuring their impact on women's decision-making abilities and confidence. Community engagement initiatives must be designed to create long-term cultural shifts rather than short-term compliance.

In conclusion, the study reaffirms that the reservation of seats for women in PRIs is a necessary but insufficient step towards achieving gender equality in governance. Empowerment requires more than just representation; it necessitates dismantling systemic barriers and fostering environments where women can exercise real authority. Punjab, with its unique socio-cultural and economic landscape, serves as both a microcosm and a laboratory for examining the broader dynamics of gender and governance in India. By addressing the challenges and leveraging the opportunities identified in this study, women leaders in Punjab's PRIs can become catalysts for transformative change, creating governance systems that are not only inclusive and equitable, but also reflective of the diverse voices they aim to represent.

REFERENCES

Ban, R. & Rao, V. (2008). "Tokenism or Agency? The Impact of Women's Reservations on Village Democracies in South India." *Economic Development and Cultural Change, 56*(3): 501-530.

Bardhan, P., Mookherjee, D. & Parra Torrado, M. (2010). "Impact of Political Reservations in West Bengal Local Governments on Anti-Poverty Targeting." *Journal of Globalization and Development, 1*(1): Article 5.

Beaman, L., Duflo, E., Pande, R. & Topalova, P. (2012). "Female Leadership Raises Aspirations and Educational Attainment for Girls: A Policy Experiment in India." *Science, 335*(6068): 582-586.

Bhavnani, R.R. (2009). "Do Electoral Quotas Work after They Are Withdrawn? Evidence from A Natural Experiment in India." *American Political Science Review, 103*(1): 23-35.

Centre for Women's Studies, Punjab University. (2023). *Report on Women's Participation in Panchayati Raj Institutions in Punjab*. Punjab University Press.

Chattopadhyay, R. & Duflo, E. (2004). "Women as Policymakers: Evidence from A Randomized Policy Experiment in India. *Econometrica, 72*(5): 1409-1443.

Clots-Figueras, I. (2011). "Women in Politics: Evidence from the Indian States." *Journal of Public Economics, 95*(7-8), 664-690.

Jayal, N.G. (2006). "Engendering Local Democracy: The Impact of Quotas for Women in India's Panchayats." *Democratization, 13*(1): 15-35.

Krook, M.L. (2010). *Quotas for Women in Politics: Gender and Candidate Selection Reform Worldwide.* Oxford University Press.

Punjab State Election Commission. (2023). *Statistical Report on Panchayati Raj Elections in Punjab.* Punjab State Election Commission.

Rai, S.M. (2017). *Gender and the Political Economy of Development: from Nationalism to Globalization.* Polity Press.

Singh, N. & Kaur, G. (2020). "Women in Punjab's Panchayati Raj Institutions: Challenges and Opportunities." *Journal of Rural Development and Governance, 12*(4): 45-63.

Surveys by NGOs in Punjab. (2023). *Empowering Women in Local Governance: Field Surveys on PRIs.* Punjab Development Network.

United Nations Development Programme (UNDP). (2020). *Gender Equality in Local Governance: Strategies and Success Stories.* UNDP.

World Bank. (2019). *Strengthening Grassroots Governance: The Role of Women in India's Panchayati Raj Institutions.* World Bank Publications.

21

Empowering the Transgender Community in Manipur through Affirmative Action

Opportunities and Challenges

Thingnam Rajshree and *Mayanglambam Lilee*

Introduction

The Article 1 of the Universal Human Rights Declaration states that, "All human beings are born free and equal in dignity and rights", but for many, being born free and equal in dignity and rights does not necessarily entail a dignified and qualified life. Many lives become undermined and undervalued because of socially sanctioned orders that decide the normal and acceptable from the rest, and anyone who does not fall into this category of being 'normal' and 'acceptable' (which can be culturally subjective) are subjected to the wrath of stigma and discrimination. The resultant effect of such stigma and discrimination is that it scrapes people of dignified lives and reduce them to a marginalized and disadvantaged position. To counter the effects of such ordeals, the state draws various policies and acts that protect the rights of such groups and for them to live in par with the rest of the populace. These acts and policies act as the anchor of the duo-empowerment and affirmative action. A report submitted by the Amnesty International on 'Colonialism and Sexual Orientation and Gender Identity' writes that "Contemporary human rights violations and abuses experienced by LGBTI people largely stem from the colonial legacy of discriminatory laws and practices" and talks about how "it has had a more far-reaching role in shaping how gender and sexuality are understood today" (Amnesty International, 2023). Across the world, the transgender population has been a stigmatized group because of their deviance from the heteronormative binary that presupposes human identity and relations which eventually leads to their discrimination and marginalization. This is not to say that all societies were heteronormative but in various societies gender variations did and does exists still. In this variation, the case of transgender in India generally and in Manipur particularly are not exception. In these views, this chapter analyses with the various measures taken up by the government to ensure Transgender inclusivity in Manipur through preferential reservation and to explore the issues and challenges at ground level in the implementation and execution of Transgender affirmative policies.

India, Colonialism and Transgender Persons

In India as well, the existence of a gender spectrum beyond the heteronormative binary as *kothi, kinnars, hijras, jogappas, aravalis* etc., has existed since ancient times. The transgender persons enjoyed certain rights and performed various 'responsible roles' during ancient and medieval era. However, as in the case of many other countries where the colonial rule has been accounted for the structural shift of pre-colonial gender variations, in India too, the British rule is seen as the onset of changes that led to the marginalization and subsequent persecution of the transgender community through various laws and policies which were 'detrimental towards the transgender persons' (Mishra, 2023). It included promulgation of the Indian Penal Code (IPC) by the colonial administrators in 1860, which included the Section 377 that criminalizes homosexuality and the Criminal Tribes Act in which the eunuchs were 'officially put under the category of criminal [caste], a dangerous outlaw', declaring [transgender] as 'criminal elements in society'. "Transgender persons were considered to be immoral, and by design their identity was undermined. The colonized population was classified in the statistics created by the British colonial administration by having just two sex categories—male and female—in their census" (*ibid.*). "Through their census classification, they sent the message that *hijra* community was unknowable and did not even have the privilege of being counted" (Gannon, 2009; Hinchy, 2014: cited in Mishra, 2023: 12). It is important to note these facts about the colonial history because the impact of such actions did not end with the end of colonialism but continued even in the post-Independence era and as Mishra puts, "the transgender people kept suffering as a legacy of the colonialism" (Mishra, 2023). The historical discrimination and marginalization of transgender has had lasting impacts and to the extent that even in the 21st Century transgender still must live with numerous multifaceted difficulties. "In India, the living conditions of transgender are still very inferior to those of binary people" (Dahiya, 2018: cited in K.G. & Keshlata, 2024: 13).

In the case of Manipur, these links have not been carved out in details yet. Manipur existed as an independent kingdom which can be evidenced in the lines of James Johnstone, 'there can be no doubt that it has existed as an independent kingdom from a very early period' (Johnstone, 1896, cited in Kshetri, 2006, 28). The kingdom, however, lost its independence and was annexed by the British on 27 April, 1891 (Khelchandra,1981; Singh, 1984, cited in Kshetri, 2006: 31). Subsequently, "on 18th September, 1891, the Government of British India appointed Churchand Singh, a six year old grandson of Rajah Nar Singh, as the Rajah of Manipur", and thus, "Manipur became a native Princely State" (Kshetri, 2006: 31). However, "the political integration of Manipur to the Indian Union took place in the year 1949 through a merger agreement" (*ibid.*). The annexation of Manipur took place in 1891 in the form of a native princely state but the merger of Manipur into the Indian Union only in 1949 and thus, it cannot be said that the Section 377 of the IPC and the Criminal Tribes Act, passed in 1860 and 1871 respectively were in force in the kingdom. Nevertheless, processes of acculturation with dominant cultures of India where transgenderism was already in the process of suppression through systematic political discrimination and persecution could have impacted the transgender culture of the state as well.

Transgender Persons of Manipur

The erstwhile Manipuri kingdom noted the prevalence of gender plurality beyond the male and female binary called the *Pheidas*. "*Pheida* is a gender that identity that exists apart from man and woman" and they "continued to exist during the reign of many Meitei kings" (AMANA, 2020). They were interpreted as per various sources as eunuchs, castrated men or as men who are like women (*ibid.*). *Pheida* was also translated as 'Eunuchs' whose "main function was to attend upon the queen" (Singh, 1976/2003: 113). The different interpretations were linked to the strong suggestion of *Pheidas* as "persons assigned male whose mannerisms and behaviour were like women" (AMANA, 2020). The *Pheidas* were "incorporated in the administration of the king, and they were fairly incorporated in the society", however, "contemporary Manipur is very different from earlier times in its treatment of gender inclusivity" (*ibid.*). The culture that was prevalent then seems to have undergone various changes because of the political and subsequent changes that Manipur has undergone. "The loss of royal patronage following the Third Burmese Invasion of Manipur (1819-1826 AD) and the consequent coming of the British colonial influence might have subsequently led to the subversion of the presence and privileges of the gender variant persons in Manipuri society." (Yumkhaibam, 2019: cited in Yumkhaibam, p.180). According to a training material on 'Inclusion of Transgender Children in School Education', *Nupa Maanba* is defined as 'Traditional socio-cultural trans masculine identity In Manipur' and *Nupi Maanbi* as 'Traditional socio-cultural trans feminine identity In Manipur' (Department of Gender Studies, National Council of Educational Research and Training, 2020-21).

In contemporary usage, the term 'transgender' in Manipur is used to define persons who do not identify with the gender they are assigned to at birth which includes transwomen and transmen. The Government of Manipur uses the term 'Third Gender' for transgender of the state for their legal protection (Planning Department, Government of Manipur, 2019). The transmen and transwomen populace has faced various issues and challenges at socio-cultural and political realm which has also led to their discrimination in the economic sphere. The *Nupi maanbi* (transwoman) community in the state have been much more visible than the *Nupa maanba* (transman) community. The *Nupi maanbi* community has been accepted historically as '*pheitas*' and yet they have undergone ostracization over time as gender non-conforming people were socially stigmatized and tabooed although they had one prominent space for their gender expression which was the stage of '*Shumang Leela*'[1] (Dutta, 2023). The discrimination that the transmen and transwomen both faced for so long eventually led them to a life of marginalization and destitution. However, the transgender community of the state have been, like other contemporaries, actively engaging in the pursuit of transgender rights advocacy. This is evident from the fact that the '*MarupIoi* Foundation' of Manipur founded in 2003 was the first Community Based Organization of the North-Eastern Region of India which functioned at the state level on transwomen and MSM (males who have sex with males) issues (Leibaklei Part-2, 2020).

Empowerment and Affirmative Action

The achievement of real empowerment is a process that must deal with the factors that inhibits it. Empowerment in a general sense means enabling a person to exercise their own agency in all matters of their individual and social life which includes but may not be limited to economic, political, cultural etc. A holistic empowerment which may enable a dignified life is what ought to be the basic right of every human being regardless of their differences. "Empowerment is not only about opening up access to decision-making, but also must include processes that lead people to perceive themselves as able and entitled to occupy that decision-making space" (Rowlands, 1995: cited in Oxaal & Baden, 1997: 3).

"The term 'affirmative action' is of relatively recent origin—the term was first used in 1961 by John F. Kennedy in the context of policies designed to promote equal opportunity or non-discrimination" (Deshpande, 2023). He delineates the purpose and scope of AA stating that it is not a 'conventional redistributive measure' rather it 'alters the composition of elite positions in society' (*ibid.*). And thus, it is not meant to be "an anti-poverty measure, nor an employment generation measure". For him, the rationale of AA is that "given the systematic and multifaceted discrimination against certain groups, the normal process of development might not automatically close the gaps between the marginalized and dominant groups because dominant groups will disproportionately corner the fruits of development" and "fulfils an important function of providing some members of the disadvantaged communities a voice in decision-making: by placing them in prestigious jobs and elite educational institutions, provides the community with say" (*ibid.*). Affirmative action in India was initially caste based in the form of quotas or reservations for [Scheduled] Castes (SCs) and [Scheduled] Tribes (STs) with the inclusion of Other Backward Classes (OBCs) which the Mandal Commission determined using "11 indicators of social and economic criteria, which were grouped under three heads: social, educational and economic" (*ibid.*). This chapter thus, engages with government's various measures for Transgender inclusivity in Manipur through reservation and to explore the transgender's issues and challenges at ground level.

NALSA 2014 and the Transgender Persons (Rights of Protection) Act, 2019

In 2014, a turning point in the history of transgender community was marked with the passing of the NALSA Judgement by the Supreme Court of India. The judgement called for various legal remedies of which the most important was the treatment of transgender persons as 'third gender' for safeguarding and enforcing their constitutional rights appropriately and self-determination or the right of the transgender persons to decide their self-identified gender and for the legal recognition of their gender identity as male, female or third gender. It also directs the Centre and State Governments to take steps to treat them as socially and educationally backward classes of citizens and to extend all kinds or reservation in cases of admission in educational institutions and for public appointments (Arjan Kumar Sikri & K.S. Panicker Radhakrishnan, 2014 INSC 275). On November 26th, 2019, [The Transgender Persons (Protection of Rights) Bill, 2019]. The Transgender Persons (Protection of Rights) Act, 2019 was legislated on the 5th December, 2019 following the Act of Parliament and assent of the President (Government of India, 2019). Subsequently, 'National Council for Transgender Persons' was formed in 2020 to advise, review, evaluate, and coordinate the Central Government, all the departments of Government and other Governmental and non-Governmental organizations with transgender related matters. The Act also declares various actions against transgender persons as criminal offences. One of the key features is that it entitles transgender persons *the right to self-perceived identity*. Under this provision, various cells for transgender community are established in Manipur.

On Transgender Persons in Manipur, Empowerment and Affirmative Action

Despite the various legal remedies and measures being taken up to safeguard the rights of the transgender persons of the country, multiple disabilities still curb them from enjoying the benefits of the same. "Our legal system frequently fails to shield trans individuals from discrimination based on our gender identification" (Dr. Konika Khuraijam, 2022). The most important right provided to transgender persons is that of the legal recognition as 'Third Gender' and their right to self-perceived gender identity. The Census of 2011 which recorded a total populace of 1343 persons in the 'Other' category not only included 'Transgender' persons but also any person who desired to record their sex under the 'other' category and states that the Census of India does not collect any data specifically on 'transgender' (Ministry of Social Justice & Empowerment, 2019). A random survey conducted by AMANA (All Manipur Nupi Maanbi Association) revealed over 4000 adult transgender population in the state (Sarma, 2024). Also, there can be many transgender persons who do not come out openly. The NALSA Judgement enabled many transgender persons in the state to claim their rights and come out openly.[2] The legal recognition of their self-perceived gender identity also allows them to change their name as per their choice and to change their identity in all official documents. However, the transgender community still faces various problems in doing so. The National Portal for Transgender Persons is an online portal where transgender persons can apply and avail Transgender Certificate and Identity Card which are nationally recognized given by the Ministry of Social Justice & Empowerment.[3] In contrast to the transgender population as per AMANA's survey, only 751 transgender certificate and ID card applications have been received of which 628 have been issued and 123 is pending.[4] Despite these provisions, a transgender person of the state Beoncy Laishram who was born biologically male and transitioned to female was informed that she needed a court order to change her name on her degree certificate by the Chairman of the Board of Secondary Education Manipur (BOSEM). The change in the HSLC examination certificate would enable change in name and gender in other educational certificates (Ngangom, 2024). Following her plea, "a single bench of Justice Ahanthem Bimol issued a notice to the educational departments to respond within three weeks" (*ibid.*).

The Government of Manipur has also mentioned about the transgender persons of the state in the 'Manipur Vision 2030' and states that "the Centre and State Governments are to take steps to treat them as socially and educationally backward classes of citizens and extend all kinds of reservation in cases of admission in educational and public appointments and frame various social welfare schemes for their betterment" (Planning Department, Government of Manipur, 2019). It also states that the population of transgender persons recorded in the Census 2011 are exclusively transwomen and that no survey for transmen has was conducted in the same. It also includes various centrally sponsored schemes formulated by the Ministry of Social Justice and Empowerment, Government of India, which includes scheme for financial support to the parents of transgender children, pre-metric and post-metric scholarship for transgender students, assistance for skill development and training and National Pension scheme for transgender persons (*ibid.*).

The educational realm has been one of the most challenging areas where transgender persons of the state face various difficulties. Starting form bullying to unavailability of a transgender inclusive social and structural space, inclusive education which is an essential component of transgender empowerment, and the act has been a challenging area. The treatment of transgender persons as 'third gender' guarantees them the rights enshrined in the Constitution of India which includes the right to free and compulsory education till the age of fourteen. But the prevalence of bullying of transgender persons by their peers, questioning upon their gender expression by educators demoralize them leading to high rate of dropouts (Lairikyengbam, Legal Hints, 2022). "Most of them (*Nupi maanbis*, transwomen) are school-dropouts and as such they are deprived of various basic rights" (Chanu, 2018). According to Randhoni Larikyengbam, Assistant Director, SAATHII (Manipur), majority of the transgenders do not possess high level of education and so skill training is very important for livelihood inclusion (Lairikyengbam, Legal Hints, 2024). Santa Khurai, a leading transgender activist of the state and author, notes that as there is no separate category for transgender in school admissions, regardless of the many things that transgender persons might want to learn, they are unable to do so because of the lack of a space that feels inclusive to them. She also states that addition of such a category would give them a 'recognition' that would provide an enabling environment where transgender persons shall enjoy going to (Leibaklei Part-I, 2020). The various other issues relating to transgender dropouts also relates to lack of support, safety concerns, proper toilets which may be designated for transgender persons or be gender neutral, uniform issues, lack of resources and others.

The Census of India 2011 records that the national literacy rate of transgender persons is 56.07 per cent which is very low as compared to the national average of 74.04 per cent (Mehta & Sharma, 2023). The literacy rate of transgender persons in Manipur is 67.50 per cent which is higher than the national transgender literacy rate, but it is still lower than the national literacy rate and that of the state's literacy rates which stands at 74.04 per cent and 76.94 per cent, respectively. It is also lower than the literacy rate of females which is 70.26 per cent. The literacy rate provided is also based on the Census data of the 1343 transgender persons and hence not inclusive of the entire transgender populace of the state. However, low literacy rate negatively influences employment opportunity that which is one of the major factors for social and economic mobility. It also has significant "economic, social and health impacts at both an individual and societal level" (Miranda, 2021). The Ministry of Social Justice and Empowerment has also produced various financial aids for transgender persons under the SMILE scheme. Although few transgender persons from Manipur have applied, there is no news about getting the scholarship yet (Lairikyengbam, Legal Hints, 2022). Till date, the Government of Manipur has issued two official memorandums which include appointment of a Complaint officer to deal with complaints relating to violation of the provisions of the Transgender Persons (Protection of Rights) Act, 2019 in respect of University & Higher Education Department (Government of Manipur, 2023) and for providing Vocational Skill development, scholarship/ entitlements, fee waiver, free textbooks and other facilities and subsidized rates for transgender students, and for all educational institutions/Universities to establish an anti-discrimination cell to monitor any form of discrimination or harassment against transgender students (Government of Manipur, 2023). There are very few transgender persons who are employed and even if they do, they are not taken into account in public spaces.[5]

In today's world, education is one of the most crucial factors that dictate employment besides others. "Lack of education and professional qualifications in addition to consequences of social barriers created by unconventional gender identity are some of the major factors responsible for such marginalisation. In due course, these [circumstances] leads to insufficient scope for socio-economic status among nupi maanbis" (Yumkhaibam, Beauty Parlour as a Scope for Socio-economic Status among Transgender Nupi Maanbis of Manipur, 2017). According to Census 2011, the portion of transgender community who are working is 38 per cent which is considered much lower to the percentage of working persons in the general population which is 46 per cent and only 65 per cent of transgender persons find work for more than six months (UNDP, 2016). Bonita Pebam, a prominent transgender rights activist of the state and a National Awardee for Path Breaker states that although the *Nupi Maanbi* community of the state do find a source of livelihood through *Shumang Leela* and the glamour world, it is not sustainable as it lacks future security and financial stability. The job opportunity and accessibility for transgender persons is also extremely limited in addition to the already existing unemployment issue that persists in the state. She further adds that there should be more focus on education to increase the employment opportunity as it is very essential. For *Nupa Maanba* persons, employment opportunity is higher as they can venture in government sector, sports, home department as security etc. Their gender expression for instance, maintaining a short hair is negligibly stigmatized. But for a transwoman to wear saree along with maintaining long hair is more tabooed.[6] On 6th February, 2024, the Scheme Guideline of Chief Minister's "*Ima Nongthangleima Yaipha Tengbang*" under Social Welfare Department, Government of Manipur was notified which aims to empower a target group of women of the state by providing financial assistance of Rs. 500 per month who are not beneficiaries of any existing government schemes whing included single transgender women above the age of 40 years to aid them in pursuing diverse livelihood options (Government of Manipur, 2024).

Conclusion

The legal remedies provided by the government have shown certain changes that favours the transgender populace. However, it is not without limitations. Affirmative action provides for preferential reservation of these categories on areas related to employment, education, electoral sphere (Deshpande, 2023). Randhoni states that there is no clear mention of reservations or percentage of reservations allotted for the community (Lairikyengbam, Legal Hints, 2022). The Calcutta High Court gave a judgement directing the West Bengal Government to provide one per cent reservation to transgender persons in all public employment in the state (Jain, 2024). But no such precise horizontal reservation is provided for transgender persons in Manipur as of now in terms of employment, education or in the electoral sphere although inclusion is advocated and encouraged.

Transgender persons who have successfully changed their gender as Male or Female shall be entitled to existing reservation for the above-mentioned categories. Nonetheless, the unclear condition on reservations, and having only 628[7] transgender persons from the state having TG Certificate/ID Card would mean that many who do not have the same shall be denied of any such benefits. Also, challenges in obtaining official documents changed to the preferred gender of transgender persons would further create issues in employment. The fact remains that even after 11 years that the NALSA 2014 judgement was passed, and six years of the Act being implemented there are still ambiguities and hurdles that curb the community from enjoying the benefits of the same. The intersectionality of the issues of marginalization and other existing issues that ails Manipur, of which conflict, unemployment or redundancy and lack of resource are prominent impacts the transgender community with greater potency making them even more vulnerable. In spite of all these issues, the community has shown immense resilience and their unwavering efforts through advocacy and coordination with various stake holders has made great impact in the implementation and execution of the Act.

To conclude, it is important to note that the transgender population of the state have seen changes and inclusion to certain extent in matters pertaining to education and health. Yet, issues with matters like employment still exist. Therefore, increasing the number of transgender persons through reservation in higher education and employment would help break the barriers of discrimination through re-socialization of both transgender and cisgender communities. Thus, in coordination with Despande's idea of giving a voice for the marginalized through Affirmative action, a distinct quota for the said community in the form of reserving their seats in respective fields shall help in empowering them even further.

NOTES

1. Shumang Leela is an indigenous form of theatre in Manipur performed in the courtyard.
2. Extracted from interview with Bonita Pebam, Transgender Rights Activist, Project Coordinator, Transgender Health and Wellness Centre.
3. Retrieved from National Portal for Transgender Persons on 11 August, 2024—https://transgender.dosje.gov.in/Applicant/Registration/Displayform1
4. Retrieved from National Portal for Transgender Persons on 18 March, 2025—https://transgender.dosje.gov.in/
5. Extracted from interview with Bonita Pebam, Transgender Rights Activist, Project Coordinator, Transgender Health and Wellness Centre.
6. Extracted from interview with Bonita Pebam, Transgender Rights Activist, Project Coordinator, Transgender Health and Wellness Centre.
7. Sourced from National Portal for Transgender Persons on 9th March, 2025, https://transgender.dosje.gov.in/

REFERENCES

AMANA. (2020). *Pheida: Gender at the Periphery.* Imphal: KK Printers.

Amnesty International. (2023). *Colonialism and Sexual Orientation and Gender Identity: Submission to the Independent Expert on Protection against Violence based on Sexual Orientation and Gender Identity.* Peter Benenson House, Easton Street London WC1X ODW, UK: Amnesty International Ltd.

Arjan Kumar Sikri, J. & K.S. Panicker Radhakrishnan, J. (2014 INSC 275). *National Legal Authority Vs. Union of Inida and others.* Digital Supreme Court Reports. Retrieved September 14, 2024, from http://digiscr.sci.gov.in

Chanu, S.B. (2018). State, Citizenship and Transgender Identity India: A Case Study of the Nupi Manbi Community in Manipur. New Delhi, India: Sodhganga.

Department of Gender Studies, National Council of Educational Research and Training. (2020-21). Inlcusion of Transgender Children in School Education: Concerns and Roadmap. New Delhi. Retrieved March 7, 2025, from https://clpr.org.in/wp-content/uploads/2022/01/Inclusion_of_Transgender_Children_in_School_Education.pdf

Deshpande, A. (2023). *Affirmative Action in India.* New Delhi: Oxford University Press.

Dr. Konika Khuraijam, D.R. (2022). A Study on Violation of Rights of Transgender in Manipur. *International Research Journal of Commerce Arts and Science, 13*(12), 50-59.

Dutta, S.B. (2023, August 26). Nupi Maanbi: Transgenders of Manipur Who Went from Being Accepted to Ostracised to Now Finding Own Voices. India: Indiatimes News. Retrieved June 5, 2024, from https://www.indiatimes.com/news/india/nupi-maanbi-transgenders-of-manipur-who-went-from-being-accepted-to-ostracised-to-now-finding-own-voices-606294.html

Government of India. (2019, December 5). *The Transgender Persons (Protection of Rights) Act, 2019.* Government of India, New Delhi. Retrieved March 8, 2025, from https://www.indiacode.nic.in/

Government of Manipur. (2023). *The Expert Committee constituted by the Central Government on Transgender, list of actions shall be taken up by the Department of Higher & Technical Education, Manipur as per the timeline, Gazette No. 563.* Directorate of Printing and Stationary, Government of Manipur. Retrieved March 12, 2025, from https://manipurgovtpress.nic.in/en/details_gazzete/?gazette=2032

Government of Manipur. (2023). *The Governor of Manipur is pleased to appoint Director, University & Higher Education, Manipur as the Complaint officer to deal with the complaints relating to violation of the provisions of the Transgender Persons.* Gazette, Directorate of Printing & Stationary, Government of Manipur. Retrieved Febraury 24, 2025, from https://manipurgovtpress.nic.in/en/details_gazzete/?gazette=2033

Government of Manipur. (2024). Gazette, Dirtectorate of Printing & Stationary,Government of Manipur. Retrieved March 15, 2025, from https://manipurgovtpress.nic.in/media/gazzete/EG-265.pdf

Jain, A. (2024, June 19). As Calcutta HC orders 1 per cent quota for transgender people, how SC ruling & 2019 law protect their rights.

The Print. Retrieved April 3, 2025, from https://theprint.in/theprint-essential/as-calcutta-hc-orders-1-quota-for-transgender-people-how-sc-ruling-2019-law-protect-their-rights/2138068/

K.G., D. & Keshlata. (2024). towards Transgender Inclusion: Apllying Sustainanble Devlopment Goals to Address and Resolve the Transgender Challenges in India, in R. Bala & M. Lilee, *BREAKING BARRIERS: Gender Disparities, Inclusion and Empowerment in India* (pp. 13-30). New Delhi-110068: Mohit Tiwary for M/s. Sunmarg Publishers &Distributors.

Kshetri, R. (2006). *The Emergence of Meetei Nationalism*. New Delhi: Mittal Publications.

Lairikyengbam, R. (2022, October 19). *Legal Hints*. (W. GuniLeima, Interviewer) Doordarshan Manipur. Retrieved November 16, 2024, from https://youtu.be/87ZbOXosuIs?feature=shared

Lairikyengbam, R. (2024, May 8). Legal Hints. (Chanchalkumari, Interviewer) Doordarshan Manipur. Retrieved November 20, 2024, from https://youtu.be/XpN1U-4Zh4Y?feature=shared

(2020, May 4). Leibaklei Part-2. *Leibaklei Part-2*. (A. Huidrom, Interviewer) Doordarshan Manipur. Retrieved March 11, 2025, from https://youtu.be/k2-UEnc20ng?feature=shared

(2020, February 6). Leibaklei Part-I. (A. Huidrom, Interviewer) Doordarshan Manipur. Retrieved March 3, 2025, from https://youtu.be/kGFyOLDuW_w?feature=shared

Mehta, D.R. & Sharma, M. (2023, January 1). "Transgender's Education in India: Status and Challenges." *International Journal of Novel Research and Development, 8*(1), a248-a246. Retrieved March 11, 2025.

Ministry of Social Justice & Empowerment. (2019, June 25). Welfare of Transgenders. Press Information Bureau. Retrieved February 20, 2025, from https://pib.gov.in/PressReleasePage.aspx?PRID=1575534

Miranda, N. (2021, July 23). *World Literacy Foundation*. Retrieved March 15, 2025, from https://worldliteracyfoundation.org/early-intervention-reduces-illiteracy/

Mishra, V. (2023). *Transgenders in India: An Introduction*. Abingdon, Oxon; New York, NY: Routledge.

Ngangom, T. (2024). *Manipur HC issues notice to state edu dept on PIL by transgender medical officer*. Imphal: *Hindustan Times*. Retrieved

March 3, 2025, from https://www.hindustantimes.com/india-news/manipur-hc-issues-notice-to-state-edu-dept-on-pil-by-transgender-medical-officer-101718519666293.html

Oxaal, Z. & Baden, S. (1997). *Gender and Empowerment: Definitions, Approaches and Implications for Policy.* Brighton,UK: BRIDGE (development-gender) Institute of Development Studies, Univeristy of Sussex.

Planning Department, Government of Manipur. (2019, November 11). Manipur Vision 2030 Leaving No-one Behind: Acheiving Inclusive Growth and the Sustainable Development Goals. Retrieved February 21, 2025, from Planning Department, Government of Manipur: https://planningmanipur.gov.in/media/filer_public/05/b8/05b8621c-943a-4682-ae5f-d02e7db7b5c9/manipurvision2030_fullnew.pdf

Sarma, K.S. (2024, January 24). Just 239 Voters? Manipur trans Community Raises Eyebrows. Imphal: *The Times of India.* Retrieved March 2, 2025, from https://timesofindia.indiatimes.com/city/imphal/just-239-voters-manipur-trans-community-raises-eyebrows/articleshow/107098382.cms

Singh, N.I. (1976/2003). *The Manipur Administration (1709-1907)* (First Edition 1976 ed.). Imphal: Ningombam (O) Ibetombi Devi.

The Transgender Persons (Protection of Rights) Bill, 2019. (n.d.). Retrieved March 8, 2025, from https://prsindia.org/billtrack/the-transgender-persons-protection-of-rights-bill-2019

UNDP. (2016). Skilling for Livelihood Opportunities for Transgenders in India. Retrieved February 18, 2025, from https://www.undp.org/sites/g/files/zskgke326/files/migration/in/Skilling-for-Livelihood.pdf

Yumkhaibam, R. (2017, August). Beauty Parlour as a Scope for Socio-Economic Status among Transgender Nupi Maanbis of Manipur. *International Journal od Research in Humanities, Arts and Literature, 5*(8). Retrieved 2018.

Yumkhaibam, R. (n.d.). Gender Inequality, Power, and Resistance: A Study of the Socio-cultural Location of Trangender Nupi Mannbis of Manipur. 180-191. Kyoto University. Retrieved February 19, 2025, from https://www.kuasu.cpier.kyoto-u.ac.jp/wp-content/uploads/2020/04/11.-Rubani-Yumkhaibam.pdf

22

Ensuring Women's Political Empowerment

The Women's Reservation Act, 2023 and the Ways Forward

Yumlembam Khogen

Introduction

India's journey towards women's political empowerment has been marked by significant milestones and persistent challenges. Despite constitutional guarantees of gender equality, women's representation in legislative bodies has remained disproportionately low. As of 2023, women occupied only about 15 per cent of seats as Members of Parliament (Singh, 2024) and some other indicators also reflect a substantial gender gap in political participation (Kundal, 2023). The enactment of the Women's Reservation Act of 2023, officially known as the Constitution (One Hundred and Twenty-Eighth Amendment) Act, represents a pivotal step towards addressing this gender disparity and this new quota creates an unprecedented demand for women candidates and it may prompt political parties to seek qualified women contenders (Kaur and Philips, 2025). The Act mandates the reservation of one-third of all seats for women in the Lok Sabha, state legislative assemblies, and the Legislative Assembly of the Union Territory of Delhi (India, 2025). The implementation of this Act is contingent upon the completion of the next census and subsequent delimitation exercise in order to ensure that the reservation aligns with updated demographic data. The reservation is set to be in effect for a period of 15 years from its commencement, however; there are provisions for extension as determined by law (PRS India, 2025). This chapter explores the multifaceted prerequisites essential for effectively implementing the Women's Reservation Act, 2023. This chapter will examine the legislative, administrative, societal, and supportive measures that are necessary to ensure increase in women's numerical representation but also empowers them to participate meaningfully in the political processes. By addressing these prerequisites, the chapter seeks to provide a comprehensive framework for translating the promise of the Act into tangible progress in terms of true political empowerment of women in India.

Legislative and Judicial Prerequisites

The Women's Reservation Act, 2023 marks a significant milestone in India's pursuit of gender equality in political representation. In order to translate the Act's provisions into tangible outcomes, a robust legislative and judicial framework is a must. Firstly, a comprehensive and transparent legal framework is necessary. The Act mandates the reservation of one-third of seats for women in the Lok Sabha, state legislative assemblies, and the Legislative Assembly of the National Capital Territory of Delhi. However, its implementation is contingent upon completing the next census and subsequent delimitation exercise, which may delay its enforcement until at least 2029 (*The Hindu*, 2023). Comprehensive guidelines detailing the operational aspects of the reservation such as the criteria for seat rotation and the mechanism for identifying constituencies etc. are essential to ensure clarity and consistency. Secondly, drafting of detailed guidelines and operational rules becomes another prerequisite for the successful execution of the Act. This includes defining the methodology for rotating reserved seats to ensure equitable representation across different regions of the country and various sections of the society. Additionally, mechanisms must be instituted to monitor compliance and address any anomalies that may arise during implementation. Retrospecting the implications of the 73rd and 74th Constitutional Amendments which provided for the reservation of seats for women in Panchayati Raj Institutions can offer valuable insights into structuring the effective guidelines for the implimentation of the Women's Reservation Act, 2023. Thirdly, robust judicial mechanisms and grievance redressal systems shall be crucial to uphold the integrity of the Act's reservation policy. Existing structures like the Department of Administrative Reforms and Public Grievances and the Directorate of Public Grievances should be leveraged to handle issues related to the implementation of the Act. India's judiciary has historically played a pivotal role in shaping and reinforcing reservation policies. In the landmark case of *Indra Sawhney* v. *Union of India* (1992), the Supreme Court upheld the validity of reservations for Other Backward Classes while introducing the concept of 'creamy layer' to exclude more affluent members of these communities from availing reservation benefits and similarly, in the *Ashoka Kumar Thakur* v. *Union of India Case* (2008), the Apex Court upheld the 27 per cent reservation for OBCs in educational institutions, emphasising the need for periodic review and the exclusion of the creamy layer (Singh, 2018). These court judgments underscore the judiciary's commitment to ensuring that reservation policies are implemented in a manner that promotes social justice while maintaining the principles of equality as enshrined in the Constitution of India. In the implementation of Women's Reservation Act, 2023 also, the judiciary must play pivotal role.

Administrative and Governance Prerequisites

The successful implementation of the Women's Reservation Act, 2023 will need a robust administrative and governance framework across national, state, and local levels. This framework must ensure seamless coordination among various administrative agencies, adequate allocation of resources, and the establishment of dedicated institutions to oversee the Act's execution. A multi-tiered governance structure is essential to operationalise the Act effectively. At the national level, the Election Commission of India (ECI) should spearhead the formulation of guidelines for the reservation of seats, ensuring uniformity across states. State governments must establish committees to oversee the implementation within their jurisdictions, adapting national guidelines to local contexts. At the local level, Panchayati Raj Institutions (PRIs) and Urban Local Bodies (ULBs) should be empowered to facilitate grassroots-level awareness and participation. The 73rd and 74th Constitutional Amendments which mandated one-third reservation for women in PRIs and ULBs was a success (Srivatsa, 2016), and it underscores the importance of decentralised governance in enhancing women's political participation. Another key element is the effective coordination among administrative agencies. The Ministry of Women and Child Development (MWCD) should collaborate with the Ministry of Law and Justice, the ECI, and State Election Commissions to ensure cohesive policy implementation. The collaboration should also extend to civil society organisations and academic institutions in order to incorporate diverse perspectives and expertise. The government's "whole-of-government" and "whole-of-society" approach, as highlighted in recent initiatives, exemplifies the need for such integrated efforts (PIB, 2025).

Next comes the importance of adequate financial, human, and infrastructural resources. Allocating sufficient resources is critical to the Act's success. Financial investments are required for conducting capacity-building programmes, awareness campaigns, and infrastructural enhancements to support elected women legislators. Human resources including trained personnel and gender-sensitised officials are essential to facilitate women's effective participation. Infrastructures in the form of dedicated offices and childcare facilities within legislative premises can help a lot in addressing practical barriers faced by women representatives. Lessons from the implementation of women's reservation in local governance reveal that women representatives know the local priorities but rotation of seats, dominance of related males, women's difficulties in interaction with external bodies, unability to maintain a balance between work and house chores, and limited resource allocation significantly influences the effectiveness of such women's reservation policies in politics (Kumar and Ghosh, 2023; Buch, 2009). Therefore, lessons from the past experiences are required. After analysing the past experiences, it becomes clear that establishing dedicated institutions and committees will be vital for monitoring and evaluating the Act's implementation and effectiveness. A central monitoring committee, comprising representatives from relevant ministries, the ECI, and civil society, can oversee progress and address the persisiting challenges. At the state level, similar bodies should be constituted to ensure localised oversight. These institutions should be empowered to collect data, assess impact, and recommend policy adjustments. The Standing Committee on Personnel, Public Grievances, Law and Justice has previously emphasised the importance of such oversight mechanisms in the context of reservation policies (PRS India, 2025).

Capacity Building, Training, and Resource Allocation

The successful implementation of the Women's Reservation Act, 2023 hinges on comprehensive capacity-building initiatives, targeted training programmes, and strategic resource allocation. These elements are crucial to ensure that women not only occupy legislative positions but also participate effectively in the political processes. Training and capacity-building programmes shall equip elected women representatives (EWRs) with the necessary skills and knowledge to perform their roles effectively. The United Nations Development Programme (UNDP) emphasises that capacity-building initiatives enhance the performance of EWRs by providing them with leadership skills, understanding of governance processes, and the ability to engage with constituents effectively (UNDP, 2012). In case of the 73rd and 74th Constitutional Amendments, the training programmes imparted by the National Institute of Public Cooperation and Child Development (NIPCCD) have been instrumental in transforming women's participation from mere representation to active involvement in decision-making processes (NIPCCD, n.d.). Moreover, the NIPCCD has highlighted the need for continuous training programmes for EWRs to address the challenges they face in governance roles. These programmes focus on developing competencies in areas such as policy formulation, budget analysis, and legislative procedures, thereby enabling women to contribute meaningfully to legislative debates and policymaking. Allocation of ample financial resources shall be needed to conduct such training programmes, and awareness campaigns that can provide monetary and logistical support not only to the trainers but also to EWRs. Previous initiatives have shown that when adequate resources are provided, women are better positioned to participate actively in governance and contribute to community development (UNDP, 2012).

Societal and Cultural Prerequisites

The enactment of the Women's Reservation Act, 2023, marks a significant milestone in India's journey towards gender equality in political representation. However, the success of this legislation hinges not only on legal and administrative frameworks but also on addressing deep-rooted societal and cultural barriers. Patriarchal norms, gender biases, and entrenched stereotypes continue to impede women's full participation in politics (Kundal, 2023). Therefore, comprehensive strategies encompassing public awareness campaigns and educational initiatives are essential to transform societal perceptions and empower women across all strata of society. Patriarchy remains a pervasive force in Indian society. Patriarchy manifests in various forms, including restrictive gender roles, limited access to education, and societal expectations that prioritise domestic responsibilities for women over public engagement (Kundal, 2023). These cultural norms often discourage women from pursuing political careers and can lead to resistance when they do (Thomas and Kaunain, 2025). Internal party dynamics often reflect these societal biases where women face challenges in securing nominations and leadership positions even within the political parties. This systemic marginalisation underscores the need for a cultural shift that values and supports women's political participation. There is also a need for public awareness campaigns to challenge and reshape societal norms. Initiatives like the "Selfie With Daughter" campaign have successfully utilised social media platforms to promote the value of the girl child and challenge traditional gender biases. By encouraging families to share positive images and stories of their daughters, the campaign has fostered a more inclusive narrative around gender roles. Similarly, more media campaigns should be initiated and play an instrumental role in initiating conversations around gender equality and contribute to a gradual shift in public perceptions

(Thomas and Kaunain, 2025). By highlighting the achievements of women leaders and normalising women's presence in public life, media and awareness campaigns can dismantle stereotypes and inspire broader societal change. Education serves as a fundamental tool for empowerment, equipping individuals with the knowledge and skills necessary to participate actively in political processes. Programmes like Mahila Samakhya have focused on women's education and empowerment, particularly in rural areas, fostering awareness of rights and encouraging community participation (Bhuwania *et al.*, 2024). Furthermore, integrating gender sensitisation into educational curricula can address biases from an early age. By educating youth on gender equality and the importance of inclusive representation, we can lay the groundwork for a more equitable society. Engaging local communities through workshops and dialogues can also foster supportive environments for women's political participation (Sharma, 2024).

Supportive Networks and Mentorship Programmes

Abled mentorship and support networks are pivotal in fostering women's political leadership particularly in a landscape where systemic barriers and societal norms often hinder their participation. These structures provide guidance, skill development, and emotional support, enabling women to navigate the complexities of political engagement effectively. One notable initiative is the "She is a Changemaker" programme launched by the National Commission for Women (NCW) in 2021. This pan-India capacity-building programmes aims to enhance the leadership skills of grassroots women political leaders, encompassing representatives from gram panchayats to parliament members. By offering training and mentorship, the programmes seeks to empower women to assume more significant roles in governance (PIB, 2021). For a guaranteed success of India's reservation policy for women in the highest political decision-making bodies, there is need for more rampant execution of such mentorship programmes. On top of formal programmes, grassroots initiatives like Self-Help Groups (SHGs) must be instrumental in shifting gender norms and promoting women's political empowerment. Creating sustainable networks involves institutional support and continuous engagement. Organisations like the Centre for Social Research (CSR) have been at the forefront, offering leadership training and advocating for women's rights. Their initiatives aim to build a supportive ecosystem that nurtures women's political ambitions and addresses challenges unique to their experiences (CSR, 2020). To make the Act successful, there is need to create more SHGs and civil organisations which shall establish sustainable networks supporting women's political ambition and participation.

Monitoring, Evaluation, and Accountability Mechanisms

The effective implementation of the Women's Reservation Act, 2023, necessitates robust monitoring, evaluation, and accountability mechanisms to ensure that the intended outcome is realised. Even after the implementation of the Act, there is a need for a comprehensive monitoring and evaluation framework to track progress, identify challenges, and inform policy adjustments. Such a framework should encompass both quantitative and qualitative indicators, allowing for a nuanced understanding of the Act's impact. It will be imperative to establish measurable indicators like percentage increase in women's representation in legislative bodies at various levels, number of women candidates fielded by political parties, extent of women's participation in legislative debates and committees, impact of women's legislative participation on policy outcomes etc. to assess the effectiveness of the Women's Reservation Act. Regular data collection and analysis will facilitate evidence-based decision-making and ensure transparency in the implementation process. Civil Society Organisations (CSOs), media, and independent institutions should play a pivotal role in holding stakeholders accountable and ensuring the Act's successful implementation. CSOs can monitor compliance, advocate for women's political rights, and provide capacity-building support to women candidates and elected representatives. The media must serve as a watchdog by highlighting successes, exposing shortcomings, and fostering public discourse on women's political participation. Autonomous bodies such as the Election Commission of India and the National Commission for Women will be instrumental in overseeing adherence to the Act's provisions and addressing grievances. Collaborative efforts among these entities can create a conducive environment for women's political empowerment, ensuring that objectives of the Women's Reservation Act, 2023 are met effectively and sustainably.

Political Commitment and the Ways Forward

The effective implementation of the Women's Reservation Act, 2023 hinges on sustained political will transcending party lines. Historically, the the Women's Reservation Bill faced multiple setbacks due to political disagreements and lack of consensus (Dhavan, 2008). Therefore, it underscores the necessity for unwavering commitment from all political stakeholders to ensure its success. To maintain continuous political support and avoid tokenism (Ban and Rao, 2008), it is imperative to integrate the Act's objectives into the broader political discourse. This involves not only endorsing the legislation but also actively promoting women's participation through party nominations, leadership roles, and capacity-building initiatives. Political parties must move beyond symbolic gestures and ensure that women are empowered to influence policy decisions meaningfully. Additionally, addressing potential challenges such as the delayed implementation due to pending census and delimitation exercises is crucial. Ensuring transparency and accountability in these processes will be vital to uphold the Act's integrity and objectives. Starting from the British Raj, discussions on reservations for women were overshadowed by caste and religious considerations (Jenkins, 1999: 59) and the debates over the implementation of the Women's Reservation Act of 2023 are continuing on the grounds of timelines (Singh, 2024), sub-quotas for OBC and Muslim women etc. Such persisting debates will only delay the effective implementation of the Act and as such, political parties must come up with a consensus on such issues as soon as possible.

Conclusion

The Women's Reservation Act, 2023 stands as a transformative step towards gender parity in Indian politics but its success depends on a constellation of interdependent prerequisites. There are crucial needs for a comprehensive legal framework, detailed operational rules, robust judicial and grievance redressal mechanisms, administrative preparedness, sufficient capacity building, and resource allocation. Equally important is societal shifts to challenge the detrimental patriarchal attitudes, and the cultivation of mentorship networks, and strong political commitment that transcends symbolic gestures. To actualise the Act's objectives, integrated and coordinated efforts are required across legislative, administrative, societal, and political domains. Legal mandates must be reinforced with administrative capacity, social awareness, and political will to create an enabling environment for women's political leadership. Institutions at every level must collaborate to deliver transparent, accountable, and sustained support for the Act's implementation. The vision must extend beyond numerical representation to fostering the meaningful and empowered participation of women in decision-making processes. Only through such a holistic and sustained approach, the Women's Reservation Act, 2023 can usher long-term democratic reform and inclusive governance. Empowering women politically is not merely a legal imperative, it is also essential for the social, economic, and ethical development of India's democracy in the twenty-first century.

REFERENCES

Ban, R. & Rao, V. (2008). "Tokenism or Agency? The Impact of Women's Reservations on Village Democracies in South India." *Economic Development and Cultural Change, 56*(3): 501-530. doi:10.1086/533551

Bhuwania, P., Mukherji, A. & Swaminathan, H. (2024). "Women's Education Through Empowerment: Evidence from A Community-Based Program." *World Development Perspectives, 35*, Article 100785. Retrieved from https://www.sciencedirect.com/science/article/pii/S2452292924000055

Buch, Nirmala. (2009). "Reservation for Women in Panchayats: A Sop in Disguise?" *Economic and Political Weekly*, October 3-9, *44*(40): 8-10. Retrieved from https://www.jstor.org/stable/25663646

Centre for Social Research. (2020, December 24). *Advocacy and Political Empowerment of Women*. Retrieve from https://www.csrindia.org/advocacy-and-campaign/#

Dhavan, R. (2008). "Reservations for Women: The Way forward", *National Law School of India Review, 20*(1), Article 1. Available at: https://repository.nls.ac.in/nlsir/vol20/iss1/1

Jenkins, L.D. (1999). "Competing Inequalities: The Struggle over Reserved Legislative Seats for Women in India." *International Review of Social History, 44*(S7): 53-75. https://doi.org/10.1017/s0020859000115196

Kaur, K.P. & Philips, A.Q. (30 January, 2025). "Sustainable Representation through Electoral Quotas: Evidence from India". *Politics, Groups, and Identities*, DOI: 10.1080/21565503.2025.2455140

Kumar, S. & Ghosh, A.K. (2023). *Lessons from 30 years of Women's Reservation in Panchayats.* Observer Research Foundation. Retrieved from https://www.orfonline.org/expert-speak/lessons-from-30-years-of-women-s-reservation-in-panchayats

Kundal, A.B. (2023, September 16). *India's Women Reservation: Kill Bill or Time to Close the Gender-democratic Deficit?* Observer Research Foundation. Retrieved from https://www.orfonline.org/expert-speak/india-s-women-reservation-kill-bill-or-time-to-close-the-gender-democratic-deficit

NIPCCD. (n.d.). *Early Watch Report. National Institute of Public Cooperation and Child Development.* Retrieved from https://www.nipccd.nic.in/ewr?utm#gsc.tab=0

Press Information Bureau. (2021, December 7). *NCW Launches a Pan-India Capacity Building Programme 'She is a Changemaker' for Politics.* [Press release], Ministry of Women and Child Development. Retrieved from https://pib.gov.in/PressReleasePage.aspx?PRID=1778787

Press Information Bureau. (2025, March 19). *Government Adopts Comprehensive Strategy for Women's Empowerment, Focusing on Political Participation and Local Governance,* [Press release], Ministry of Women and Child Development. Retrieved from https://pib.gov.in/PressReleasePage.aspx?PRID=2112762&utm

PRS India (2025). *Women's Reservation Bill 2023 [The Constitution (one Hundred Twenty-Eighth Amendment) Bill, 2023].* Retrieved from https://prsindia.org/billtrack/the-constitution-one-hundred-twenty-eighth-amendment-bill-2023

Sharma, A. (2024). "Empowerment of Women through Gender Sensitisation." *International Journal of Research and Analytical Reviews, 11*(1): 813-820. Retrieved from https://ijrar.org/papers/IJRAR24A3171.pdf

Singh, J. (2018). "Role of Judiciary on Reservation Policy in India". *International Journal of Research and Analytical Reviews, 5*(4): 199-204. Retrieved from https://ijrar.org/papers/IJRAR19D3593.pdf

Singh, T. (2024). "Women's Reservation Act of 2023: A symbolic

Gesture or a Significant Stride towards Empowerment?". *Economic and Political Weekly (Engage)*. Retrieved from https://www.epw.in/engage/article/womens-reservation-act-2023-symbolic-gesture-or-0

Srivatsa, P. (2016, October). "Political Empowerment of Women: Women and Panchayati Raj." *Yojana.* Retrieved from http://yojana.gov.in/public-account_2016sep.asp

The Hindu (2023, September 20). *Women's Reservation Bill will be Implemented only after 2029: Amit Shah*. Retrieved from https://www.thehindu.com/news/national/womens-reservation-bill-will-be-implemented-only-after-2029-amit-shah/article67327038.ece

Thomas, V. and Kaunain, S. (2025). "The Intersection of Culture and Politics: Understanding Women's Underrepresentation in Indian Democracy." *Journal of Asian and African Studies, 60*(1): 578-592. DOI: 10.1177/00219096231176738

UNDP. (2012, January 21). *From Reservation to Participation.* Retrieved from https://www.undp.org/india/publications/reservation-participation?utm

Index